*Living Christian Science*

# LIVING CHRISTIAN SCIENCE

## Fourteen Lives

*by Marcy Babbitt*

PRENTICE-HALL, INC., *Englewood Cliffs, N.J.*

Library of Congress Cataloging in Publication Data
Babbitt, Marcy.
Living Christian Science.
1. Christian Science—Biography. I. Title.
BX6990.B3        289.5′092′2 [B]    74-20673
ISBN 0-13-538884-8

# Foreword

*This is a stirring book.*

Many of the people who have told their life stories to Marcy Babbitt have accomplished notable things. They tell, explicitly and with explanations of the process, how Christian Science has enabled them to manifest a substantial measure of good in their lives.

There is tremendous earnestness in these narratives. Some of the people have walked through deep shadows. Nearly all of them have been students of Christian Science for many years. Most of them found Christian Science at times of great need.

Six continents are represented by the lives recorded here. There is rich diversity. There is no pattern of profession or life style. What is shared is the fact that Christian Science has entered and transformed the lives of all the people here included. In essence it is an awareness of God, a sense of His ever-presence, an application of the divinely scientific Principle of living and healing which run through all the lives.

The far-flung episodes are dramatic. Something catches the breath and lifts the heart in almost every one of them. A young Indonesian dancer in a World War II prison camp, a distinguished American diplomat facing severe political challenge, a space scientist and administrator coping with the challenge of travel to the moon, an eager Nigerian yearning for a worthy career after being deprived of opportunity to go to university, an American black deeply involved in practical, constructive urban politics, an Argentinian agrarian reformer seeking to serve his people, a fashion designer striving to express beauty and function, a girl enmeshed in the heavy drug scene: these are only some of the vivid human experiences in which the power of God to solve all problems is understood and demonstrated.

While Christian Scientists may glow pridefully in these accomplishments and love to read about them, the book's real utility should be to those who need fresh spiritual horizons in their lives. They can learn just how Christian Science has worked in the human experience of all these people. It can work for them as they seek earnestly to reflect God's goodness in the face of their own need. They will find how the Bible and the insights of Mary Baker Eddy have transformed and spiritualized human experience in these explicit cases. Obviously, a great many more similar life stories could have been told. These are enough to let people know that many individuals of accomplishment and worth in these times are eager to explain the privilege that has been theirs.

It is a book of sharing, of gratitude. It has the aroma of joy. It should not be read by anybody as if smugness of self-righteousness were being expressed. There is a danger that the deep sense of privilege which Christian Scientists feel may be misunderstood. It should not be so. God's goodness is an open fount. The Christian Scientist's approach is not exclusivist. Nor elitist. Christian Science is not some fancy formula for "success." It is a way of bringing any of us into a deeper sense of sonship with God.

For every Christian Scientist who became an ambassador or an opera star or a business leader there are many, many others who are living its precepts simply, lovingly, and in what may seem to be obscurity. Their lives are just as significant as those recorded here. Each of them could also help enlighten the seeker, and many do with each weekly or monthly issue of the Christian Science periodicals.

It is perhaps more "authentic" for the lives in this book to be recorded with names and dates, chapters and verses. But personality is not the essence of Christian Science. Everything in this book would have just as much meaning if the names were left off. But here they are, people, many of whom are known and recognized in the world of affairs, telling of the blessings they have received—perhaps reluctantly as far as the personal identification is concerned—so that people who need to learn of this truth may find their way more readily into the understanding of God's love for them through the application of Christian Science.

*Erwin D. Canham*

# Preface

*Living Christian Science: Fourteen Lives,* illustrates how dedicated Christian Scientists individually live their religion in various careers and professions. The book presents the lives of fourteen Christian Scientists from different countries and working in different fields: law and business, diplomacy and youth, music and the sciences, politics and the civil rights movement, cattle breeding and global grain trading, communications and fashion designing, and Christian Science healing and teaching.

Through these lives the reader is able to view the universal spectrum covered in the teachings of Christian Science, to see into the inner spiritual lives of people who live close to their concepts of God, and to comprehend the practical, healing influence of Christian Science on individual and collective experience.

For these biographic sketches, I personally interviewed and wrote the life stories as told to me by Adele Blok, Howard Palfrey Jones, Homer E. Newell, Deborah Appleton Huebsch, James A. Jordon, Marion Jordon, William Howlett, John Reardon, and Adele Simpson. Lord Gore-Booth wrote his own chapter. The remaining chapters of Rodolfo A. Weidmann, N. Leonard Alderson, Elliot O. Yemitan, and Ellis Gulliver, were based on material provided to me. It was a privilege to work with these devoted Christian Scientists, and I am everlastingly grateful to them for their generous giving of thought and time.

My gratitude extends to The Christian Science Board of Directors for permission to quote from the writings of Mary Baker Eddy—the woman who stands among the great spiritual thinkers of all time—and to The Christian Science Publishing Society for use of material published by it. I am also grateful to John Beaufort for the care with which he read the manuscript and for his editorial advice, and to George Nay, former associate editor of the *Heralds of Christian Science,* for his experienced editorial counsel.

Finally, I dedicate this book to youth, whose high and pure

concepts of God, Science, and their own being can lead them into the vast ranges of Mind, where all reality, power, and vision exist, and where all lasting achievement takes place—before it is shared with the world.

*Marcy Babbitt*

*New York, N.Y.*

# CONTENTS

*Living Christian Science*

# EXPLANATIONS

Christian Science teaches that God's nature is defined by seven synonyms: Mind, Life, Truth, Love, Spirit, Soul, Principle. These are always capitalized when referring to Deity, as they are throughout this book.

*Abbreviation: Science and Health with Key to the Scriptures* by Mary Baker Eddy is frequently abbreviated to read *Science and Health.*

*Miss Adele Blok (6th from left) with young Indonesians outside the Christian Science Church in Jakarta*

# SEARCH AND DISCOVERY IN INDONESIA

## ✒ *Adele Blok*

CHRISTIAN SCIENCE TEACHER AND PRACTITIONER OF
JAKARTA, INDONESIA

✒ My search for truth began long before I came into contact
with Christian Science, and I now tell the story of my spiritual
progress in the hope that it will be helpful to others.

I was born in the city of Bandung, Java. My father was of
Dutch nationality and had a Dutch name. My mother was also
of Dutch nationality and had a French name. But my family is
of European, Indonesian, and Chinese blood. So although we
lived in what was then called the Dutch East Indies and were
Dutch citizens, we had dark skin. And a perpetual question
faced me: I was not really Dutch, nor Indonesian either, so what
was I? Because of this, from young girlhood I kept searching for
my identity.

My father died when I was six. My stepfather was manager of
a tea and rubber estate so we had ample funds, had a beautiful
villa set into the mountainside of Bandung, moved in good
social circles in Holland and Indonesia, and my sisters and I

went to excellent schools in both countries. We enjoyed all the advantages of the good life in Indonesia. But the divisions in my race and nationality, and the contrasts between the wealthy elite and the impoverished millions, troubled me. I yearned to find my way to God and have Him give me answers to humanity's injustices.

The books to which I turned for understanding opened a world of ideas. I read Nietzsche, Tolstoy, Dostoevsky, Hermann Hesse, Thomas Mann. I read Chinese philosophies, books on Islam, the poetry of many nations. I read the works of Multilati, a protester against colonialism. But my absorbing interest became works on metaphysics, philosophy, and religion. I believed that the world's thinkers would teach me the Great Cause of life and assure me that there is beauty, order, and purpose in God's universe. While discovering many beautiful truths, I never found a book that stated a system of thought I could apply to problems when in need. As a result—until I was twenty-five years of age—I remained uncommitted to any faith. Then I found Christian Science.

&✒ For hundreds of years Indonesia has been 90 percent Muslim, 6 percent Hindu, and 4 percent Christian and other religious and nonreligious groups. Ever since I could remember, I had heard the prayers of Islam issuing from the towers of the Muslim mosques over the community. Reverence for God was deeply rooted in my Indonesian heritage, but my Western heritage demanded that I understand my individual purpose in God's universe.

I was sixteen years old when I found a book in a library containing beautiful pictures of great Indian masters. Their faces were pure and serene; they looked as if they had found truth. So I prayed fervently that God would send me a master who could lead me to an understanding of Him. That night I had what I have since called a vision. It was not a dream, nor was I awake. But suddenly I was on my knees, with my forehead touching the floor, bowing before my Master. I tried to see him, but I was unable to lift my head and saw only the hem of his garment. Keenly disappointed, I realized I was seeing Jesus in my vision. I rejected this Master, just as I rejected Christianity.

At that time my concepts of Christianity were vague. My parents claimed to be Protestants, but we neither went to church nor read the Bible. As a child I had gone to Sunday School but Christianity, as presented, lacked appeal for me. To my immature understanding, Jesus didn't appear to be a strong spiritual leader such as the world needed. When he was struck on one cheek, he turned the other. I decided I would never surrender that way to evil.

The next morning I remembered the vision vividly, remembered rejecting it, and still did. Years later I was to understand what I had rejected.

ॐ My academic studies in Holland and Indonesia were finished and I had graduated as a primary school teacher; but teaching school was not what I wanted to do. From early childhood I had taken dancing lessons. My older sister and I now wanted to teach modern dance and physical culture in Indonesia, and our parents sent us to Vienna to study.

Throughout all Asia, including Indonesia, dance often has a religious connotation; the dance patterns and symbolism are a way of expressing the highest ideas of Asian traditions and culture. But modern dance, portraying the ideas of the Western world, had captivated my thought. Isadora Duncan, Mary Wigman, Rosalia Chladek were projecting a message of new freedoms through the art of dance, and I wanted to bring this message to our young people.

While I was studying modern dance and gymnastics in Vienna, Hitler marched into Austria, and I saw the tragedies which had befallen the Jews; saw the devastating effects of Fascism; saw the poisoning of thought which overnight turned friends into enemies; saw how Jews, who had been self-assured artists and professors, were stripped overnight of their dignity and human worth and became nonpersons, committed suicide, and withered away in fear.

It was shattering to meet nice young Germans and find them unperturbed by the attacks and bloodshed in the streets and the vaunted destruction of a people, while at the same time they were reaching for spiritual truths. I remember asking one of them, "Why are you persecuting the Jews?" He answered that he didn't know the difference between a Jew and a non-Jew. It was a state policy. These words revealed to me the tragedy of a country under complete despotic control. I believed at that time, and I still believe, that every citizen is responsible for his nation's policies, whether they are good or bad. If a policy is evil, as in the case of Nazism, a whole nation is held responsible, and all the people pay the penalty.

The year of the *Anschluss,* my sister and I left Austria and went to Paris to continue our studies. In both Vienna and Paris we met pupils of many nations—Hungarians, Poles, French, English—and I came to the conclusion that we were all alike in our ideals. Our faces and clothes were different, we spoke different languages, but the thrust of our inward search was toward the goal of equality among people and a standard of universal good. And if you ask me what today's young people are searching for, I recognize the same goal, with this exception: today there exists a world community of youth seeking spiritual truths, and I believe that their love for mankind is leading them to universal answers.

When World War II broke out, France was hiding behind the Maginot Line, feeling certain the Nazis couldn't get through this barrier. But Paris wasn't the same any more. Everything was geared for war and many people left the capital for the country. My sister decided to remain in Paris but I went to Capri, overlooking the beautiful Blue Grotto, and stayed with Dutch friends for three months.

At that time fierce fighting on the Western front had not yet started, but there was no doubt it would and that nothing could divert it. I was torn apart by feelings of sorrow and rebellion. It seemed incredible that people would slaughter one another when they could spend their time improving this world and enjoying the earth together. I knew God is good, but in this turbulent time He seemed remote from life's practical realities. My question to myself and to God was: Why and what is evil? Europe held too many problems without answers.

My sister left Paris and I Capri, both returning to Bandung where we opened our school of contemporary dance. Here we were involved with many young people. Training in dance requires intelligence and is physically very demanding. I found that the stricter the discipline, the more the young people liked it; but it was self-discipline, not discipline imposed from the outside.

Pursuing further my spiritual search, I looked into the systems of mysticism. But I found I could not surrender my individual consciousness to an unknown power which I didn't know beforehand was fundamentally good and leading me to ultimate truth. I was told I was not open to the mystic faith.

I looked into the social world but found it a lie. I kept a diary and every night would write in it, "Everything today was a lie." You had to be polite to people whom you despised. When you tried to be honest, people attacked you. When you were hypocritical and went along with the crowd, they despised you. There was no standard of truth in this way of life.

While I was in this state of discontent and disenchantment, Hitler invaded Holland, and the Netherlands joined the Allies in their war against Germany, Italy, and Japan. When Holland fell, Indonesia, as its colony, was at war only theoretically, since Germany and Italy were too far away. Although the attack from Japan was long expected, for two years nothing happened. Then Japan invaded our shores and we became an occupied country.

This was a deeply moving time for me because I was caught between two different political viewpoints. One was the Dutch way of looking at the situation, which argued that Indonesia was under the rule of the Netherlands and consequently was expected to support the mother country. On the other side was the Indonesian point of view, which had been gathering strength, especially among the youth: that Indonesia should regain its national independence and be free at last of three hundred years of Dutch colonialism.

My parents were loyal to the Dutch viewpoint and expected the same patriotism from their daughters. But a question had lodged in my thought for a long time: Don't the Indonesians have a right to their national independence, their individual identity? To assume either attitude was treachery to those holding the other opinion.

So even though our nation was firmly under Japanese rule at that point in history, the political views of Dutch and Indonesian populations clashed violently. With the fiery zeal of youth, disregarding caution, my sister and I voiced our political opinions. Rumors spread. Several times we were arrested and put into prison for interrogation.

My first three days of imprisonment were spent in solitary confinement. There was nothing in the cell except a small board of wooden slats used in Indonesia for shower purposes. The window had been hammered shut, no light entered the cell, and I had no way of measuring time. Also during those three days I was not given any food.

But strangely, this imposed hunger made my thinking very acute. What helped me most was an Asian proverb: "Regard what men do to you as an act of God toward you; and whatever you do to men, as an act of yourself toward God."

I asked myself, 'Why has God done this to me?' I knew God is good, so there must be something in me that deserved this kind of treatment. Looking within myself for the reasons, I found many. I had been a deeply dissatisfied human being, but my most prominent fault was ingratitude for life. Ungrateful for the sunshine, I could see now what it meant to me. The beauty of the universe, the heavens, the trees, the grass—I hadn't thought of them as I went complainingly through life. I had not been grateful for the food and would often throw it away; now I had none.

Beginning to purify my heart and mind, I promised God I would be different. Then one night I saw it was futile to judge others because in reality all humanity was joined in a search for freedom and happiness. I decided that when released from prison I would devote my life to helping mankind find freedom from oppression. How to do this, I didn't know, but my dedication brought me close to God.

After three days my sister and I were put into the same cell under somewhat better conditions, and our Japanese interrogators began to demand that we give them information about people who were involved in political action. By this time I was so deep in meditation that I felt detached from world conflicts and no longer saw enemies anywhere. And because of this I believe my interrogators began to have compassion for us. They would come in the night and hand us some fruit or a piece of bread through the bars, and then rush away as if they didn't want the others to see their kindness.

But no matter how many questions our interrogators asked or how vehemently they shouted at us, we didn't give information about anyone we knew to be still in Java. After they read our report—which we confined to people who had escaped to Australia—the chief intelligence officer threw it back at us, saying, "We want information on people who have *not* gone to Australia." But somehow they never forced us. After several months' imprisonment, I told my sister that I felt purified to the extent that I was ready to go out into the world again. That same night we were released from prison.

When we returned home to our dancing school, we learned that many of our Dutch friends had been put into prison camps. The Japanese considered all Dutch Indonesians suspect and we were under constant surveillance. Again my sister and I were arrested, interrogated, and released. The peace and hope I had gained in the solitary prison cell during that first imprisonment became submerged in a turmoil of endless questioning: What am I to do?

One day while sitting with one of our assistants in the pavilion of our school, I heard a voice saying "Batavia," the name for Jakarta at that time. It was the still, small voice of Truth speaking to my consciousness, but it sounded so loud that I asked my assistant whether she had heard it; of course she hadn't.

From that moment I felt driven to leave Bandung and go to Jakarta, 100 miles distant. From many standpoints it was a difficult decision. I would have to leave my sister. Also we were an occupied country, and finding a place to live in the heavily populated capital city seemed impossible. Neither I nor my two assistants who had decided to accompany me had any friends there. For me to open a school of contemporary dance seemed unrealistic. But I had to obey that inward voice, and this is what I did. In this city of extreme unrest and uncertainty I rented a house and started my own school of dance. I shall always be grateful for my obedience to that inner urging, because it was in Jakarta that my spiritual mission in life eventually became clear to me.

Located near the coast of the Java Sea, the city just falls short of being a port, having a harbor to its north called Tandjung-priok. In a few more years it would be considerably expanded and emerge as one of the few international cities of Southeast Asia. But at that time it bore the marks of military occupation, and to me it had an atmosphere of foreboding. Our school was in our home, and we seldom ventured from it.

Besides running the school, I had a job teaching physical culture to a group of Indonesian artists. One day an artist told me he had been sent by his master to teach me the way to find God through mysticism. Although my former search into the mystic systems had not proved successful, I was still seeking to find truth. So while the man didn't impress me as spiritual, I was curious and agreed to let him teach me.

My first lessons were on meditation. He would ask me to think of a lily and of nothing else, and while I was sitting beside him meditating, unnatural thoughts assailed me. One day he gave me a present all wrapped up. He told me it was a drawing and asked me to hang it in my room and write underneath it the words, "I must pray." When I reached home and removed the wrappings, I saw it was a drawing of his face. I had been raised in a rather Puritan manner and this seemed an invasion of privacy. I disliked hanging the picture in my room, but did so.

Then one night soon afterward, just before falling asleep, I became dizzy. I felt my sense of place disappear, and from a corner of the room some fearful dark thing seemed to be approaching me. It looked like a monster, bearish and black, and I felt it wanted to overpower me. With all the mental effort I could command I said No to it, again and again, until it moved back and disappeared.

The next morning when I awakened and saw the picture of that man with my handwriting underneath it, I suddenly understood that he was trying to get control of my thinking and use my consciousness for his own purpose. This type of domination was a form of *guna guna*, as such practice of black magic is known in our part of the world. The drawing landed in the wastepaper basket, and I ended the lessons.

֍ The war was not yet over. I had just found a better location for my school and moved my furnishings into it when I was arrested again, this time by the military police.

Crowded into a tiny cell with seven other women, vermin crawling over everything, I came close to the mental breaking point, going through all the stages of despair, revulsion, self-pity, with one argument repeating itself: Give in. You have seen enough to know there is no justice on earth and no sense in trying to live a good life. Why not give up the effort and accept evil as fact? Or, let your mind go. Escape from reality, escape from consciousness. Without an ideal, I felt I couldn't endure, and oblivion was preferable to anguish.

Suddenly I had a mental picture of what my future would be if I didn't resist the temptation to go insane. At that moment, deciding never to admit that evil is stronger than good, I regained my poise. Removed from the Jakarta prison, I was transferred to one in Bandung, and shortly thereafter was released.

Back home in Jakarta, the father of one of my pupils told me he had seen me when I was under police guard during the trip to Bandung. Then he asked me if I had read *Science and Health with Key to the Scriptures* by Mary Baker Eddy. Though I thought I had exhausted all books on metaphysics, this one was unknown to me. I borrowed the book.

At first there were many parts of it I didn't understand, and other parts with which I disagreed altogether. But halfway through the book, when I came to the chapter "Science of Being," where Mrs. Eddy makes the distinction between Jesus and the Christ, everything suddenly fell into place.

For the first time I understood that Jesus was the human man, but Christ was the divine Truth—Christ was the way Jesus thought, lived, and taught! And this Christ, Truth, was the savior of mankind from all its troubles. To follow Christ meant I was to know this Truth as Jesus did, and to let it guide my life.

I glimpsed what Paul meant when he said to the early Christians: "Let this mind be in you, which was also in Christ Jesus." [1] And I learned that it was what Paul called "the mind of Christ" that enabled the early followers of Jesus to heal for 300 years after the Master's advent on earth—until Jesus' simple concepts of truth became lost in the complexities of ritualism, and the letter of the law obscured the grace and spirit of Christ-healing.

[1] Philippians 2:5.

The many questions I had had about God and man began to crystallize in my thought. Answers of truth for which I had been searching most of my life began to appear—answers to the problems of what and why is evil, and how evil is to be overcome in man and the world.

Not mere faith in the person of Jesus, and not even mere faith in God—although faith was needed—enabled the early Christians to heal the sick, cleanse the sinners and lepers, raise the dead, and advance the new theology of love, health, and brotherhood. A more spiritual understanding of God and man than had ever before been presented under the religious concept of one God was required. The divine truth of man's original, divine nature as the child of God was the truth which made man free.

I found myself agreeing with the book's logic: that Jesus knew man to be God's spiritual manifestation of Himself; knew man not as a sinner, although he appeared physically to be so; knew man not as sick, although he appeared physically to be so; knew man not as deprived, although he appeared physically to be so.

Jesus knew man as God had created him, the perfect child of God. Multitudes who came within the compass of the Master's thought stood bathed in the radiant light of their Godlike selfhood. In this light the Christ blessed them. Blessing them, it healed them. And in healing them, it taught them eternal truths about themselves and God, inspired them to lay down their physically based lives for the spiritual life in Christ, and led them to join the great army of Christian healers.

Was this healing Christ power of good over evil possible to man in this age? Was this consciousness possible to me, as this book claimed? As I continued to read, there followed many unforgettable and holy moments in which I knew I was the child of God and knew I could behold others in their spiritual identities as God's children. In humility I had begun to open the door of my thought to the understanding of the Christ.

In *Science and Health* I read these words: "The advent of Jesus of Nazareth marked the first century of the Christian era, but the Christ is without beginning of years or end of days. Throughout all generations both before and after the Christian era, the Christ, as the spiritual idea—the reflection of God—has come with some measure of power and grace to all prepared to receive Christ, Truth." [2]

Gradually I grasped the idea that God, the Principle of the power of Christ, which Jesus understood, did not belong exclusively to him, any more than the principle of music belonged exclusively to Mozart or the science of higher mathematics belonged exclusively to Einstein. It was possible, through this book, to learn the Principle of Christ, Truth, and when I obeyed God's laws and identified myself with Christ as the nature of my own thought, I could perform cures and help oppressed humanity.

Even a glimpse of these truths at that first reading seemed like such a great revelation that I rushed out of the room and announced to my assistants, "I have found the Truth." I had indeed found the answer to good and evil. I had found the way to my spiritual identity.

My assistants went to the secondhand book stalls and bought several copies of *Science and Health,* and we began to study this beautiful book every day. We thought it was an old book, something forgotten. But whatever we understood seemed too vital, too important, to be lost to the world, and we felt that many could be helped by it. We decided to start a Christian Science church. We didn't know that Mrs. Eddy had already founded a worldwide movement, or that in 1925 a Christian Science church had been established in Jakarta, and others in Bandung and Surabaja earlier than that.

Then I remembered the schoolgirl vision of long ago. God had indeed answered my prayer that night, and I had seen my Master. But it was not a person I was to follow. My Master was the universal Christ, and to follow Jesus meant to enter the Christ ministry, a calling that exceeded anything I had ever imagined. Jesus' greatness became magnified to my view as I understood why he could offer his other cheek to men. No human blow had the power to touch his Christly thought or turn him from his sublime destiny.

Today the name of Mary Baker Eddy fills me with an inward surge of awe. All I know of the Christ, Truth, and of the laws of the harmonious government of man and the universe has come

[2] *Science and Health with Key to the Scriptures,* p. 333.

from her books which opened the Bible to me in its spiritual splendor and significance. Mrs. Eddy was a great prophet and the day will come when mankind will acknowledge more widely her contribution to the spiritual freedoms of the age.

ᔥ After World War II ended, the Japanese left our country and we resumed our normal activities. But Indonesia, as it was soon to be called, would never be the same as it had been before the war. The drive for national independence was advancing. A bloody revolution began and Indonesians fought with everything they had. In retaliation the Dutch wiped out whole villages. But the revolutionaries pressed on, with the young Sukarno emerging as the powerful leader of our country.

Convinced that many of my countrymen were searching for the freedoms inherent in the teachings of Christian Science, I met with other Christian Scientists in Jakarta and we decided to reorganize the Christian Science church in our city. Although we later moved to other quarters, the first Sunday services were held in May 1946 in the big hall of my dancing school. We started at the very beginning, and the process was slow because we had much to learn. Around us the storm of revolution continued to rage. Curfews were imposed, and we couldn't go out at night. But all through the years of Indonesia's struggle for national sovereignty our church stood, endured, and grew.

After their release from prison camps in 1945, most of the Dutch Christian Scientists left Indonesia. Later, when the Indonesian people revolted against the Dutch government and Sukarno began his political power struggle, still more Dutch Scientists left the country, further reducing our membership rolls. By the time all the Dutch were finally expelled from the country, the church had become sufficiently Indonesian to carry on. Having by now renounced my Dutch citizenship and accepted Indonesian nationality, I could stay, and gradually more Indonesians began to come to our church services.

There lived in Jakarta and its environs many Indonesians not practicing any religion. Among these were suffering and discontented people, and when some of them heard that Christian Science heals, they came to the church. These first Indonesians who came to our church services knew very little about our religion. For an Indonesian steeped in Asian religions and philosophies, the transition to a workable understanding of Christian Science is usually a difficult one. But when they read the books of Christian Science and when their diseases were healed and their problems solved, they became consecrated students and joined the church.

Once, after a church service, a young man who was in need of Christian Science treatment, which is prayer, approached me. He looked very sick and said that his mother, not a Christian Scientist, had sent him to a doctor who recommended an operation. The young man considered himself a Christian Scientist and didn't want an operation, but he had not been able to heal himself through his own prayers.

When I asked him, "Do you accept the basic message of our religion that now you are the child of God?" the young man said he accepted the message in principle but that now he was very sick. Of course I had compassion for his suffering. But I pointed out to him that his belief that he was the perfect child of God and his belief that he was also sick were contradictions. Now what *did* he believe? Using the metaphysical logic of Christian Science, I asked him, "Were you the child of God yesterday?" He answered, "Yes." "Will you be the child of God tomorrow?" "Yes," he answered. "Then, if you were the child of God yesterday and well, and will be the child of God tomorrow and perfect, can you, as the child of God, be sick *now?*"

The light of this metaphysical truth broke through, and the fear of his disease left him. The next day when he awakened he was completely healed. The law of Christian Science Mind-healing had operated successfully for him. Then he understood that sickness is a mistake of thought, just as two times two equals five is an error of thought. When thought is corrected, then health appears in the body.

&ᐧ When I became a Christian Scientist, I knew that the practice of this religion was going to be my work for the rest of my life. While realizing that the vast majority of Indonesians would remain faithful to the teachings of Islam, I knew there were others—especially young people who were uncommitted to any faith—whom Christian Science could reach, and I wanted to help them.

When more people turned to me for Christian Science

treatment and were healed—of blood poisoning, brain concussion, pneumonia, poverty, and other maladies—I gave up my school of dance and realized a goal for which I had long been preparing. I entered the public practice of Christian Science. After nine years of much work in church and further growth of my practice, I was made a Christian Science teacher.

As a practitioner, I was dedicated to the healing and spiritual development of my patients. Now, as a teacher, my work took on an added dimension. My pupils were to be taught in a systematic manner, from the Christian Science textbook, *Science and Health*, the metaphysics of God's universal laws which would prepare them for the healing work of Christian Science and eventually lead many of them also into the public practice.

&✒ National sovereignty did not instantly solve Indonesia's problems. The nation needed economic, military, and technological help from the great powers, and under Sukarno's leadership Indonesia was moving toward Communism.

During this period I came into contact with young people who despaired of the economic and educational limitations of their life and believed that Communism was the only answer. The Communists infiltrating our country were organizing youth groups and indoctrinating them in dialectical materialism.

One young man told me that young people were turning to Communism because of impatience. Indonesia needed change, and only violence would bring quick reforms. Religion, they said, was a myth, causing people to be resigned to injustices rather than fight them.

It was understandable that these young people wanted to improve their own and their country's circumstances. But I disagreed with them that Communism would lead to equality of justice for themselves or their country. What they were proposing would result in a shifting of power, whereby one group of people rises to the top while the other group is oppressed, so that eventually much the same situation emerges—the dominating and the dominated. Perhaps along the way some of these young people would gain a better education and material comforts. But ultimately Communism would mean giving up their primary freedom: to think for themselves.

The real revolution is a spiritual one, as I have had to learn.

The great conquest is to gain dominion, not over someone else, but over one's own self-centered materialism. This is the pure idealism Jesus and other spiritual leaders have taught. And its practicality is seen as it produces better men. Christian Science could show the youth of our country how to be truly free and to possess the courage to fulfill their Christly mission, no matter what the cost. In that spirit they would be empowered to prove God's promise in their lifetime and contribute meaningfully to the progress of the Indonesian people.

The Republic of Indonesia is established on five basic principles: belief in God, national consciousness, humanism, social justice, and sovereignty of the people. Religious freedom in Indonesia enables the Church of Christ, Scientist to carry on services. Membership is growing gradually, but the Sunday School is full.

It has been said that if all Christian churches withdrew from Asia, they would not leave more than a dent on the consciousness of the Asian people. But there is undoubtedly renewed interest in the Christ teaching all over the world including Asia, and while Christendom today may be stripped of much of its formalism and ritualism, this only serves to let the vital Christ message come through more clearly and be better understood.

For my countrymen and others, Christian Science presents a universal concept of Christianity. It says that whether we are of the East or the West, God has given to every man the full measure of his divine heritage. No man on earth can give us anything we don't already have by divine right, and no man on earth can deprive us of anything that is ours by divine right. But each of us has to take possession of our birthright as a child of God, and think and act like one.

Indonesia is a country of 4,000 islands strung like a magnificent girdle of jewels across the Indian Ocean, spanning the earth in a breadth as wide as the United States. It slumbered for a long time, lacking national independence and the freedom of its people to forge ahead. But now it is awakening and discovering its intellectual and physical resources. Indonesia has a great contribution to make to the world. In natural resources, it stands third among the world's nations. And I believe that spiritually and practically, there is the same enormous potential of development in its people.

Mrs. Deborah Appleton Huebsch addressing the International
Youth Meeting at the Christian Science Center in Boston, 1974. Mo
than 30 countries were represented.

# YOUTH
# AND
# RELIGION

## ॐ Deborah Appleton Huebsch

WITH CHRISTIAN SCIENCE YOUTH ACTIVITIES SECTION IN
BOSTON

ॐ One of the greatest things I have learned in Christian
Science is the difference between sensuous, human love and
divine Love.

Human love, I have found, can be treacherous; it can be
worship and adulation; it can be difficult to control; it is subject
to outward conditions and circumstances. Human love sometimes can bless, but by itself it can never heal. On the other
hand, divine Love always blesses and always heals, and it never
fails.

My yearning for human love failed me, resulted in frustration,
broken relationships, bitterness, hatred, depression, drugs, and
suicidal urges. My finding of divine Love through Christian
Science freed and regenerated me, showed me direction and
purpose, and the Christian Science church opened channels for
me to help mankind.

When The First Church of Christ, Scientist, in Boston, appointed me representative of its College Organization Section for the Southeast area of the United States, I visited annually for two years about 125 campuses in nine states. I met with university officials and chaplains and spoke with hundreds of college students and other young people in Christian Science branch churches. I knew the campus scene well. Only a few years back I had been a student at the University of California at Berkeley, later at the University of Oregon, and also a faculty member at Oregon.

On the campuses I visited I found most students apathetic about traditional religion. They felt a great discrepancy between what was preached to them about love and what they saw as being practiced. They were not being taken into the structure of the churches' activities nor were their energies utilized for healing mankind's problems. I found that these students had a yearning to help the world, a yearning to love it and be loved by it, and many of them found no way of fulfilling such longings.

So often I found students involved in promiscuity, drugs, communal living—all in a desire, it seemed to me, to find this thing called real love. I heard a Governor's Council on Drugs in Tennessee report that much of the drug usage could be attributed to a lack of love in the family or among peers. It is often the unfulfilled desire for love that motivates promiscuity and the craving for drugs. But students soon discover that these substitutes for real love are empty and meaningless. Finding themselves in a dead-end situation, many of them drop out. Others turn to hard drugs. Yet, despite the disillusionment, youth's idealism persists. I learned that while orthodox church attendance was decreasing, college religion classes were filled with students who wanted to learn about the varieties of religious experience in the hope that they might find a religion that would give them answers.

I don't mean to leave the impression that religious organizations in the traditional sense have disappeared from American campus life. Societies representing a variety of faiths function at most universities and colleges. I found many Christian Science students doing important healing work for themselves and their friends, curing nervous breakdowns, malignancy, and other ills, as well as drug addiction. Many other young people wanted to know the fundamentals of Christian Science and how it heals. As one whose life offers abundant proof of this religion's healing power, I was able to furnish satisfying answers to such questions out of my own experience.

ᢒᴥ From early childhood to the age of twenty, I was driven by a yearning for love. When I was five years old my parents were divorced. When my mother left our home never to return, I was raised by my father. We had a series of perhaps fifteen housekeepers who came and went until I was twelve, and by that time I had been given most of the cooking and housework to do. Though my father did his best to care for my sister and me, his efforts were woefully inadequate. I became increasingly bitter and resented the absence of a mother to whom I could turn and confide my hopes for a career in the arts. My father understood nothing of this desire and did everything he could to discourage me. When it was time for me to go to college, I chose a school far from home. I wrote seldom to my family, feeling no bond between my father or my sister and me. I hated them and believed they hated me. Going home was always a dreaded experience.

After three years of college, I became very depressed. I was broken up over a relationship I had with a man I loved. I was doing poorly in my courses, drank heavily, used several kinds of medication, and began taking Speed and sleeping pills in increasing doses. At times I had memory lapses, and I began having suicidal urges. I had very few friends and felt terribly alone. My life was devoid of purpose. Unable to face a day without the stimulus of Speed, I became more and more locked into a dependency. After a sleepless night, I could see only two choices open to me. One was suicide; the other, hard drugs.

My chosen career was ballet, and I had often found the ballet studio a refuge from the storm. So in desperation I went to the studio, hoping to find someone to comfort me. It was early, and there was no one around. In terror, frustration, and loneliness, I stood in the hall, crying bitterly. The director of the ballet company came out of her office to see what was wrong. Inviting me in, she asked what was troubling me. Out poured the whole story of frustration, fear, and depression. After listening quietly, she said, "I think what you need is religion."

Since I had left an orthodox church several years before, feeling that religion had no real answers and that there could not be a God because there was so little evidence of law and love in the world, my response to her remark was, "I don't need religion, I need some practical help." She pushed a book across her desk and told me I might enjoy reading it. This book was *Science and Health* by Mary Baker Eddy. Not wanting to offend her, I took it.

But I was insulted by this offer of religion, which to me seemed a crutch for people too weak to stand on their own feet. In anger I walked down the street and into the nearest bar, slammed the book on the bar, and ordered a drink. As I stood there, it occurred to me I could help this woman by pointing out to her that religion, especially Christian Science, had no practical value. Then I thought, How can I do that when I don't know anything about Christian Science except that Christian Scientists "don't believe in doctors"? I decided to read the book as a source of some good ammunition.

It didn't make much sense to me as I read, and much of it antagonized me, except for one phrase that contained the most beautiful words I had ever read: ". . . Love supports the struggling heart until it ceases to sigh over the world and begins to unfold its wings for heaven." [1]

But this didn't alter my determination to refute Christian Science. I went to the ballet director's office several times a week to point out to her the fallacies of Christian Science, asking questions in a spirit of belligerence, convinced that each question would knock the props out from under her religion. She answered each question satisfactorily, and her great love neutralized my venom. After several weeks I began to ask

[1] *Science and Health*, p. 57.

questions that had really been perplexing me and had not been answered by my previous religion: Who am I? What is my identity? Where am I going? As she patiently answered my questions, I felt a growing sense of purpose, a reason for being. My feelings of loneliness and fear began to abate.

One day I had a healing. I was running down the stairs of my apartment building and scraped my hand severely on the brick wall. I remember standing on the stairs, looking at my bleeding and bruised hand and thinking: Of course Christian Science doesn't work, but if it did work and I were a Christian Scientist, what would I do right now? Then I thought: If I were a Christian Scientist, it would be simple, because Christian Science teaches that God is good and is all-presence, so all has to be good, and there is nothing outside of good. That was all there was to it. When I looked at my hand there wasn't a mark on it. I was awestruck because I didn't understand what had happened. But for the first time in my life I felt the presence of something greater than myself and knew that somehow I could learn to utilize this healing power.

Continuing to read *Science and Health*, I saw clearly that its author had compassion for mankind's yearnings and search for truth when she wrote: ". . . man, left to the hypotheses of material sense unexplained by Science, is as the wandering comet or the desolate star—'a weary searcher for a viewless home.' " [2] Because Mrs. Eddy desired to help mankind in their search, God revealed His answers to her, and she gave these answers to the world. I began to see my life as immortal because it always was inseparable from God; in fact, God Himself was my life and I was His image and likeness. I now understood what Christ Jesus meant when he said, "Before Abraham was, I am," [3] and what Paul meant when he said, "Your life is hid with Christ in God." [4] With the realization of my eternal identity as a child of God, I rose in the dignity of man's immortal selfhood.

By the time I had finished reading the book, I was a Christian Scientist. I couldn't remember the last time I had taken Speed.

[2] *Science and Health*, p. 121.
[3] John 8:58.
[4] Colossians 3:3.

The need had left, and I was free. There were no struggles, no anxieties. As cynicism and bitterness dropped away, I was transformed. This Christian Scientist who had given me *Science and Health* had literally loved the hell out of me.

The first Christian Science service I attended was in the branch church in the Haight-Ashbury section of San Francisco, an area where drugs were openly sold and hippies thronged the streets. At my first Wednesday evening testimonial meeting I felt a little uncomfortable because the things I had associated with church were not visible, such as an altar, vestments, choir. At the same time I felt a wonderful sense of spirituality and warmth. The sincerity which the people expressed in relating their gratitude for their healings was very moving to me.

After the service I was rushing out when a little lady came running after me and said, "We're so glad you came tonight." In my embarrassment of not knowing what to say, I remarked about a flower she had pinned on her coat. "What a lovely gardenia," I said. She took the flower off her coat, pinned it on me, and said, "I hope we'll see you again." I learned a great deal about the Christian Science church that night. The love expressed to me seemed overwhelming, and even now I often ask myself, Am I giving my gardenias as freely as this lady gave hers? I know of several young people on drugs who were healed while attending services at this Christian Science branch church.

ॐ  From then on Christian Science became a deep study. I learned that it is the Science of Life embracing every aspect of man and the universe: the sciences, art, music, business, law, astronomy, communication, industry. It is the Science that harmonizes earth and sea and sky. All this had to be grasped in the vastness of this great religion. But I had to start with the simple understanding of it, and divine Love was the foundation stone.

The next important lesson I learned was the meaning of my relationship to God and therefore my relation to man. God, I came to understand, was not only the Father but also the Mother of creation, not as two but as one infinite Being, the creator of all. Forever at one with my creator, in reality I was never without a spiritual Mother; and since I was God's child, I could never be separated from the family of man any more than I could be separated here on earth from the law of gravity.

I wanted the freedom and joy that my newfound religion presented; I wanted to be loved and loving, to belong, to be respected. I wanted security; I wanted a sense of family. As I came to see that these attributes were mine as a gift from my Father-Mother God, who cared for me wherever I was, I met a family in the branch church who took me into their home life; and for the first time I felt loved by a family, felt the warmth and joy of a close, sharing relationship.

At this point it was necessary for me to spend a summer at home and I knew I had to resolve the hatred I still entertained for my family. I decided I would find something I could appreciate in my father, and this was difficult because he seemed opposed to everything I cared for. I started with a little thing: he has excellent taste in art. So every time I talked with him or thought about him, instead of letting the blind hatred sweep over me, I would say to myself, "Remember, he has wonderful taste in art, he has spiritual discernment of good." Through the summer months I found that I could add other good qualities, such as intelligence, kindness, consideration, until by the end of the summer I could see the whole man as the child of God, and there was not a vestige of hatred left. I could put my arms around him and say, "Daddy, I love you," something I hadn't been able to do before. We have had a marvelous relationship ever since. I appreciate what he is doing and he appreciates what I am doing.

For many years I had tried to love him because he was my father and I owed him a certain amount of respect and love, but all I experienced was rejection and alienation. When I learned how to utilize the healing power of divine Love, the emotion of hate was washed away, and the shortcomings and foibles were replaced by man's innate nobility. That summer the breach between my sister and me was healed also.

As a psychology major, I had begun work in a psychiatric

ward, but I became disillusioned by the inadequacy of the treatment given to help people. It was at this point that I became interested in Christian Science, and discovering that this science offered to me a better way of helping others, I saw I had to rechart my directions. I left school and spent a year and a half studying Mrs. Eddy's writings and the Bible, and learned all I could about Christian Science. Then I returned to Berkeley and finished my studies in another field—the theater.

᭞ Around graduation time I met a young man who was a Christian Scientist and we became engaged. I was learning how to love purely, openly, and my love was based on my understanding of God. This was so different from the previous relationship, in which I had experienced all the degradation, selfishness, and rejection of human, sensual love and had felt deeply a sense of failure in love. This new, spiritually based love was a fulfillment of all that the other relationship was not. In it I found compassion, kindness, unselfishness, and faith. We were married and had a very happy, growing experience. We moved to Oregon, where I entered the University of Oregon, received my Master's degree, and became a faculty member; my husband was working there for his Ph.D. We became active members in a Christian Science branch church.

After a year my husband suddenly became sick, was taken to a Christian Science sanatorium, and passed on. Again I was plunged into deep waters and faced with the searing question: Had Christian Science failed me? During those few days following my husband's passing, I began to grasp what Christian Science is—the full implication of it as the reality of all being.

The subject of the Lesson-Sermon that week was "Christ Jesus," and it included the story of Jesus raising Lazarus. I thought a great deal about that story, asking myself the question: Why did Jesus raise Lazarus from the dead? Was it because Jesus needed proof of life? No. Jesus knew and proved that life is eternal, so he didn't need the physical proof to convince him. Did Lazarus need the proof? No. Lazarus' life was going on, so he already knew life as eternal. But the people who were standing around were the ones who needed proof, and Jesus gave it to them.

I applied this story to my own situation. Although my husband was no longer at my side, did I doubt—did I need physical proof—that man's life is eternal? No, I really believed what Jesus said. Did my husband need proof that life is eternal? No, for in reality he was still alive in God's spiritual universe. Therefore I did not need to see activity come back to a physical body to convince me that life is eternal.

I thought about what Jesus said when he raised Lazarus: "Lazarus, come forth." And I said mentally, "Dave, go forward. I am not going to hold on to you." Then Jesus said, "Loose him and let him go." And I received the command, "Let go of the concept that man, the son of God, lives or dies in a material body. In reality, man's life has always been in God, and so was never limited to matter." That was my healing. I saw that the affection, the joys, the hopes we shared were still alive because their source was God. I understood the immortality of divine Love, because for Love to cease would be for God to cease. Therefore there is no death in Love.

I was able to go back to Oregon and complete another year on the faculty, living in the apartment Dave and I had shared. With the help of the church members, I was able to prove what Jesus said, "He that believeth on me shall never see death." I didn't see death, and neither did the church members, whose support and love were an enormous help in sustaining me through those months. Church became to me an expression of divine Love meeting the human need, a sense of belonging, of having a spiritual family.

The lessons I learned and the spiritual insights I gained through this experience brought me to the point where I was, to an extent, able to rise above materialistic desires and ambitions, and prepared me for the public practice of Christian Science which I in due course entered. The rock-bottom proof that the king of terrors has no power, and that no material circumstance could interfere with my joy and productivity, really convinced me that Christian Science is the Way; and I hoped to bring this conviction and proof to others.

To those who need healing, Christian Science offers more than physical relief. It does that, but it also offers a way of peace and joy and a full salvation. It offers freedom from pressures and fears of every kind. Fear and bitterness often appear as disease, and in Christian Science healing, when the cause of disease is destroyed, the body becomes free.

Let us suppose that a man has an ulcer which the doctors have told him is caused by anxiety. He might take tranquilizers to quiet the pain, but it is quite clear that unless his anxiety is removed, the ulcer will not be healed. Christian Science destroys the predisposing cause of disease not merely by treating physical symptoms but by dispelling the anxiety with the confidence-inspiring consciousness of God as Love, the divine Mind, the All-in-all of man.

Everyone has before him the possibility of learning to heal through Christian Science because every man, woman, and child is in reality God's child, His perfect, spiritual expression. The moment one glimpses his God-given heritage and learns even the simplest rules of the Science of Christianity, he is able to utilize this knowledge to free himself and others from limitation and sickness.

᭞᭞ From my first encounter with the ballet company director who introduced me to Christian Science, and on through all the subsequent experiences I have told about here, I had been on the receiving end of Church. I decided the time had come for me to be on the giving end. So I wrote to The Mother Church, The First Church of Christ, Scientist, in Boston, and asked for employment. I also began setting aside an evening a week for public practice. At the conclusion of my contract with the University of Oregon, I came to Boston and was given a job in the College Organization Section of the Youth Division of The Mother Church. Since then I have corresponded with college students all over the world (there are approximately 500 Christian Science College Organizations). I have given talks at college campuses and to many other young people in Christian Science branch churches, and have coordinated and addressed Christian Science regional youth meetings throughout the world. During this activity, I have continued in the healing practice.

If there is one major idea that the Christian Science church offers young people, it is the understanding of the nature of divine Love's healing power, the understanding that helps to shape the destiny of the individual, the church, and the world. Divine, impartial, and universal Love wipes out racial discrimination, educational snobbery, and social injustice. When we base our lives on divine Love, then our lives will furnish proof of healing and spiritual power.

Many denominational churches are dying because they rejected the qualities of youthfulness expressed by their members whatever their age, and the reach for progress has been discouraged. One of the most important motivations in young people today is their basic desire to see progress for all mankind. Christian Science provides a practical channel for their idealism.

੨● The desire for progress and healing, and its fulfillment, are two different things. As a graphic illustration, let us imagine that we have a solvent that will dissolve any substance on earth. At the same time we have a substance that needs to be dissolved. No matter how powerful the solvent is, it cannot act on the substance until the solvent is applied. A dynamic, vital church isn't limited to theories about progress and change but utilizes the solvent of divine Love to act upon humanity's problems. Youth's qualities possess the potency to help bring this about.

In a world crying for spiritual progress—in government, law, politics, business, military organizations—youthful freshness, vigor, and vision are what will make significant changes. Patience and persistence are needed, but even a single life dedicated to the universal Principle, Love, can effect a lasting change for good. Jesus' life is still revolutionizing the world.

The most valuable, the most practical contribution young people can make to mankind is Christian Science healing; and increasing numbers of them in many nations are studying the textbooks, *Science and Health* and the Bible, in order to reach out with love to others and learn how to become effective healers.

The healing work in Christian Science is a great discipline, demanding purity of thought and action. When young people break the moral law, they can be healed in Christian Science because its Principle is universal Love, which excludes no one. But these young people can heal others only as their own lives are purified. Through immorality and sensualism, their spiritual light has become shadowed and Christ's healing power doesn't shine through. If young people's mission is to bring healing to the world, what alternative do they have but to obey the moral and spiritual laws of life?

ঌ When I really wanted to let God's will, and not mine, be done, and to live the kind of unselfish Christianity that Christ Jesus taught and practiced, more and more people came to me for help. I had to learn to be ready at any hour of any day or night. I needed to be able to give help when help was needed. Then, without my seeking it in any way, a wonderful friendship with a man came into my life. Our companionship developed and this man became my husband. With this marriage has come a boundless sense of love, of support, of courage, of balance, which I feel is very good and has given each of us a greater freedom to fulfill our destinies as children of God.

Youth's important role in the world today is well understood by leaders in politics, business, education, government, the arts, the sciences, and the church. All of these fields are beckoning to young people to contribute their enthusiasm and idealism in behalf of reform and progress.

Many years ago, in an address to the Christian Scientists, Mrs. Eddy said: "Beloved children, the world has need of you —and more as children than as men and women: it needs your innocence, unselfishness, faithful affection, uncontaminated lives. You need also to watch, and pray that you preserve these virtues unstained, and lose them not through contact with the world. What grander ambition is there than to maintain in yourself what Jesus loved, and to know that your example, more than words, makes morals for mankind!" [5]

[5] *Miscellaneous Writings*, p. 110.

Howard Palfrey Jones (at left) after his swearing-in ceremony as Unit
States Ambassador to Indonesia being congratulated by Secretary of
State John Foster Dulles.

# THE LIFE OF
# AN AMERICAN
# DIPLOMAT

## ৯ Howard Palfrey Jones

FORMER AMBASSADOR TO INDONESIA

৯ The event that made the greatest impression on me as a boy and influenced the course of my life was my mother's dramatic healing of tuberculosis through Christian Science. My earliest memories of my mother are always of her in bed or sitting in a wheelchair. The day came when the doctors said she was in the last stages of the disease and wouldn't live more than two months. At that moment someone recommended Christian Science. Only five years old, I accompanied her to the home of a Christian Science practitioner, where she had to be helped up the stairs. An hour later I saw her walk out of the practitioner's office on her own power. In two weeks she was completely healed. Our family became Christian Scientists and joined the Christian Science church. Mother became a Christian Science practitioner, healing and helping many people. When I was eighteen years of age I took class instruction from a Christian Science teacher—teachings which committed me to follow the words and works of the Master, who said: "He that believeth on me, the works that I do shall he do also; and greater works than these shall he do." [1]

Consequently, as I moved forward into professional life, I knew that the power of prayer was equal to any emergency and would solve any problem with which I was confronted. Christian Science has been a way of life, a way of thought that influenced everything I have done. I have made many directional changes in my life, all of them in response to Truth's still small voice within me. The power of God was not something one theorized about but actually applied in facing a crisis or working out a solution to a problem, whether physical, financial, political, or situational. As the years unfolded and my life as a diplomat brought me into decision-making roles in Europe and Asia, I came to understand that among the "greater works" Jesus spoke of were collective ones—the healing of the nations.

᠑ At 24, I was sent out to be managing editor of a Scripps-Howard newspaper in Evansville, Indiana. Being a crusader and reformer at heart, my philosophy coincided with that of the publishers, who believed that the role of the press was to promote the cause of reform and progress.

The Ku Klux Klan, representing one of the most vicious forms of American racism, bigotry, and anti-Semitism at the time held a dominant position in Evansville. Its members were burning crosses in the hills, destroying statues in front of Roman Catholic churches, and boycotting Jewish stores. This was during Prohibition, when rum-running was one of the biggest businesses in the area. The newspaper discovered that the Klan had a tie-up with rum-running, gambling, and prostitution; also that the Klan had gained control of nearly all the law-enforcement machinery in county and state by having a Klansman in every important agency post. Behind a facade of virtue and 100 percent Americanism was rot and corruption.

For months the Scripps-Howard organization debated whether or not to attack the powerful Klan. Finally a decision was made to run an editorial on the front page exposing the Klan—eight forceful columns across the top of the page. The

[1] John 14:12.

paper had been made up and the front page was on press when my phone rang. "This is the Grand Kleagle of the Ku Klux Klan," the voice said. "You have now in type in your composing room an editorial attacking the Klan. I warn you, don't publish that editorial. If you do, you'll regret it."

The newspaper's publisher and editor was out of town, so the decision rested with me. I was familiar with Mary Baker Eddy's words, "When the press is gagged, liberty is besieged." [2] So I said to the Grand Kleagle, "Thank you very much for your call, but that editorial will run."

The editorial ran. That night the Klan burned fiery crosses. Next day, under Klan pressure, almost half of the paper's advertisers canceled their advertising contracts and a third of the subscribers canceled their subscriptions. The Klan was engaged in a major campaign to drive the paper out of business. Even my getting home safely at night became a question, since the Klan's method was to beat up people who opposed them. But I had no fear, nor did my young wife who had been raised in Christian Science. We knew that truth coincides with the power of God; therefore truth has its own protection. I was not harmed.

Within a year the newspaper not only had won the battle with the Klan but had become the leading newspaper in Evansville. Most of the subscribers came back. Advertisers renewed their contracts. People had confidence in the paper. By this time most of the Klan leaders had been caught or left town.

Surely all right-minded persons will agree with Milton's perception of the power of Truth when he wrote: "Let Truth and Falsity grapple; whoever knew Truth put to the worse, in a free and open encounter?"

&ell; At this point the University of Michigan invited me to teach a journalism course. I accepted the offer and also did postgraduate work at the University. Following this, I became editor-in-chief of a chain of nine small newspapers in Michigan. The papers successfully campaigned for the city-manager plan of municipal government, and to some extent contributed to the elimination of corrupt government in the communities where the papers operated.

[2] *Miscellaneous Writings*, p. 274.

After about two years, not satisfied that I had enough education and feeling that I was writing with seeming authority on subjects about which I knew very little, I made the decision to sell my interest in the newspapers and go back to school. At New York City's Columbia University I did postgraduate work in public law, constitutional law, and public finance, preparing myself for a career that would eventually involve the guardianship of public monies in the United States and many other nations.

I had a family to support—we had a little daughter—so I had to work while studying at Columbia. I took on many interesting jobs, one of which was writing for the United Press, then as now a leading newspaper wire service. But my most important job was Director of Public Relations for the National Municipal League, a research and educational organization whose purpose was improvement of state and local governments in the United States. Soon I was acting as consultant for municipalities and states on the drafting of basic laws, city charters, state laws, and home-rule laws for cities, as well as civil service legislation and recommendations to the New York State Constitutional Convention.

Considered a specialist in my field by now, I was named Director of Research for the New York State Commission on Revision of Tax Laws. This was during the Depression, when government revenues decreased because people couldn't pay their taxes, while the demands for government expenditures increased because of the needs for unemployment relief. Government at all levels was coping with a desperate economic situation.

One day I received a telephone call from Governor Herbert Lehman asking me to come to Albany. "Don't talk to anybody or tell anyone you are coming up, because this is a very confidential matter," said the Governor. The purpose of the Governor's call was to offer me the job of New York State Civil Service Commissioner. The Democratic and Republican machines had worked out a bipartisan deal and had agreed to place their man in the position of New York State Civil Service Commissioner. The New York State Constitution required that the job be filled on the basis of merit.

"If I appoint you," the Governor said, "you are going to have both political machines against you, and your nomination will be attacked. If there is anything in your past life that you wouldn't want to appear on the front page of newspapers, don't for a moment think of accepting the job." I accepted the job.

The Court of Appeals had recently mandated the government of New York State to extend its civil service. So far Buffalo and New York City were the only municipalities in the entire state that had civil service, and the Governor wanted me to take on the job of bringing it into all the other 4,000 municipalities. He needed a man, he said, who understood municipal relations and was thoroughly familiar with civil service law and administration; I was able to satisfy these requirements, visiting almost every county in the state. As civil service jobs became available to them, thousands of people went back to work, unemployment relief rolls decreased, and more people were able to pay their taxes.

&» Just about the time the job of bringing civil service into New York State's municipalities was completed, the Second World War came along. I had been a reserve officer and was called into service as a major. The Army wanted me for military government, and my first job was to teach public administration at the famous Charlottesville School of Military Government at the University of Virginia. I wasn't convinced that this was to be my role in the war, so after one semester I asked to be sent overseas. Soon I was assigned to General Eisenhower's staff as head of public finance for Supreme Headquarters' mission to Belgium, and I went to London to work with the Belgian Government-in-Exile. In that beleaguered city, with bombs falling all around us, we developed plans for reestablishing the legitimate government when the Allies drove the Nazis out of that country.

One of the problems was currency conversion. The Nazis had been denuding Belgium of its goods by paying for them with pieces of paper printed on the Belgian government's printing presses. It was necessary to replace that fake money with legitimate currency as quickly as possible after Belgium was liberated. Otherwise the Germans could still use their illegitimate currency to buy goods and take them into Germany, leaving Belgium in economic poverty.

Our plan was to make a currency conversion just as soon as there was a legitimate government in Belgium. In readiness for this move, 143 tons of Belgian currency—286,000 pounds—had been printed in England. In September 1944 news reached London that the British 21st Army Group had liberated Brussels. The same day, I received the assignment to transport the 286,000 pounds of currency across the English Channel to the continent and into Brussels.

The Belgian Government-in-Exile and I ordered the currency —labeled "Wild Dog" and packed in small wooden boxes for easy handling—to be loaded on fourteen trucks. Then, in a morning of mist and fog, accompanied by only two representatives of the Banque Nationale Belgique, I headed up the convoy and drove from the engraving plant to the port of Southampton. Under cover of night we boarded a small coastwise vessel, loaded all the boxes on it, and headed across the Channel to Dieppe, the closest harbor the Allies controlled at that time.

A torrential rain swept over the Channel as our vessel ran the German blockade—German submarines lurked in the water, German planes patrolled the skies. All that night I stayed up on the bridge with the captain, watching out for submarines and torpedoes. At no point—and this is true throughout the entire war—did I have any sense of anxiety or fear whatsoever. I held to the words of Proverbs: "Trust in the Lord with all thine heart; and lean not unto thine own understanding. In all thy ways acknowledge him, and he shall direct thy paths." [3] I thought also of what Mrs. Eddy writes in *Science and Health*: "Under divine Providence there can be no accidents, since there is no room for imperfection in perfection." [4]

Toward evening of the following day we finally sailed safely into the Belgian harbor, unloaded the hundreds of boxes of currency onto trucks, and took them to the railroad station. There we assembled a bombed-out freight train whose caboose was missing nearly one side. With a small Army detachment as a

[3] Proverbs 3:5–6.
[4] *Science and Health*, p. 424.

guard for the train, we arrived in Brussels after three days and four locomotive breakdowns. At two o'clock in the morning we were relieved to see every box unloaded and checked off. Not one was missing; 286,000 pounds of currency could run the entire country of Belgium.

So Belgium had a successful conversion of currency, which established the basis for that country's prosperity, and enabled her to be the first nation to recover from wartime destruction. The Belgians were great financiers, not needing the United States except for operating the organizational changes. When the Belgian economy had been organized and public finances turned over to the able Minister of Finance Gütt, I was transferred to the Ninth U.S. Army under General Simpson and put in charge of military government finance in Germany.

ও The job of military government finance didn't mean financing United States armed forces. It meant organizing banks across Germany, sector by sector, as the United States Army advanced in its victorious course. It meant making arrangements to pay German coal miners, workers in industry, school teachers who would be phased in to get the schools going again, city employees wherever they could be found, to get water works, electricity, telephones—civilization and human society—reorganized. This was the job.

The war was at its fiercest when I was dispatched on an urgent mission to the city of Recklinghausen, through which United States armed spearheads had rolled the night before. In a jeep, my driver and I rumbled over the Rhine on a makeshift pontoon bridge. In city after city we drove through dismal scenes of destruction. Suddenly we emerged into a peaceful countryside where birds sang, pear trees were in bloom, women worked in the fields. There were no signs of American troops, no scars of war. We had, it seemed, taken a wrong turn, and in wartime, wrong turns can be serious. Right then I knew it was important to rely on the spiritual law of Christian Science which says that man is under Mind's direction, and under His guidance man makes no wrong turns.

We drove on until we came to a small village where a girl stood on a corner. Whirling up to her, I asked how to get to

Recklinghausen. "You are on the right road," she said. "Go straight ahead." I thanked her and we drove on. But at the next corner, a sign four feet high said "Recklinghausen. Turn right via autobahn."

We drove back to intercept the young woman. "What do you mean by telling us to go straight ahead?" I demanded angrily. "There's a big sign at the next corner saying 'Recklinghausen, turn right.'" The girl's eyes looked steadily at me. She said quietly, "There are two ways to get to Recklinghausen. You can turn right and go via the autobahn, or you can go straight ahead." She paused a moment. "The road straight ahead is the better road."

I sensed she was telling me the truth. Regarding her thoughtfully, I tried to fathom the meaning behind her words. Finally I understood, smiled, thanked her, and drove on. She was right. We had no more trouble. Later we learned that on the autobahn we would have run straight into enemy machine guns. Nazi troops still controlled the main artery. To me, it was an instance of the protecting power of Truth, of right thinking. I had made no wrong turns. And it is impossible for us to make wrong turns in moments of crisis if we rely upon the truth about man and his eternal relationship to God.

 

&#8258; When the Ninth Army came into Aachen, a city of 150,000 people, 85 percent of it had been bombed. The Nazis had followed a scorched-earth policy and by actual count only 1,100 people emerged from the rubble. In a final, desperate effort, Hitler had sent his toughest generals to the front with orders to defend Germany to the last house, and in advancing, the United States Army had no choice but to bomb some of the most beautiful cities and landmarks of that country. The miracle was that, although the great Cathedral of Aachen was very badly damaged, the beautiful little chapel where Charlemagne had been crowned—one of the first chapels built by the early Christians—remained untouched.

As a sequel to this, I remember vividly one of the many amusing incidents that happened during the war. Ninth Army Headquarters had appropriated Field Marshal Herman Goering's former quarters in Braunschweig. One rainy night, when I was the officer on duty, a corporal came in and said, "Sir, I have Charlemagne's crown, his sceptre and all his jewels outside. What do you want me to do with them?" Thinking that some of my fellow officers were playing a joke on me, I replied sharply, "For heaven's sake, bring them in out of the rain." The corporal replied, "I don't know whether I should, sir. There's a German goes with them. We found these jewels and this German at the bottom of a salt mine, and he has orders from his church not to leave them night or day."

"Bring him in and let me talk to him," I said. A little German was brought in, soaking wet. He had been assigned, when the bombing of Aachen commenced, to remove Charlemagne's crown jewels from the front and guard them with his life. I said, "Bring them in and let me look at them." With superb dignity the little man replied: "Sir, I cannot do that. These are sacred relics of the Church, and I can display them under proper conditions only. If you will give me the proper place, I will show them to you." "That's fair enough," I said. "What do you require?" He replied, "I need a big, long table."

So I ordered the jewels and the German brought into the officers' conference room. And here were Charlemagne's crown, with great nugget jewels almost as big as eggs, his sceptre, the sword with which he had been tapped when made emperor, and all kinds of brilliant relics. And the little man had them all displayed on black velvet.

&ral As the war drew to an end, General Lucius D. Clay was in command and I was asked to serve on Clay's staff as head of public finance of all military government in Germany. The job was to get society moving again, and the problem was money. In the early stages of recovery, American currency was used to spearhead operations. Hitler had closed the banks and it was some time before the United States military government was able to get all the German marks it needed to get the economy working.

The responsibility for the uses of money in Germany rested with our department; our decisions demanded great wisdom, and I constantly had to turn to divine intelligence for guidance. What misuse of power could have been curtailed, what wars could have been avoided, if Jesus' teaching, "Seek ye first the kingdom of God, and his righteousness, and all these things shall be added unto you," [5] had been applied in the economics of nations.

When Germany finally surrendered, I went into Berlin with Allen Dulles, then head of OSS; with Gero von Gaevernitz, American underground intelligence officer; and with Colonel von Schlabendorf, a member of the top German intelligence staff that had planned the assassination of Hitler.

General Clay named me as chairman of a committee to select candidates for various cabinet posts and other important positions in Germany. This committee classified the Nazis whom they wouldn't employ as the black Germans; the gray Germans were the doubtful ones; the white Germans were the ones who had opposed Hitler. Many of the people on the list we submitted held cabinet posts in Germany later, the famous Chancellor Ludwig Erhard among them.

We began drafting constitutional provisions and laws to establish the policies that were to govern Germany's reconstruction. We also started negotiations with the Russians who had taken over East Germany, trying to adopt uniform policies in all of the respective zones.

ॐ When the time came for me to take off my soldier's uniform and go home—I was now a colonel—my staff and I had been negotiating with the Russians for two years. The State Department asked me to stay on in Germany. I considered this for a long time. New York State had kept my job available for me, and now I was Deputy Comptroller under Governor Thomas E. Dewey, who wanted me back.

After weeks of prayer, my direction finally became clear, and I said to the people who were urging me to stay: "All my life I have believed deeply in the career diplomatic service. I have also believed deeply in the merit system of government appointments. If I could enter the career diplomatic service on the basis of merit, then I would be interested, but not in a political appointment." I was flown to Washington to take the examina-

[5] Matthew 6:33.

tion for the diplomatic system, passed it, and was thereupon appointed a career diplomat. So I resigned as Deputy Comptroller of New York State and moved over to the diplomatic foreign service.

My first job as diplomat—Director of the Berlin Element of the United States High Commission for Representatives—was to continue the work of negotiations with the Russians on the financing of Germany. This meant moving that country from military to civilian life, and into a new era. General Clay had retired as Commander, and John J. McCloy, former president of the Chase Manhattan Bank, replaced him as United States High Commissioner for Germany.

Germany's future was being weighed in the balance, and United States policy was an important factor. Should Germany be reduced to an agricultural state and never again have the industrial and economic power to wage another major war? Or should that nation, with its tradition of greatness in manufacture, literature, music, and art, be restored under new leadership to its former peacetime economy?

General McCloy asked me to go to Berlin to make a survey and recommendations as to whether Berlin could be saved. Could that city be a viable economic entity or not? During the airlift and blockade, during the final months of war, not a wheel had turned in Berlin. The United States military government could feed the city; they could send in tons of coal and keep the people alive. But they couldn't do more than that. There was no production to keep the economy going.

So I came to Berlin with my assignment. It was a time for prayer among the nations' leaders, a time for knowing that the destiny of a nation cannot safely rest upon human authority or human planning. A higher rule than economic calculations had to be invoked, a higher power had to speak. In the eyes of the world, Germany had sinned against God and man. Should that nation be saved? Only a philosophy rooted in universal Truth could provide answers that would advance peace in the world.

The design of war had been worked out with great skill by the Allied military leaders. The design for peace, requiring greater skill, had still to be worked out. The philosophy that the victor in war had sovereign right to impose sanctions against the vanquished had proved disastrous following the First World War. The resentment of the oppressed had erupted in a Second World War of unbelievable horror and genocide. Repression was not the answer.

In this postwar period, one wrestled with these questions. I felt that before I could arrive at any honest decision to bring back to General McCloy, I had to be sure of my own base of thinking. The philosophy of Christian Science to which I was committed is based on salvation, on the premise that the spiritual element in men makes regeneration possible. Jesus said: "The Son of man is come to save that which was lost," [6] and Mrs. Eddy says in *Science and Health*: "For victory over a single sin, we give thanks and magnify the Lord of Hosts. What shall we say of the mighty conquest over all sin? A louder song, sweeter than has ever before reached high heaven, now rises clearer and nearer to the great heart of Christ; for the accuser is not there, and Love sends forth her primal and everlasting strain." [7] From the Christian viewpoint, salvation, not condemnation, had to be embodied in any lasting design for peace involving the destiny of a nation, a people, a city.

After all this thinking had sifted down, a plan began to unfold to me for saving Berlin economically. I presented the plan to General McCloy who, after some deliberation, approved it and asked me to fly to Washington and make our recommendations to the State Department. This plan required a large appropriation from Congress, but mainly it was a question of United States policy. The decision was: the United States would attempt to save Berlin. I was asked to go back to Berlin and set up an organization to implement the program I had outlined.

General Maxwell D. Taylor had just been appointed United States Commander in Berlin, and I went into that city to work with him. We functioned well in a difficult situation. Berlin was an island in a Red sea. Constant harassment of one kind or another prevailed, both personal and economic. It was a period of tension. We thought of it as opportunity. The United States was making progress, and it was an exciting, gratifying, and very important time.

[6] Matthew 18:11.
[7] *Science and Health*, p. 568.

During the war all Christian Science churches in Germany had been closed. Many German Christian Scientists, torn between loyalties to their Fatherland and the Church, decided to support the Führer. Others rejected Nazism and were thrown into prison. Now the Christian Science churches began to reestablish themselves according to the provisions by which Mary Baker Eddy had founded The Church of Christ, Scientist. My wife and I recall with special affection our friendship with the loyal teacher of Christian Science, Friedrich Preller, and his wife.

ॐ Then, in 1951, after Generalissimo Chiang Kai-shek was forced out of mainland China onto the island of Taiwan, I was appointed Chargé d'Affaires at Taipei. I felt my job in Germany was done. The groundwork had been established and the foundation laid; there were able people to carry on. Cecil Lyon, later the United States Ambassador to Ceylon, succeeded me. My decision to leave Germany was motivated by a rule I have followed in my career. Always I have been interested in doing a job, not holding a job. As long as you are doing your thing, you have a sense of involvement and achievement, and this is great. But as soon as you reach a point where you think your particular contribution has been made, then I feel it is time to let somebody else take over. This is one of the reasons I liked the foreign service so much. You could advance within the diplomatic service, but when your job was done, you moved on.

A British ambassador once remarked to me: "Americans are often accused of being brash and aggressive. But no matter where you are, the first thing you ask yourself is, 'How can I improve it? How can I make it better?'" I think this is the essence of the American attitude toward life. We don't always live up to it, and we sometimes don't make things better. But in my experience, wherever I have landed, I have had a philosophy of progress. In Christian Science progress fulfills the law of God.

ॐ Communist planes were passing overhead when I arrived in Taiwan to work with Chiang Kai-shek. The United States' and Chiang's policies were intermingled at that point. The threat of a Sino-Soviet bloc of international Communism dominated American thinking. As a consequence, the United

States was interested in building up Taiwan as a showcase of free enterprise in contrast with the Communist system, and also in building a United States military force in that part of the world that could, if opportunity arose, participate in establishing a democratic government in mainland China. The United States had a substantial aid program to Taiwan, and this was one of the things to which I gave great emphasis.

Chiang Kai-shek is a towering figure in Chinese history of the past fifty years, a very strong man, a very stubborn man. But I find that men who have long-range objectives are invariably stubborn men. They don't yield to obstacles readily. The best of them can be flexible at intermediary places, but the one who really succeeds is the one who knows how to be flexible without giving up his goals.

The Chiangs are Methodists and Madame Chiang, who occasionally preached a sermon in the church at Taiwan, likened the Nationalists' trials to those of the Israelites in the wilderness. Certainly there was more of the Old than the New Testament in the Generalissimo's fierce intensity. My relations with Chiang were excellent, and I saw him quite frequently. But although the United States was supporting his government, we frequently found ourselves in strong disagreement as to policies or their implementation. Regardless of how unpleasant the message might be, however, or how strong his own convictions, Chiang invariably listened to me with courtesy and patience.

The haughty imperial image of Madame Chiang Kai-shek was not reflected in my, or my wife's, friendship with her. Mrs. Jones and I lived in an attractive Japanese house in Taiwan on the slopes of Tsao Shan (Grass Mountain), overlooking the residence in which the Generalissimo and his wife spent six months of the year. One morning the bell of our house rang, and it was Madame Chiang Kai-shek at the door. She came in, visited with Mrs. Jones for a few moments, and then walked over to look at the dramatic view from our window: rice paddies like silver mirrors cascading into the fields, and in the distance five ranges of mountains, each higher than the other.

Three days later there was another ring at the door. It was Madame Chiang's number-one boy bearing a painting Madame

Chiang had made of the scene from our window. The painting still hangs in our home and is one of the treasured mementos of our two and a half years in Taiwan.

The groundwork of the United States aid program was laid during my two years in that country. While I was there, American aid kept Taiwan alive. Now Nationalist China is so prosperous it no longer needs aid. As a matter of fact, it has over twenty programs of aid to other nations.

ॐ In 1954 I was appointed Ambassador to Belgium. My wife and I had our tickets and were scheduled to sail for Europe in a few days on the S.S. *United States.* I was having luncheon at the University Club in New York when the phone rang. It was John Foster Dulles, then Secretary of State, asking me if I would trade Belgium for Indonesia. I flew down to Washington and was told: "If you still want to go to Belgium, that is all right with us. But you have never served anywhere except in a hardship post. Let me tell you what the story is."

The United States mission was in trouble in Indonesia. It needed a new program. The State Department said: "People talk of the domino theory of Communism in Asia. We don't agree. We call our theory the leapfrog theory. We think the Communists are going to leap over Thailand in Southeast Asia and concentrate pressure on Indonesia, the largest nation in Asia except for China, and the third richest in the world. If the Communists should succeed in taking over Indonesia, or establishing a Communist government in Indonesia, the rest of Southeast Asia would be caught in pincers between Communist China on the north and the second largest Asiatic country on the south. The rest of Southeast Asia would be seriously threatened by Communist domination. So Indonesia is the key to saving Southeast Asia."

My answer was: "You've said enough. Send me to Indonesia." So I went to Indonesia in 1954, not as Ambassador this time but as head of the United States aid program.

ॐ When my wife and I arrived in Indonesia, as we drove from the airport to our home, every tree and telephone pole had a hammer and sickle on it. And later, driving across Java, we saw arches of hammer-and-sickle streamers fastened to trees on either side of the highway everywhere.

After a few days, "Pepper" Martin, correspondent of *U.S. News and World Report* and then regarded as dean of foreign correspondents in Asia, called on me. "It looks as if it's all over but the shouting, doesn't it?" he said. "It certainly looks that way," I replied, "but I think there is a little to be said yet." It wasn't all over, but this represented the first of the big drives by the Communists to gain total power in Indonesia.

After nearly 300 years of Dutch colonialism, and four years of revolution from 1945 to 1949, Indonesia finally regained its national sovereignty. Then began the fierce power struggle for the kind of government Indonesia would have. Could that country maintain its republic on the basis of democratic rule with religious freedom for all, or would she be forced into a Communist type of government? This was the battle being waged, and the future of Indonesia and possibly all of Asia would depend on the outcome. Many nations were involved in giving foreign aid to Indonesia, the largest contributors being the United States and the Soviet government.

In 1954 the Indonesian official responsible for handling all foreign assistance was Dr. Djuanda Kartawidjaja, head of the Planning Bureau, who later became his country's Prime Minister. While the United States could not help Indonesia for the time being in some politically sensitive areas, there was no controversy in one area: Dr. Djuanda recognized American preeminence in technology—physics, public administration, education. These fields were all underdeveloped in Indonesia, and five years after independence Indonesia's major problem was paucity of trained personnel. Only 120 engineers existed in the entire country, as large as the United States. In the entire Ministry of Agriculture, with 4,000 employees, there were just two college graduates.

Dr. Djuanda and I agreed on a formula for the United States aid program. To the degree that its aid budget made possible, America would take as its major responsibility the technical education of Indonesians. Both Djuanda and I were tacitly aware of the by-products, namely, understanding of the United

States by Indonesians, who would presumably return to their country with increased technological knowledge, and more importantly perhaps, with an appreciation of what a free society was like, some comprehension of the American dynamic.

I believed strongly that if sufficient future Indonesian leaders could visit America long enough to understand us, not only would our relations with this important country benefit, but Indonesia might be less likely to abandon democratic concepts. I foresaw that Indonesia's youth was to play an important role not only in the political and spiritual destiny of that nation, but in the destiny and peace of the world.

As the gears of the United States aid program began to mesh, United States relations with the Indonesian government improved. It was not that America was giving them more aid. It was that the United States was working with them, abjuring the attitude that "Papa knows best." The Indonesian, who had been treated as a second-class citizen for so long, resented the slightest tinge of paternalism, and he was very adept at recognizing it. Depending on one's attitude toward him, his reaction would be one of passive resistance—or cooperation.

Reorganizing the mission, we developed a new aid program with a new philosophy. In June 1955, after my first year in Indonesia, a telegram summoned me back to Washington as Deputy Assistant Secretary for Far Eastern Economic Affairs. It had been a good year. My wife Mary Lou and I had come to love Indonesia, and we were leaving a host of friends behind. Hundreds turned out at the airport to say *Silom Djalan*—Go with God.

As my wife and I flew over the Java Sea headed for America, I had no premonition that within three years I would be returning, this time as Ambassador, to share in a more turbulent period than the country had known since its revolution.

ঌ The job of Deputy Assistant Secretary for Far Eastern Economic Affairs covered the entire rim of Asia—Japan, Korea, China, the Philippines, Taiwan, Indonesia, Singapore, Malaya, Thailand, Burma, Australia, New Zealand, Laos, Cambodia, and Vietnam—all of East Asia except Pakistan, India, and Afghanistan. I traveled a great deal and had three fascinating and exciting years as part of the decision-making process. And during those years, I was learning about the Asian people, their history, religion, government—but mostly their aspirations. God was preparing me for the most challenging experience of my life as a diplomat.

ࢶ In 1958 President Eisenhower nominated me as Ambassador to the Republic of China at Taiwan. Then a turn of events in Asia changed my course again. While the Senate was considering my nomination, revolution broke out in Indonesia. John Allison, former Ambassador to Indonesia, had just been transferred to Prague, and the State Department was looking for an ambassador to replace him. They came to me and said: "You are the only senior officer who has had the needed depth of experience in Indonesia. Would you be willing to change countries?" I answered yes and went off to Indonesia with the words of John Foster Dulles ringing in my ears: "We have given you one of the toughest assignments in the world today."

The second time I went into Indonesia, I went as an old friend aware of a nation whose people were seeing the same stars, dreaming the same dreams people dream in every nation in the world.

In 1954 my dealings had been mostly with Dr. Djuanda, who had become Prime Minister. Now, as United States Ambassador, my negotiations would be mostly with President Sukarno. And here began for me an extraordinary friendship that lasted for a period of almost eight years. Each of us was steeped in the history of war and revolution. Each was dedicated to freedom. But each viewed the means to freedom from a different base: I from my conviction that Indonesia's national freedom could be preserved only if that nation remained spiritually and economically free from the web of dialectical materialism; President Sukarno from his conviction that in revolution, in his country's drive for independence and progress, both democratic and Communist concepts were acceptable.

A rebel leader as far back as the 1930's, Sukarno had kindled in the minds of his people the flaming idea that national sovereignty could be an actuality in their time. For this the Dutch officials had imprisoned and exiled him for a total of twelve years. During those years of prison and exile friends smuggled to him the books he most wanted to read: books on socialism and revolution that would teach him how to organize against the Dutch, that would give him a philosophy of revolution, that would teach him how to build a nation. Sukarno read them all, from Danton through Marx to Paine and Lincoln. "I met in the world of the mind with these leaders," he later wrote. "Well, having met—having spoken with all those great leaders—I became convinced that mankind is one."

In its reach for freedom, mankind is indeed one. But in this amalgam of concepts, Sukarno believed that he could mix political oil and water. He refused to admit that there are contradictions in political philosophy that cannot be resolved. He was convinced he could unite conflicting social forces by merging Communism with anti-Communism. And here, in my judgment, Sukarno was naive and made his greatest political blunder.

From this base of political philosophy proceeded years of discussion and many diplomatic moves between Sukarno and myself. The issue at stake was Indonesia's destiny. I had faith that the first of the five principles of the Republic of Indonesia's Pantja Sila—*Belief in God*, not Communism—would govern the next crucial step in that country's political and economic history. As future events proved, I was right in believing that Communism would not be acceptable to its dedicated and most influential political and religious leaders.

૭ঌ At this point, after taking the periodic physical examination required in the diplomatic service, the physician who had examined my X-rays said, "I am terribly sorry, Mr. Ambassador, but you will have to return to the United States for hospitalization." My first thought was, "This can't be true! Man is spiritual and perfect, as the image and likeness of God. Error has no power to fasten such a claim on God's man." Aloud I said, "Doctor, I just can't believe it. Furthermore I cannot return to Washington immediately." And I explained that I was due at an important conference the following week in a neighboring country. "Give me a week," I said, "and another examination." He agreed to this.

My wife, who has been a strong support throughout my years of public service, joined me in prayer. It was prayer based on the conviction that in this hour of need, as in former times, Christian Science would heal me. We were sure God had led us to this post of service, therefore no obstructive influence could prevent His power from being operative in our life and work. We relied heavily on Christ's law of Mind-healing permeating these words in *Science and Health*: "A spiritual idea has not a single element of error, and this truth removes properly whatever is offensive." [8] We also asked a consecrated Christian Science practitioner to pray for us.

I attended the conference in the neighboring country, and then, as arranged, went for another medical examination. "I've got good news for you," the physician said after examining me thoroughly. "There's nothing wrong. You are perfectly healthy." I had expected nothing less. Later when I reported to the regional medical director that I had a clean bill of health, he congratulated me, and then added, "Sounds like Christian Science."

❧ The civil war that had brought us to Indonesia went on for some time, and there were constant bombings and demonstrations over foreign intervention. Not many months after our arrival in Indonesia I received a telephone call at my office from a neighbor who had a house across the street on Embassy Row. "There is a big crowd demonstrating outside your house," she said. Calling for my car, I hastened home. Approaching our residence, I could hear angry voices from a block away, and turning the corner, I saw a crowd of perhaps a thousand outside our gates. They were shouting denunciations against SEATO and American intervention in Sumatra.

The crowd was too large to get through, so I drove around to the rear entrance and walked up on the veranda. In full sight of the mob, my wife was sitting there calmly reading a magazine. I asked her why she wasn't upstairs. "Do you think I would let those people think I was afraid?" she asked. "Not on your life!" I grinned. "Then let's both sit down," I said.

[8] *Science and Health*, p. 463.

Soon the yelling became louder and more menacing as the iron gate to the garden clanked open. Within seconds the mob was streaming into the garden and racing up the driveway to our house. Some of them were tough-looking thugs, others obviously were university students.

Turning to God in prayer to show me how to handle the angry crowd, I walked out to meet them. Taken by surprise, the crowd slowed down to a halt. Managing a smile, I held out my hand. Shaking hands with half a dozen or more, I asked them to select one man as their spokesman. They selected a handsome university student who made a speech against America. I explained that America was interested in the preservation of Indonesia's independence, as I assumed they all were. Then I shook hands with all I could reach, after which the crowd slowly broke up and departed.

A few days later a young man whom I knew to be a Communist said to me: "Ambassador, I have just had a report from one of the demonstrators at your house. Apparently you made quite an impression. Congratulations!" By Indonesian standards I had done the right thing. I had acted in the correct tradition of preserving the appearance of Javanese nonchalance in the face of danger. Actually I believe it was more than that: my confidence in God's disposal of events.

ॐ Amid the political turmoil and revolution, I set out to explore the many facets of Indonesia: its religions, artifacts, and architectural heritage, its natural splendors, its venerable art and haunting music. In this exploration I came to admire the beauty, intelligence, and gentleness of the Indonesian people.

At times when American-Indonesian relations were considerably strained, I found it possible to maintain friendly relations with the President and his officials by following the commandment of Jesus, the great Ambassador for Christ, who said, "Thou shalt love thy neighbor as thyself." [9] Operating on the basis that friends can disagree and still remain friends, my continuing disagreements with Sukarno didn't affect my friendship with that charismatic leader. Sukarno was aware of my love for his

[9] Matthew 19:19.

country and knew that I was doing what I thought best for Indonesia as well as for America. Diplomacy is a two-way street.

Out of affection for the brilliant Sukarno and in appreciation of his years of struggle to win independence for his country, I joined with Indonesian leaders in trying to persuade the President to turn from the destructive course he was pursuing as he drew closer to a dictatorship under Communist rule. Believing mystically that he was the immortal embodiment of his people's aspirations, their only true mouthpiece, Sukarno was lulled into a state of self-delusion. Failing to keep in touch with his people, their voices no longer reached him. His dissolute way of life tarnished Indonesia's image abroad, and more and more it alienated him from his countrymen. He lost contact with much of the youth, who no longer respected him.

Almost imperceptibly at first, the great Indonesian leaders drew away from Sukarno and began to chart a new political course for their country, founded on democratic rule and dedicated to the principles of Pantja Sila. As I saw this happening, I pleaded with Sukarno to turn from his suicidal course. But by that time Sukarno was committed to Communism and he could no longer reverse his destiny.

In January 1965, catching most if not all Indonesian leadership by surprise, Sukarno withdrew from the United Nations. Among the Indonesian elite the conviction soon developed—and I shared it—that Sukarno had to go.

Ironically, at the moment of one of Sukarno's greatest mistakes—his withdrawal from the United Nations—he announced one of his greatest single achievements: his country's freedom from illiteracy. This represented one of the outstanding educational achievements anywhere in the world. An estimated 60 percent of Indonesians were illiterate when Indonesia became independent in 1945. Nineteen years later there were schools in almost every village, and those in cities like Jakarta were operating on three shifts. Virtually all Indonesians between the ages of 13 and 45 could read and write.

᭞᭞ Several months before Sukarno's dramatic withdrawal from the United Nations I was offered the job as Chancellor of the East-West Center in Honolulu. I couldn't take it because I was Ambassador to Indonesia. "But," I said to them, "if you are willing to wait until the State Department establishes my successor in Indonesia, the answer is yes. I am tremendously interested in this concept. I think the East-West Center is the most significant experiment in international education that we have."

When the State Department finally released me as Ambassador on June 30, 1965, events in Indonesia were already turning in a healthy direction. Strong and dedicated leaders like General Suharto, Dr. Djuanda, and Foreign Minister Adam Malik were moving into positions of power, and I was confident that these great statesmen would lead Indonesia away from Communist control into an era of democracy. Having seen the leaven of progress stirring in the hearts and minds of the Indonesian people, I was convinced that nothing could stop their growth. I felt that the groundwork had been laid for sound relationships between Indonesia and the United States. After eight and a half years in that country which I loved, I felt my job was done. So my wife and I left Indonesia, trusting it in our prayers to God's government.

ࠔ On July 1, 1965, the day after I was released as Ambassador to Indonesia, I took over my position as Chancellor of the East-West Center. Three joyous years followed in a very creative and constructive experiment in education.

The Center was first established by United States legislation in 1960. Actually it didn't get started until 1962, so the groundwork had just been laid, the buildings had just been finished. It was still feeling its way as an institution, still having to prove itself, though strong supporters like myself felt it had already done so.

This was a postgraduate program. Two-thirds of its students were Asians and one-third Americans. The only institution in the West where Asians outnumbered Americans, it was designed to instruct young people who would be the future leaders of that continent. They would go back to their countries in Asia and apply what they had learned. This is a great institution, it is one of the roads to peace.

One day I asked a young Pakistani with two years at the

Center, "What have you gotten out of this?" He answered: "I came to the Center because I wanted two things. First, I wanted to advance myself in my own field, of course. Second, I wanted to learn more about your dynamic American society. Both of these objectives I have accomplished. But there is another dimension that to me may have proved to be even more important. Do you know that before I came here I had never met an Asian of another Asian country? I had never realized that we Asians are so different from each other. Most Asians don't know this. Asians are much more different from each other than Americans are from Europeans.

"In these two years I have been learning about Asian cultures and histories, and I have made closer friends among my fellow Asians. Some of my best friends are Indians. When I go back I will have intimate friends in every country in Asia; and when problems in government come up, we can trust each other, we can communicate with each other. And I think we can prevent wars."

ॐ In 1968 the Hoover Institution on War, Revolution, and Peace at Stanford University honored me with a senior research fellowship, and I left the East-West Center to write a definitive book on Indonesia under the Institution's auspices. Before beginning my book, I took a "sentimenal journey" with my wife back to Indonesia. We were warmly welcomed by the Indonesian officials and the new United States Ambassador. During the three years since our departure many dramatic changes had taken place in Indonesia. Sukarno had been ousted, Communist control had been overthrown, General Suharto had become the new President, Indonesia had rejoined the United Nations, and cordial relations had been reestablished with the United States. The leaven of progress had indeed been working in Indonesia, and the physical alteration in Jakarta alone was impressive— handsome boulevards and neat walkway bridges, a hundred new schools, new parks, and paved roads.

Upon my return to the United States I was invited to be a member of the Board of Trustees of The Christian Science Publishing Society, and I accepted this opportunity to serve my

Church. While in Boston, I finished writing *Indonesia: The Possible Dream*, which was published in April 1971.* The publisher, Harcourt Brace Jovanovich, called it "a love letter to Indonesia." Later, believing I had finished my special contribution to the Church, I returned to the Hoover Institution, where I set to work on a book titled, *Swords Into Ploughshares: War in Modern Society.*

* Editor's note: In his book review in *The Christian Science Monitor*, Guy J. Pauker, former chairman of the Southeast Asia Center at the University of California, commenting on the dramatic sequence of events after Ambassador Jones left Indonesia, wrote: "Ambassador Jones' forbearance, empathy and understanding had prepared the groundwork for this most successful episode in recent American diplomacy in Southeast Asia."

*Lord and Lady Gore-Booth with Mrs. Indira Gandhi upon their departure from India, 1965*

# THE LIFE OF
# A BRITISH
# DIPLOMAT

## ৯ Paul Gore-Booth

FORMER PERMANENT UNDERSECRETARY OF STATE
FOR FOREIGN AFFAIRS, LONDON

৯ Ever since I learned to read Mary Baker Eddy's writings quietly to myself, I have been fascinated by a discourse on the world's destiny in *Science and Health* which continues for nearly two pages. Two extracts read as follows: "This material world is even now becoming the arena for conflicting forces. On one side there will be discord and dismay; on the other side there will be Science and peace." After describing some of the symptoms and features of such a period, she continues: "During this final conflict, wicked minds will endeavor to find means by which to accomplish more evil; but those who discern Christian Science will hold crime in check. They will aid in the ejection of error. They will maintain law and order, and cheerfully await the certainty of ultimate perfection." [1]

The first thing to notice about these sentences is that they were written at the high tide of confidence in material progress

[1] *Science and Health*, pp. 96–97.

toward the end of the nineteenth century. Mrs. Eddy clearly foresaw that the next century would bring about convulsions of the nature and intensity that we are now beholding. But while writing in these cosmic terms, Mrs. Eddy also speaks with comfort and encouragement to the individual. So I believe that the individual, in whatever his activity, can help toward the consummation of victory over the more violent, devious, and lawless ideas current in the world.

Obviously diplomacy has a role to play in this if you believe, as I do, that diplomacy, or the conduct of relations between states, is not wholly cynical. A French diplomat once observed to me that nation states are cold-blooded and selfish; to a degree, yes. But I remain convinced that there is in much of foreign policy at least an element of idealism.

Of course it depends on people, and this again depends on upbringing, conviction, standards, and indeed religion. If there are no ethical standards, "the people perish."

So Christian Science has produced a standard, not only of ethics, but also of practical application and demonstration. It behooves the Christian Scientist, whatever activity he pursues, to do his best to understand and uphold that standard.

᠅ I was born before World War I in the Yorkshire town of Doncaster, famous at that time for the manufacture of railway locomotives and for the second most important horse race "on the flat" in Britain, the St. Leger. Doncaster—or Danum, to use its Roman Empire name—is surrounded by the rich South Yorkshire coal field. Its industry has now diversified, the town has grown and its industrial smoke abated. But thanks to a geography governed by the configuration of the River Don valley, Doncaster retains much of its older character and the people remain doggedly Yorkshire men and women.

We lived in Yorkshire because my father had come from Lissadell, the family home in the west of Ireland, to work as an engineer in a Sheffield steelworks. He was the younger brother of two remarkable Irish beauties, the poetess Eva Gore-Booth and the Irish nationalist Constance Markievicz. My mother, Evelyn Scholfield, grew up in the agricultural country of East Yorkshire. I am thus naturally concerned to maintain that Ireland and

Yorkshire make a good combination. In proof of this my parents lived to enjoy a golden wedding. We stayed in Doncaster until I was six and then moved eight miles west to a more spacious house and garden on the outskirts of the coal mining village (now town) of Maltby. We stayed there for eleven years. Such is the roving nature of diplomatic life that these eleven years were the longest consecutive period I have ever lived anywhere.

The family connection with Christian Science was originally through my great-aunt, Mrs. Mabel S. Thomson. This very remarkable woman was one of the original members of First Church of Christ, Scientist, London. Through her healing work she interested a number of members of my mother's family and, as is not uncommon, scared others. My mother and my grandmother were impressed, as was my uncle Ralph Scholfield, who in 1935 became a First Reader in The Mother Church in Boston and later served as a lecturer and teacher of Christian Science. He was also, for a time after World War II, manager of The Christian Science Publishing Society office in London.

Since we were, by the standards of time, remote from any church, my mother was not able to attend services while we lived at Maltby. In any case my father was, and always remained, skeptical about everything to do with Christian Science and understandably did not want his gardening Sundays to be disturbed by a repetition of the twelve-mile journey to Sheffield which he made every weekday. This did not mean there was a blank in religious upbringing. Bible stories, told and read, gave me a great admiration for Old Testament figures, notably Elijah, Daniel, and Nehemiah. From the family nanny, or "Nana" as we called her, I learned many Scriptural passages by heart, especially verses from the Psalms. When we went to stay with my grandmother at Christmas each year, I read with her over and over again a large illustrated volume which we called "the Jesus book." One hoped each time that the sadder parts of the story would somehow disappear, but the tranquil happier ending brought consolation.

ॐ It was very much the custom in those days for a family that could manage it financially to send their sons to preparatory boarding schools in the south of England. After one unsuccessful venture, I went to St. Michael's, Uckfield, in Sussex. The headmaster was an Anglican clergyman and held Anglican services; but he also permitted Christian Science services to be held. The school, which lay on high ground with a wide view, had a feeling of welcome informality. Years later, during World War II, it moved, since it lay on the direct path of enemy aircraft attacking London. There were two successors to St. Michael's, and one of them, on a new site in Surrey, is Fan Court, the highly successful preparatory school for the children of Christian Scientists.

When the time came to leave St. Michael's, I gained a scholarship to Eton College, which I entered in 1922, and where I studied for nearly six years. It was hard keeping up with my scholarship contemporaries, but I managed to do so, discovering in the process that history was the subject at which I made out best. It satisfied my desire to know what happened and why, and who contributed to events in an important measure. This spontaneous interest was strongly reinforced by good elementary teaching at St. Michael's and Eton, and inspiration added to it by a great scholar and future Eton headmaster, Robert Birley. Serious interest in foreign languages began to grow at this time also, but there was not much opportunity for application and I had no idea what I should be doing when I grew up. In any case, there was the university period still to come.

Fairly soon after I had arrived at Eton, my uncle Ralph Scholfield, himself an old Etonian, obtained permission to hold Christian Science Sunday School classes in some rooms near the school, and this meant that by leaving St. Michael's I was not in any danger of losing touch with my religion. During this time I had what was perhaps the most remarkable healing I can recall. There was an outbreak of mumps just before a most important examination. Those about to take the examination went away for a few days' rest, and on the first evening I did not feel well. I rapidly developed symptoms of the disease accompanied by much fear, because if I missed the exam I should lose my place in the school order, and this would have other unfortunate consequences.

A Christian Science practitioner was asked to help. On the third morning, a Sunday, I experienced a great convulsion and then went to sleep. The next morning I was taken to see a doctor. In a puzzled tone he explained that I had had symptoms akin to those of mumps, but they had been coincidental and I could go back and take the exam. I did so, with success.

But it took me years to understand how much this incident had proved the permanent effectiveness of Jesus' teaching. As recorded in John 14:12, Jesus said: "He that believeth on me, the works that I do shall he do also; and greater works than these shall he do; because I go unto my Father." Centuries of history have sidestepped this promise. But with her discovery of Christian Science, Mrs. Eddy revived its reality. She writes in *Science and Health*: "It is not well to imagine that Jesus demonstrated the divine power to heal only for a select number or for a limited period of time, since to all mankind and in every hour, divine Love supplies all good." [2] Every Christian Scientist accepts an obligation to prove, as far as he or she is able, the healing efficacy of this religion.

From Eton the natural step was to Balliol College, Oxford, my father's old college, where I won a history scholarship. As already explained, I was attracted to history by curiosity about what happened and who did it. With study, this interest broadens into a desire to know more about the history and influence of economics and ideas, the whole field of what the Romans neatly called *rerum cognoscere causas* (learning the causes of things).

The Founder of Christian Science was a keen student of history, and particularly of the interaction between strength and weakness of societies and their ethical and religious standards. The trend of my life, which has brought me into dramatic historical events, has shown that these standards are not so remote from day-to-day events as it has become somewhat fashionable to suppose, and this thought leads straight to Mrs. Eddy's challenging statement in *Science and Health*: "The true theory of the universe, including man, is not in material history but in spiritual development." [3]

The transition from a school routine, however liberal, to

[2] *Science and Health*, p. 494.
[3] *Science and Health*, p. 547.

university freedom was pretty drastic, and it naturally took some time to work out one's priorities. In my studies, instead of pursuing history as such, I took on the stiff challenge of a three-year course in philosophy and ancient history. I felt I ought to grapple with what the best human minds from Plato onwards had thought about the essence of reality as opposed to appearance, and about the nature of good and evil, of principle and expediency, as understood by philosophers through the ages. It was an absorbing exercise in thinking about thinking and, although it did not bring top degree honors, I considered it an invaluable reinforcement of mental capacity.

But the study of the pursuit, through purely human philosophy, of ultimate reality or a perfect ethic leaves in the end a feeling of unsatisfied effort. Each great philosopher provides reasons why his predecessors were not quite right and adds reflections of his own. But at the end there remains a quest for something more positive, more certain, more applicable, and more effective. Perhaps the search for true wisdom (and philosophy means the love of wisdom) involves more than intellect and concentration, and embraces the whole of experience including inspiration and demonstration. In that case the Christian can only turn to the philosophy of Jesus and Paul, of which Mrs. Eddy writes in *Miscellaneous Writings*: "This philosophy alone will bear the strain of time and bring out the glories of eternity; for 'other foundation can no man lay than that is laid,' which is Christ, Truth." [4]

᳕ As employment prospects in the Depression year of 1931 were poor, I did a fourth-year mixed course with emphasis on economics, with much the same academic result, but further fortified with useful equipment for the future.

Priorities did not include only studies. Those were great days for organized games and I played both Rugby and tennis for the college. There was the great attraction, to me, of the Oxford Union (debating) Society at which I spoke for two years, but then had to cut it out because preparation of speeches took too

[4] *Miscellaneous Writings*, p. 365.

much time from study. And in the beginning of the summer vacation there was a fortnight's tour in the West country with the Balliòl Players presenting English translations of Greek classical plays. I directed Euripides' *Rhesus*, a tragedy of the Trojan War, and one year took the part of Oedipus in Sophocles' overwhelming *Oedipus the King*.

There was of course at Oxford a total freedom of religion. I joined the Oxford University Christian Science Organization. In my time it had among its members three people, Clayton Bion Craig, Erwin D. Canham, and Peter Henniker-Heaton, who have since done outstanding work at the headquarters of the Christian Science movement.

Perhaps the most exciting event in the Organization during my time at Oxford was the holding of the first Christian Science lecture ever sponsored by it. I was asked to see whether Balliol College would agree to the use of their hall. A friendly Bursar said, "Of course. The usual ash trays, I suppose?" Since Christian Scientists don't smoke, I could reply, "Not even those." The lecture was well supported by both undergraduates and people from outside, and the Organization's lecture program has continued ever since. The Organization survived the difficult days of World War II when universities ran at half-strength, if that, and it now continues its steady progress, deriving its membership both from British students and from students from the United States, the Commonwealth, and other countries.

Although I was undecided about a career, it became quite clear that I wanted to do something which would mean working with people from other countries. The experience of my mother, who had a remarkable knowledge of French and German, had no doubt something to do with this decision, as did also the brief periods which I had spent in France, Austria, and Germany. Events moved both naturally and dramatically when another uncle, Alwyn Scholfield, Librarian of Cambridge University, suddenly presented me with a gift enabling me to study German seriously. Looking some months later into requirements for admission into the Diplomatic Service, I realized that if I also studied French intensively for the two and a half months remaining before the next exam, I might make it. I did, even if my accelerated French was only just good enough.

It may seem from the narrative so far that a great deal of chance entered into the process by which I became a diplomat. Whether you accept this or not depends on your general outlook. I find myself agreeing with Shakespeare's Hamlet that "There are more things in heaven and earth, Horatio, Than are dreamed of in your philosophy." And as I think back on this period, I am constantly reminded of the statement by Mrs. Eddy about exchanging our belief in chance to a proper sense of God's unerring direction. In other words, as one came to think more deeply in terms of man's relationship with God, there was growing comfort in the conviction that, far from being subject to caprice and accident, I could trust always in God's law of direction and protection.

ॐ In 1933, at age 24, I entered the Diplomatic Service. The choice of diplomacy as a career does not normally relate to one's attitude concerning current policy. Nor had I any very clear idea of what I would be doing or how I would fare. But it seemed at the time that, while British policy in the wake of economic crisis seemed hesitant and uncertain, Britain was a great power with certain responsibilities, aims, and ideals, the furtherance of which would offer a lifetime of interesting service. What could not in the least be foreseen was the range and depth of experience the mid-twentieth century would provide.

In the Foreign Office in London I was assigned to the desk dealing with the United States. There my work was a mixture of following the progress of the Franklin Roosevelt New Deal and handling small but sometimes complex problems which arose between the two countries. Work on American affairs soon led me to visit the United States for the first time in my life. I found that more of America was like a Hollywood movie than I had supposed, but most of it was not like that at all.

I took the opportunity to attend the 1934 Annual Meeting of The Mother Church. (Christian Scientists from all over the world gather together each year to hear reports from the officials of The First Church of Christ, Scientist, in Boston, concerning progress in the movement.) Christian Science was growing throughout the Western world and many new churches were forming. I have never forgotten the exalted moment when, in the beautiful Mother Church Extension, 5,000 Christian Scientists—most if not all of whom had had healings in Christian Science—joined in the repetition of the Lord's Prayer. One felt that Christ's healing power on earth was being affirmed.

ॐ In 1936 I was transferred from London to the British Legation in Vienna, Austria. Life in Vienna was very pleasant. The music was wonderful, but diplomacy was uphill. The Austrians were friendly enough, but there was strong Nazi pressure against Austrian independence, and the effort to preserve that independence, without any guarantee of British and French armed support, was bound to fail.

Before this happened and the Nazis took over, I was posted to Tokyo, Japan, in December 1937. Here the tension between Japan and the West, particularly Britain and the United States, first raised by the Japanese invasion of Manchuria in 1931, rose inexorably as Japan's expansion over China and then Indochina proceeded. This expansion, combined with Japan's involvement in the so-called "Rome-Berlin axis" before and after World War II broke out, meant continuous Japanese pressure against British political and commercial interests. Diplomacy consisted in trying to protect these interests without giving the Japanese the pretext for entering the war on the enemy side. Eventually the military element in Japan took over, and seeing that American friendship for China would preclude continued Japanese expansion there, brought about the attack on Pearl Harbor.

During this period of tension I met Patricia Ellerton. She was born in Kobe, Japan, of an English father and an Australian mother, and had been to school in Australia. Having returned to Japan, she came on the outbreak of war to work in the British Embassy, and finding ourselves working together, we decided to make the arrangement permanent. When we first met she had never heard of Christian Science, but she found this religion, with its reassuring message for every individual, a natural, helpful, and practical one. Her first healing occurred at this time with the disappearance, almost unnoticed, of a hitherto tiresome skin complaint.

The attack on Pearl Harbor and Southeast Asia meant the immediate involvement of Britain in the expanded war, followed by internment of the British Embassy staff in the Embassy compound. Ninety people were concentrated where thirty had lived before. As government officials, we had the right to repatriation and therefore had better expectations than those British nationals who were to spend up to two and a half years in captivity. But the exchange operation, which normally takes at most a few weeks, took eight months and our small community had to cope with all the problems of isolation from family and country and of organizing life in a compound from which no exit was allowed.

During those eight months Pat and I were, from the religious point of view, thrown back very much on our own resources. But such understanding of Christian Science as I had gained over the years greatly fortified us in the conviction that no harm could come to us as captives in material bonds, since the consciousness of things spiritual transcends all such limitations. Pat and I adopted as a kind of family motto the text in Joshua 1:9: "Be not afraid, neither be thou dismayed: for the Lord thy God is with thee whithersoever thou goest." Perhaps we helped thereby to make our contribution to general good morale at a time when the fortunes of war were at their lowest.

During internment we received a message through the Swiss Embassy that my next post would be Washington. When evacuation finally came at the end of July 1942, we traveled under safe-conduct ships to a Britain that was embattled but in resolute spirits. Homecoming meant also a reunion with my parents after nearly five years' separation. After about two months in wartime England, we sailed for America in December 1942.

We began our stay in Washington with the memorable wartime hunt for a house and discovered one remarkably near the British Embassy. We looked for a Christian Science church and found one—Fifth Church of Christ, Scientist, Washington —three doors away. So we joined a young and active membership. If ever you want to know what Paul meant when he said, "There are diversities of gifts but the same spirit," try joining a church, or for that matter any form of rather intimate society, in a country not your own.

Five months after our arrival, our first children, twin boys David and Christopher, were born.

ॐ By the beginning of 1943 it was clear that the Allies would win the war in the end, though there was no way of estimating how long the grim struggle would last. My job in Washington consisted in the main of keeping in touch with the growing amount of work being done both in Britain and the United States on the problems that would arise in the postwar period. This involved constant contact with the State Department and attendance at a number of conferences, such as the Hot Springs Food and Agriculture Conference of 1943, the first conference held under the title of "United Nations," and the Chicago Civil Aviation Conference of 1944. My capacity was that of a diplomatic adviser to the many political and technical experts who made up our delegations. By early 1945 the time was ripe for the political climax, the San Francisco Conference to draft a charter for the United Nations and to prepare for the setting up of the United Nations itself.

The conference lasted from April until the end of June and was attended by the representatives of 51 nations. My role was again that of adviser to our political spokesmen, with the difference that, as a general election was called in Britain less than halfway through the conference, I moved into the front row. Thus I was British spokesman in discussions on the purposes and principles of the Charter and a number of other items including the position of the Secretary-General. There was hard arguing, word by word, especially between the greater and smaller powers, but eventually, on June 26, 1945, the United Nations Charter was signed.

The performance of the United Nations is an immense subject for judgment. There have been great achievements. But the ideological conflict and other influences have made it difficult for a body representing practically all the nations to accept the disciplines which the founders hoped would be adequate and acceptable for world security and world development.

What great wisdom is contained in Mrs. Eddy's words: "The suppositional world within us separates us from the spiritual world, which is apart from matter, and unites us to one another. Spirit teaches us to resign what we are not and to understand what we are in the unity of Spirit—in that Love which is faithful, an ever-present help in trouble, which never deserts us." [5] How long it will take for humanity to arrive at this wisdom, we cannot know. Let us hope that we have at least started along that path.

 

🦆 After the San Francisco Conference, I was transferred back to London, where we went through the rigors of immediate postwar life in Britain. Our daughter Celia was born that winter, making us a family of five. I continued to work on United Nations matters, particularly on the first U.N. Assembly meeting in London in January 1946, and on economic and social questions.

In 1947 a new and frightening problem burst over Europe. A mild winter in 1945–1946 had created the illusion that Europe, including Britain, was industrially convalescent. The exceptionally severe winter of 1946–1947 dispelled this illusion. The United States responded with that great enterprise, the Marshall Plan of June 1947, under which American resources would be made available to help Europe to help itself. When the necessary research work had been done, an International Convention had to be drawn up as the instrument under which American aid would be administered.

So once again, as in San Francisco, I was sitting at the negotiating table, this time with representatives of eighteen other countries, working out an international agreement. (The Soviet Union had declined to take part and the rest of Eastern Europe had therefore no choice but to follow suit.) There were naturally national differences, but the purpose was urgent and unanimous, and in April 1948 the Convention was signed in Paris, setting up the Organization for European Economic Cooperation. This organization presided over the elimination of scarcities and frictions in the West European economy—thus, in

[5] *The First Church of Christ, Scientist, and Miscellany*, p. 167.

a sense, working itself out of a job. Twelve years later, in 1960, the member governments decided to reform it into something corresponding to newer needs, including finance in the age of development. As I happened to be available in London, I was one of the four people who met, again in Paris, to draw up a new draft Convention setting up the successor organization, the Organization for Economic Cooperation and Development.

&ᴥ Meantime, my four years in London meant that a move must be impending, and somewhat to my surprise I was assigned back to America, this time as Director-General of British Information Services in the United States. Before World War I official information about Britain had been difficult to obtain in the United States: it was available only at the Embassy in Washington (which had no specialist information setup) or at the British Library of Information in New York. Lord Lothian, in his remarkable year as British Ambassador at the beginning of World War II, began to break down these barriers. By the end of the war a large organization existed in New York with a Director-General in Washington and branches in other leading cities to put out information about British performance and policy and to conduct public relations for important British visitors.

By 1949, when I returned to the United States, the organization had naturally somewhat decreased in size, but it still employed some 200 people, many of whom were exceedingly skilled professionals in the conduct of relations with the media and with individual personalities. It was my somewhat daunting task to assume, under Ambassador Sir Oliver Franks, a real but not an interfering or officious leadership of this team. Pat and I also had a direct public relations function in visiting as much of America as we could, often with separate programs: while I was addressing a Rotary lunch, she might be doing a women's radio interview. One high point of this job was the handling of the public relations of two visits to the United States by Winston Churchill. Another such climax came at the time of the Coronation of Queen Elizabeth II when, during the service at Westminster Abbey, Pat advised the Columbia Broadcasting

System about the ceremony and I helped the National Broadcasting Company.

Both these occasions gave one a strong feeling of the friendship between all that is best in the United States and Britain. My public relations assignment greatly clarified this friendship for me and the purpose which it has in the world as a whole.

⁊❧ After the racing and chasing of those public relations years, the next assignment was a total contrast. I was transferred in the fall of 1953 to Rangoon, Burma, as Ambassador. I had never been to Burma and I knew exactly one Burman. Moreover, there was and still is something especially privileged and especially delicate about being the British representative in a country once ruled by Britain (in Burma, Britain had peacefully relinquished power in 1948). But the experience proved altogether delightful. The Burmese are naturally a cordial and friendly people with a direct and blunt approach. The country is beautiful and despite insurrections by Communist groups and by racial groups who objected to the predominantly Burmese composition of the government, life was reasonably safe if one was careful not to overstep the limits of travel set by the authorities.

Our younger daughter, Joanna, was born easily and happily in Rangoon in February 1954. Our Burmese hosts were delighted and, as she was born on a Thursday, gave her the Burmese name of Myint Myint, signifying the "day of Thursday."

Service in Burma was of special interest for its proximity to active Buddhism. I represented the British government at the celebration of the 2,500th anniversary of the Buddhist religion. Buddhism has a great attraction in that it demands two things from which the world could well profit: a conscious rejection of materialistic aims and standards, and a cultivation of quiet reflection for its own sake. For the Western Christian, Buddhism takes too little account of the individual person, or identity, and this sublimation of self into a kind of abstraction may explain why Buddhist society finds it difficult to practice the tough political arts, and why in early Indian history it was swept away by the more practical forms of worship embodied in Hinduism.

I should recall here that I had an illness in Burma which put me out of action for several weeks. My health was completely restored, and for the remaining fifteen years of my diplomatic career I never lost a day's work through illness. I should emphasize that this was not a mighty effort of human will; it may seem just to have happened. But Christian Science equips one with the mental wherewithal to be more active and effective than simply waiting for what comes next. Speaking of the person who has "made the Lord . . . even the most High, his habitation," the Psalmist wrote, "There shall no evil befall thee, neither shall any plague come nigh thy dwelling." [6]

All Bible readers will remember that Daniel, as chief adviser to that most talented and difficult monarch, King Nebuchadnezzar, retired three times a day to pray and worship. I think any dedicated religionist would like to have the calm and self-discipline to do what Daniel did. Most of us probably don't. But Daniel's practice gives the rule and the incentive. There can be no doubt whatever that some reading each day of the Bible and of Mrs. Eddy's works (which most Christian Scientists do) steadies and clears the thought and adds inspiration to it, and that this action shows itself in its effect on health of body as well as of mind. This is not a selfish withdrawal; it is bringing spiritual conviction into daily life with its helpful effects upon oneself and others.

ᔥ After slightly less than three years in Burma, in 1956 I was transferred back to the Foreign Office in London to take up a newly created post of Deputy Undersecretary (roughly speaking, No. 2 level on the civil service side) in charge of Economic Affairs, with a general watching brief over relations with the United States.

My wife and I took a one-room apartment while we searched for a house, found a delightful one in Chelsea with a small back garden, and early in 1957 were settled again with a complete family for the first time after six years. These separations are

[6] Psalms 91:10.

unavoidable in diplomatic life; and even when we were in England, the three older children were at boarding school. One can only give absolute priority to keeping in touch by letter during the prolonged absences and to profit by those chances that do occur to do things together at home. We took the opportunity in 1958 to introduce the older children to Europe by means of a camping tour—the one kind of family tour possible under the exchange control regulations.

My new job was in large degree one of argument and interpretation; it was important both to convey the Foreign Secretary's views and wishes to the several other British Government departments concerned, and to make their views and interests clear to him before he engaged in discussion at the political level. There was also to be a constant stream of negotiation, consultation, and day-to-day business with other governments, whether bilaterally or with groups such as the emerging European Economic Community.

I have already sought to explain the sustaining power of religious conviction in circumstances of preoccupation and responsibility. There was one specific case in a negotiation with a friendly country where retirement from the active scene for purposes of deeper thought brought a happy response. The negotiations started with cordiality and progress; then, as often happens, a deadlock ensued. I could momentarily see no way round and retired to reflect and read to myself from the Bible and Mrs. Eddy's writings. I came upon the passage in *Science and Health* where Mrs. Eddy says: "Love inspires, illumines, designates, and leads the way. Right motives give pinions to thought, and strength and freedom to speech and action. . . . Wait patiently for divine Love to move upon the waters of mortal mind, and form the perfect concept." [7] I waited. Sure enough, in a short time "the waters" responded and, while there was still much argument to come, we were past the worst.

᠅ In 1959 I was asked whether, unless the Government wished to make a political appointment, I would accept an invitation to be British High Commissioner in India. It was a

[7] *Science and Health,* p. 454.

surprising proposal in the sense that the appointment came under the Commonwealth Relations Office and not the Foreign Office. But it happened that, in addition to the appropriate seniority, I had considerable Asian experience and it was felt that this justified the Government in going outside the normal procedure.

So Pat and I were off again, accompanied only by Joanna from the family, to a country away from Europe, a country which in 1947 had obtained its independence from Britain but had ingeniously invented the concept of remaining within the Commonwealth as an independent republic in an organization of which the British sovereign is the head. When I joined the service in 1933, there were, apart from Britain, just four independent members of the Commonwealth—Canada, Australia, New Zealand, and South Africa. By the end of the 1950's the number was eleven, and this number was to be more than doubled in the next decade. All this happened in the course of peaceful development. Meantime, partly through this process, the centers of power had moved from Western Europe to America and the Soviet Union, and a doctrinal conflict pervaded the world, sometimes acute and sometimes muted, between those who placed the highest value on the freedom of the individual to speak and worship as he pleased, and those who did not.

ॐ Everybody these days is familiar, through television, if not through more direct experience, with the India of immense crowds in the cities, of the giant beauty of the Himalayas, the dryness of much of the landscape, and the poverty of too many of the people. Less well known are the industrial achievements of India and the brave efforts made, with outside help, to improve the economy. And even less familiar, though immensely important, is the feeling of individual Indians and Indian families for real and lasting friendship.

When I arrived, Pandit Jawaharlal Nehru, the nationalist leader and the first, and until then, only Prime Minister of India, still had three and a half years of his premiership and his human life to run. This most impressive man was an incredibly hard worker, and for over two years of my time in India he was his own Foreign Minister. This perpetually put one into some indecision whether to ask to see him personally or whether to spare him at least one additional chore to the immense job of being Prime Minister of India. His moods were totally varied and unpredictable: he could be merry, cross, or silent—one never quite knew what to expect. But it was a unique privilege to be dealing with one of the great men of our century.

The British had exercised effective government in parts and later the whole of India for nearly 200 years, and the imprint of British presence will never quite die away. The long connection with Britain meant an acute sensitiveness in India to British opinion and comment on Indian affairs, which could arouse strong public reactions very quickly.

Because of the historic relationship and the peaceful nature of the transition to independence, the British High Commissioner was able to be a public figure. This is an important variant on the usual discretion of diplomacy. Internal air communications being very good, we traveled far and wide, calling on state authorities, addressing meetings, visiting factories, especially those which were British subsidiaries or British-Indian partnerships, calling on British Council (cultural) offices, and keeping the British communities as well informed as we could about affairs and policies at home.

India had passed through many difficulties in 1961 and 1962, and sadly, in 1963 Prime Minister Nehru's health and activity began to decline. He refused to give up, and in May 1964 he died, still in harness as undoubtedly he would have wished. His successor, Lal Bahadur Shastri, a diminutive man of great modesty and total fairness, was in his wholly different way a pleasure to deal with, particularly when gusts of public ill temper blew up, though not with the intensity of the days before the Chinese invasion of 1962 and British, American, and Commonwealth aid to assist it. A great deal of business was done all the time with what were called in the Ministry of External Affairs "the Secretaries," top officials of great ability and accessibility, trained in the British system of speaking with considerable authority when a member of the Government was not available or matters could be settled at the civil service level.

And so by the end of 1964 we felt ourselves very much at

home in India with many friends from different walks of life, a lovely house and garden, and some more visiting of antiquities to be done. There was also opportunity for organized worship, for the small informal group of Christian Scientists had increased enough to graduate into being recognized by The First Church of Christ, Scientist, in Boston, as a Christian Science Society.

Regardless of how small the group of Christian Scientists, or in whatever country I have been stationed, I have been grateful for the statement Mrs. Eddy makes in her book *Miscellaneous Writings*: "God is universal; confined to no spot, defined by no dogma, appropriated by no sect. Not more to one than to all, is God demonstrable as divine Life, Truth, and Love; and His people are they that reflect Him—that reflect Love." [8]

᠅ In the autumn of 1964 there was a general election in Britain, which the Labor Party, under the leadership of Mr. Harold Wilson, won by a very small majority. It was known that whichever party won, there would be changes in top posts as soon as the new Government had had time to work them out. In the last week of the year came the news that I was to be the next Permanent Undersecretary of State at the Foreign Office.

The Permanent Undersecretary is a civil servant, not an elected official. His permanence ceases when he reaches the statutory retiring age of 60. He has two main functions. He is the top adviser on foreign policy to the Secretary of State, who is always a senior member of the Cabinet, and he is responsible to him for the good functioning at home and abroad of the "machine" which executes the Government's policy. There are various ways of handling the second function. You can do a lot directly yourself, you can choose items which particularly interest you and do them in detail, or you can broadly trust the "machine" to run efficiently, injecting ideas, initiative, or caution whenever and wherever you think they are needed. As one of my political chiefs, Mr. George Brown (now Lord George Brown), has pointed out, the machine is a very professional one. I therefore chose broadly the third alternative, which is much

[8] *Miscellaneous Writings*, p. 150.

the most satisfactory for the team and enables the Permanent Undersecretary to maintain a balanced knowledge of policy and action as a correlated whole. But to do this safely and effectively you need to be very well and promptly informed on everything. I was able to achieve this through the excellent internal communications system in the Foreign Office and by short daily operations meetings with my senior colleagues. I also presided over all top-level official planning meetings.

But in exercising this degree of control one must constantly be aware that one is handling not a personal policy, but the policy of the Government of the day, determined by the Foreign Secretary with the agreement of his Cabinet colleagues as necessary and subject to such interventions as the Prime Minister may decide to make.

I occupied this post from May 10, 1965, to January 31, 1969. During this period the international scene presented a series of agonies, many of which evoked emotional storms in Parliament and conflicting public opinion. There were among many other things Vietnam, President de Gaulle's attack on NATO and his second veto of Britain's membership of the European Community, the Middle East Six-Day War, the Nigerian Civil War, and the forcible Soviet occupation of Czechoslovakia, to mention only a few. On the home front were student riots, increased violence, and other forms of overreaction to events, often carefully organized. The department had to try to discern calmly the rights and wrongs of each crisis, the national and international interest, and the capacity of Britain, no longer as great a power as before, to influence international events. There were double dangers of thinking in traditional terms or, at the opposite extreme, falling for a current intellectual fashion of supposing that less influence in the world meant no influence at all.

There remained, and still remains, an important role for a country of proved political and diplomatic ability with a veto in the United Nations Security Council. Whether the British Foreign Office emerges with a good record from that period is for others to judge, and perhaps not yet. But those years were a manifest challenge to one's ability to "hold thought steadfastly to the enduring, the good and the true",[9] when there was so much in the general atmosphere that seemed unbalanced, ephemeral, and unreal. And it is right to add that the service to which I had the privilege of belonging manifested a constant steadiness and mutual loyalty which was outstanding.

At midnight on Friday, January 31, 1969, I was able to become a retired diplomat.

ॐ When one reflects over what has been done and what is left undone, one is reminded of Mrs. Eddy's words: "We are all capable of more than we do."[9] At least my professional life afforded plenty of opportunity for "doing." I am grateful for the job satisfactions and the happiness of family and friendship that it afforded. Beyond that, Christian Science has taught me that man is forever in the service of his Maker—and in His service, there is no retirement. Since concluding my work as a diplomat, many opportunities have unfolded for me to serve the Christian Science church in England; also to serve in other capacities, and to do some writing for publication. One's vision of God's universal love for mankind continues unobstructed.

The conflict described in Mrs. Eddy's words at the beginning of this chapter may rage around us now. But we must always seek to look beyond it to the fundamental hope for all mankind, expressed in the words of *Science and Health*: "One infinite God, good, unifies men and nations; constitutes the brotherhood of man; ends wars; fulfils the Scripture, 'Love thy neighbor as thyself;' annihilates pagan and Christian idolatry,—whatever is wrong in social, civil, criminal, political, and religious codes; equalizes the sexes; annuls the curse on man, and leaves nothing that can sin, suffer, be punished or destroyed."[10]

[9] *Science and Health*, p. 89.
[10] *Science and Health*, p. 340.

*John Reardon of the Metropolitan Opera Company*

# THE
# OPERA
# SINGER

## ᔰ John Reardon

BARITONE, METROPOLITAN OPERA COMPANY IN
NEW YORK

ᔰ The Metropolitan Opera Company's 1972–1973 season
had finished on a high point of success—although the year had
begun with unforeseen problems. After 22 years of distinguished
service as general manager of the Met, Rudolf Bing had retired
when the 1971–1972 season was over. The talented Goeran
Gentele of Stockholm was appointed to succeed him. Before
Mr. Gentele could manage a single Met production, he was
killed in a tragic automobile accident, and Schuyler Chapin,
assistant manager, was made temporary manager. Despite the
upheavals usually attending such drastic management changes,
the Met had staged some of the most beautiful productions of
any year, most of the performances being sold out, some to
overflow audiences. Mr. Chapin subsequently became the Met's
general manager.

That season I had sung the roles of Mercutio in *Romeo and
Juliet*, Papegano in *The Magic Flute*, Tomsky in *Pique Dame*,

and Escamillo in *Carmen*, with Marilyn Horne in the title role. This highly successful production concluded my eighth year with the Metropolitan Opera Company.

Now in the role of artistic director of the Wolf Trap Company—having been director of the opera workshop the previous year—I was on my way to Washington, D.C., to direct and teach the young students who were coming from every part of the United States to Wolf Trap Farm Park, the country's first national park devoted to the performing arts. Usually an opera singer teaches voice when his career as a performer is over. This was not the case with me. I envisioned many more years of active singing performances. Under the general managership of Schuyler Chapin, the Met had renewed my contract and I was to take part in the 1973–1974 season in *Carmen, Madama Butterfly,* a new production of Rossini's *L'Italiana in Algeri* and *L'Elisir D'Amore.* I also had singing commitments outside New York. But I was deeply interested in helping build a national foundation that would develop the musical talents of young artists in this country. Wolf Trap had become a big step in that direction, and although the Wolf Trap opera workshop is intended largely for the college student, the enrollment includes college graduates, some of whom are 30 years of age or older. The thousands of applicants represent major universities and small colleges, big urban centers and provincial towns. Joseph Leavitt, executive director, Frank Rizzo, production coordinator, and I auditioned approximately 500 singers. We chose 40 gifted young artists on the basis of talent, stage presence, and a willingness to accept small parts or sing in the chorus.

Music of every type is either taught or performed at Wolf Trap—rock, classical, experimental, musical comedy, pop. There is also a program for dancers. A large open-air theater in the park's Filene Center seats 3,500 people and can accommodate 3,000 more on the lawn. Throughout the summer these large audiences throng to a program of musical comedies and special entertainments. Added to this entertainment, Wolf Trap produces one or two operas or musical comedies in which the young artists perform.

The summer of 1973 I directed and introduced two evenings of scenes from *The Magic Flute, Cosi Fan Tutti, La Traviata,*

*Manon, Madama Butterfly, The Barber of Seville, Pagliacci, Albert Herring, Gianni Schicchi,* and *Faust.* We also had a double-bill evening of *Man on a Bearskin Rug* by Paul Ramsier and *Trouble in Tahiti* by Leonard Bernstein.

Among the 40 young singers who performed that season were some beautiful, thrilling voices. Some of them already displayed a high level of professionalism, holding promise of their future artistry and achievement. Such talent exists today throughout the world.

&#8253; In 1972, preparing for my first season as director of the opera workshop and teacher at Wolf Trap, I had searched within myself for an approach to this assignment. I realized that my value to the young singers with whom I would be working derived from my knowledge of opera-singing techniques, study of languages, and some comprehension of conducting and directing. This was the musical investment I wanted to share. But as a Christian Scientist, I had something more fundamental.

In *Science and Health*, Mary Baker Eddy writes: "Love for God and man is the true incentive in both healing and teaching."[1] Although Mrs. Eddy intended this to mean the teaching of Christian Science, I took this statement literally to apply to my teaching work at Wolf Trap. *All* people respond to love, and this love was to be applied in my teaching by a deep desire to be interested in every one of our singers and to let them know it. I found that this principle worked wonderfully in the opera program. In an increasingly mechanized society, the simplest touch of someone who cares can inspire—with lasting effect, I believe—the careers of striving young musicians.

I had seen this truth proved by Leonard Bernstein, one of the great conductors with whom I enjoyed working. Bernstein had that spontaneous welling-up of love that was felt by everyone. He loved the music; he loved the musicians; he loved the audience. It was his deep, overflowing love to which I responded, often being lifted to new heights of performance. Bernstein is quoted as saying that music is spiritual—something with which most musicians agree. Being a spiritual outpouring,

[1] *Science and Health*, p. 454.

music partakes of the nature of God, the great Spirit of all harmony.

 

&#x218; Christian Science teaches that in his spiritual selfhood, the singer is the expression of God, Soul. So he naturally reflects Soul's beauty and perfection, embodying melody, pitch, grace, poise, and the power to express them; he cannot be limited. In directing and teaching at Wolf Trap—patiently and with perseverance—I held my thought to this concept of the singers' spiritual selfhood—the image and likeness of God. As a result of this approach, I found it was possible to bring out with these young artists the performances whose beauty and high professional quality I have already mentioned.

 

&#x218; Most of the young artists in the program understood that there is more to a career in opera than singing. During the 1973 program John Moriarty of the Boston Conservatory of Music, among his other duties, gave daily classes in diction of the major foreign languages. I considered these of great value because I believe the subject of languages is next in importance to vocal development for a career in opera. It is essential that a young singer learn to pronounce the language in which he is singing (*including English*), and he must understand the words if he is to give proper color and interpretation to the music.

He must also be as much a master of his body as a dancer—if he is to act an opera role with grace and distinction. For many years *Science and Health* has given me wise counsel along these lines: "Take possession of your body, and govern its feeling and action. Rise in the strength of Spirit to resist all that is unlike good. God has made man capable of this, and nothing can vitiate the ability and power divinely bestowed on man." [2]

 

&#x218; One often hears that there are not enough opportunities for singers in the United States. I disagree. There are today more scholarships, endowments, fellowships, and grants than there have been in the past. And equally, there are more professional opportunities today. So I can only say that a singer with talent and desire, who has prepared himself well, will succeed.

[2] *Science and Health*, p. 393.

Competition seems to be a grueling factor in the music world. Through Christian Science, I have overcome the fear of competition. I have grasped that in God's universe, creation evolves in an orderly way, and competition does not exist. Being an idea of Love, I dwell in complete harmony with every other idea. God supplies my needs, without depriving anyone else of his rightful rewards. Nor can I be deprived by anyone else's success, since God has placed me—as He places each one of His children—in our rightful roles.

This concept of man occupying his individual place in God's universe has, to a large extent, freed me from jealousy, envy, or the desire to beat someone else to a job. It has kept my relationships with fellow singers on an harmonious level. It has brought me close to God's love and made me receptive to His guidance.

&» I was born into a family made up almost entirely of musicians. My maternal grandmother had been a singer and voice teacher. My grandfather was an orchestra conductor at Poli's vaudeville house in Waterbury, Connecticut, where the family settled; he also headed up the town band bearing the family name—Fulton's American Band. They had five children and all became musicians. One of my uncles played the flute with the NBC Symphony Orchestra under Toscanini. My mother and one of her sisters did a sister singing act at Poli's Theater, with my grandfather conducting the orchestra.

After her marriage, my mother gave up the idea of a career, but she and her sisters had beautifully trained voices, and the sound of arias ringing through our home was one of my earliest memories. I can remember my mother singing "Pace, pace, mio Dio" from Verdi's *La Forza del Destino*, and my aunt singing "Mi Chiamono Mimi" from Puccini's *La Boheme* and the Act II aria of the "Queen of the Night" from Mozart's *Magic Flute*. So as a young boy soprano I thought nothing of going around the house singing opera arias in the coloratura repertoire!

I studied the piano and learned to play it fairly well. But in my teens I was determined to break the family tradition—I would not become a professional musician. I would be a businessman.

With the exception of two years when we lived in Glen Cove, Long Island, most of my growing-up years were spent in Lake Worth, Florida. My mother was a Christian Scientist and I attended the Christian Science Sunday Schools both in Glen Cove and Lake Worth.

The Sunday School teaching was from two books: the King James version of the Bible and *Science and Health with Key to the Scriptures* by Mary Baker Eddy. I was taught the Ten Commandments, the Lord's Prayer with its spiritual interpretation given in *Science and Health*, and Jesus' Sermon on the Mount—the great spiritual laws of Life, Truth, and Love which Mrs. Eddy said were basic to a knowledge of the Science of Christ by which Jesus performed his mighty healing works. As soon as we could read, the children discussed the lesson-sermons from the same Quarterly from which the adults studied, being taught the simpler meanings of Christian Science as they related to our daily lives. We learned how to heal ourselves in Christian Science. From the ages of twelve to twenty (when attendance ends), I frequently played the piano in the Sunday School, and on occasion the organ for the church services. I later studied the organ at college.

֍ Graduating from Lake Worth High School in 1948, I enrolled as a business major at Rollins College in Winter Park, Florida. It took me only three days to realize that business was not my calling, and I switched all my courses to music. I was beginning to see that a higher power than human will must direct my life. At that point I still didn't consider a career in voice, but decided to major in piano with the intention of concentrating on musical composition. In my junior year the composition professor discouraged me. "I think your talent lies elsewhere," he said.

So I went to see Dr. Harvey Woodruff, director of the Rollins conservatory, and told him that I was casting about for a new major. Dr. Woodruff, who also directed the choir, said, "I think you have the potential for a singing career and should major in voice." So I again changed my special field and decided to take my degree in voice.

Rollins College is widely known for its annual Bach Festival, held every winter for nearly 40 years. It was at Rollins that I first developed my reverence for Bach's great musical literature— especially his cantatas, masses, and oratorios. Shortly after enrolling in Rollins, I joined the choir, occasionally singing a solo part. Subsequently I was assigned solos at the annual oratorio festival, singing the stirring parts of Pontius Pilate and Peter in Bach's *Saint Matthew Passion*, considered by most musicians the most perfect oratorio ever written.

In my senior year I substituted as soloist at First Church of Christ, Scientist, Orlando, Florida, and was regular baritone and soloist at the Congregational Church in Winter Park. Over the years I have continued as soloist in the Christian Science churches. I occasionally sing the solo at the Sunday services of Second Church of Christ, Scientist, in New York City, which is located near Lincoln Center.

Some of the world's greatest music has been written on religious themes, and the profound spiritual feeling it evokes transcends denominationalism. The religious music of Bach, Handel, Haydn, and Beethoven stir us, I believe, to the unspoken realization that we are all the children of the one Father-Mother God.

ॐ After graduating from Rollins College in 1952, I was recommended to Martial Singher, who taught in summer musical programs in Aspen, Colorado. Singher is a famous French baritone who sang with the Metropolitan Opera Company in the 1940's and 1950's. I began studying with him on an off-and-on basis at Aspen, continued later at the Mannes School in New York City, and subsequently worked with him for several years. He taught me many valuable lessons in the technique of producing a tone large enough for opera.

At Rollins I had concentrated on French songs and lieder. Consequently, when I went to Singher, he informed me that I might have an opera career in France, but my voice was not robust enough for the opera stages of the rest of the world. He then proceeded to develop the fulness inherent in my voice. Through the years I have continued this process of development with Margaret Harshaw, once a famous singer at the Metropolitan Opera, who now is on the faculty of the conservatory of

Indiana University. This training dealt with the support of the voice, focusing of vowels, and vocal coloration.

But there was much more to be done than mere physical development of vocal capabilities. I needed enlightenment on the spiritual source of development. Turning to the Christian Science textbook, I read: "God expresses in man the infinite idea forever developing itself, broadening and rising higher and higher from a boundless basis." [3] Grasping the fact that God is the underlying Principle of all development, I made good progress in my vocal studies.

⋛◈ When the summer program in Aspen was over, I came to New York City to find work as a singer. I saw an ad in *The Christian Science Monitor* stating that First Church of Christ, Scientist, in Jackson Heights, Queens, was holding auditions for a soloist. So I went over to Jackson Heights, auditioned, and was selected as soloist for the church.

A few days earlier one of the students at the opera workshop at the Mannes School had said to me: "They're holding auditions for the Paper Mill Playhouse. Why don't you go?" Paper Mill housed a musical stock company in New Jersey that did two-week runs of musical comedy. It had an excellent reputation. Leading Broadway musical stars like Stephen Douglas, Dorothy Sandlin, Ted Scott, Rosemarie Broncato, Patricia Bowman, and others often performed at Paper Mill in between their Broadway commitments. Seventy-five baritones auditioned, and I was the one they selected. So I felt I was proving that "Love inspires, illumines, designates, and leads the way," [4] as *Science and Health* states.

⋛◈ At Paper Mill I was immediately given understudy roles, and after two or three shows I began to do small parts. My first assignment was the understudy of Eisenstein in *Rosalinda*—a part I was totally unprepared to sing, and I was fortunate not to be called upon to attempt it (although Eisenstein was a role I later did many times in *Die Fledermaus*, both at the New York

[3] *Science and Health*, p. 258.
[4] *Science and Health*, p. 454.

City Opera and at the Met). At Paper Mill I sang Cascada in
*The Merry Widow*, Pish Tush in *The Mikado*, Poldi in *The
Great Waltz*, and roles in *Blossom Time*, *On Your Toes*,
*Brigadoon*, and *Call Me Madame*, among others. Singing at the
Paper Mill Playhouse led to my years with the New York City
Opera Company. This is how it happened.

I was in a production of *Carmen* at Paper Mill, singing the
part of Dancairo, when John White, the assistant general
director of the New York City Opera Company, visited the
Playhouse to hear another singer. Mr. White asked someone to
tell me to write for an audition with the City Opera Company,
which I did. As a result, I auditioned for Mr. White, Julius
Rudel (who at that time occupied a minor position), and Joseph
Rosenstock, then general director. When I had finished singing
"Avant de Quitter ces Lieux" from Gounod's *Faust*, I was told
City Opera would like to engage me immediately. A few days
later the contract arrived, stating that I was engaged as
*comprimario*, a singer of small parts. But at the age of 24, the
size of the opportunity meant more to me than the size of the
roles.

ॐ The opera season being a comparatively short one, I
began to accept parts in such Broadway shows as *New Faces of
1956* and *Do Re Mi*—work for which my Paper Mill experience
had prepared me. But I soon found that opera managers
throughout the country began to classify me as a Broadway type,
while Broadway producers thought of me as an operatic singer.
Heeding Jesus' admonition to "Let thine eye be single," [5] I
affirmed my commitment to opera and classical singing, and
turned away from performing in Broadway musicals.

Soon other opportunities presented themselves in the form of
concerts and TV opera productions. I have sung with the
National Symphony Orchestra in Washington, D.C., in Britten's
*War Requiem*; with the New York Philharmonic in Haydn's
*Creation*; with the Cleveland Symphony Orchestra in *The
Seasons*; and in the great Bach and Handel oratorios with other
distinguished symphony orchestras. Many times I have felt that

[5] Matthew 6:22.

the sacred music I was singing opened my eyes to perceive what the Revelator meant when he said: "I saw a new heaven and a new earth."

᳁ I was with the New York City Opera Company for twelve exciting years. The company started as a poor struggling organization. But determined to bring opera to the people at popular prices, it fought for its survival and managed to outlive considerable financial and managerial turmoil. The audiences who came to City Center on West 55th Street—many of them young people—were deeply interested in opera and there was a wonderful feeling between audience and musicians that musical progress was being made in New York. During those years I sang the roles of the Don in *Don Giovanni*, Count Almaviva in *Marriage of Figaro*, Danilo in *Merry Widow*, Papegano in *Magic Flute*, Eisenstein in *Die Fledermaus*, and many other traditional opera roles.

By this time, the New York City Opera Company was under the directorship of the brilliant and enterprising Julius Rudel. In addition to its regular fare of standard opera, the company began to branch out in thrilling productions of modern opera. Once more came the opportunity for new experiences and the growth that comes with them. I sang the lead roles of Belaev in the world premier of Lee Hoiby's *Natalia Petrovna*, Miles Dunster in the world premier of Douglas Moore's *Wings of the Dove*, and Heathcliff in the New York premier of Carlisle Floyd's *Wuthering Heights*.

On the occasion of world or New York premieres of new opera productions, Met administration people like Rudolf Bing, Robert Herman, and other Met managers, came to City Center. Several of them I knew on a first-name basis, and I had met Mr. Bing a number of times. But I had no impatience to be at the Met. I felt that God was unfolding the right time and the right situation for me, and I was happy in my work. From time to time my manager would phone and say, "Do you want me to arrange for an audition at the Met?" Invariably my answer was, "I don't think I should ask for an audition. The Met people know my work, they know what I can do. Let's wait."

Christian Science had taught me that progress comes when we

are ready to receive it. Consequently I never felt it was necessary to go after anything. Everything in my career has led naturally to the next step. I have known many fine singers who were frustrated because they were not at the Met. Often this prevented them from doing their best work in their current assignment—because they were thinking, "When I get to the Met, I'll do my best." In my experience, wherever the engagement was, I have felt that it deserved not only my best singing but also my best attitude.

ও~ On a spring day in 1965, John Gutman of the Metropolitan Opera Company called me at my home and said the Met was hiring several singers. Would I mind coming down and singing for them so that the Met people could hear what my voice sounded like on their stage? At that time the Metropolitan Opera Company was located at Broadway and 39th Street, and the Metropolitan Opera House was a magical name. The spectacular voices of Caruso, Galli-Curci, Farrar, Schumann-Heink, Pinza, Flagstad—all had echoed through those hallowed halls.

I had prepared five difficult arias. Knowing that the Met was scheduling a new production of *Pique Dame*, one of my arias was from that Tchaikovsky work, in Russian. Several years earlier, with Thomas Scherman conducting, I had done a concert version of the opera at Carnegie Hall and the Brooklyn Academy of Music.

Mr. Bing was present at the 1965 audition. On the Met stage, I announced that I was going to sing the Yeletski aria from *Pique Dame*. "Although you are doing the opera in English," I said, "I know it only in Russian." After I had sung the aria, Mr. Bing thanked me and said, "Will you go back and see Mr. Herman." When I saw Robert Herman, the assistant manager, he told me that the Metropolitan Opera Company was offering me a contract.

That fall I made my debut in *Pique Dame* in English, singing the role not of Yeletski, but of Tomsky. (Many times since then I have sung Tomsky both in English and Russian at the Met.) That same season I also sang Madryka in the Richard Strauss opera *Arabella*.

The following season, 1966, the Metropolitan Opera House on 39th Street closed its doors forever. The Metropolitan Opera Company moved into the glamorous new Lincoln Center building with its exquisite crystal chandeliers, its lovely, winding red-carpeted staircases, gold and crystal decor, and its monumental Chagall murals. An opera era had closed. Another was about to begin.

֍ That same year the Metropolitan went to Paris on tour, taking two productions, *The Barber of Seville* and *The Marriage of Figaro*. I felt it was a great honor to have been assigned the role of Count Almaviva in *Figaro*. As it turned out, the Met was not well received in Paris. We had come at a period of strong anti-American feeling in France. Furthermore, we inadvertently offended the Parisians by choosing to do two operas based on the plays of Beaumarchais. French feeling was that their native dramatist should not have been presented by an American opera company—even by the Met with its international reputation.

*The Barber of Seville* opened first at the beautiful Odéon Theater. Not being in the production, I attended the premiere. To my consternation, the performance was followed by catcalls and boos. The following night *The Marriage of Figaro*, in which I sang, was performed, to the same hostile response. A pall of gloom began to settle on the cast, and I felt the depression beginning to envelop me.

As Christian Scientists frequently do when they are confronted with problems, I sought out a Christian Science Reading Room—this one located on the Rue de la Paix. There I began to pray for a clearer concept of God's love for man. John's words were comforting: "God is love; and he that dwelleth in love dwelleth in God, and God in him." [6] I knew that my job was to continue to dwell in the consciousness of love, and not in the consciousness of hostility and depression. Soon my peace returned. That following Sunday I attended First Church of Christ, Scientist, in Paris, and felt again the healing love that permeates Christian Science churches all over the world.

[6] I John 4:16.

A friend, who was singing the Countess in *The Marriage of Figaro*, told me that she found the hostile reception in Paris difficult to bear. I began talking to her along the lines of Christian Science: We needed to see through the mask of a hostile man in a hostile city to the man of God's creating, dwelling in the city (the consciousness) of God, Love—and not the city of mortal animosities. Finally she said she could accept this spiritual concept of love, and would carry on her performance in the knowledge that man is made in the image and likeness of God.

The second performance of *The Marriage of Figaro* received a quiet response. Our last performance, however, was a triumph; it was a complete turnaround. The audience applauded for ten or fifteen minutes. To me it was proof that when the musician understands that divine Love alone governs man, audience hostility is overcome. I was in Paris for about a week and had a glorious time in that beautiful city of centuries-old art and culture, visiting the Louvre and Montmartre, walking along the Seine, eating at the little cafes. The Met's Opera tour had not lost its luster.

From Paris, I went to Spoleto to take part in Gian Carlo Menotti's Festival of Two Worlds, singing the role of Pelléas in *Pelléas et Mélisande*, Debussy's only opera.

 

&#8666; The year before, 1965, at La Fenice in Venice, I had sung the title role in the Italian premiere of Mr. Menotti's own work, *The Last Savage*. That year brought yet another memorable experience—singing the lead role of Nick Shadow in the recorded performance of Stravinsky's opera, *The Rake's Progress*, with the composer conducting. I had appeared in the opera under Stravinsky's supervision when it was given in 1960 and again in 1962 at the Santa Fe Opera Company in New Mexico. So I was excited about being asked by him to record it.

Stravinsky, I believe, is the greatest composer of our time and I think *The Rake's Progress* is our greatest contemporary opera. This is not belittling Menotti's fine work, but Menotti and Stravinsky compose from different standpoints. Menotti writes theater-oriented opera, musical theater. Stravinsky wrote as a great composer. I feel about Stravinsky as I do about Mozart, and believe *The Rake's Progress* to be on an equal plane with the music of the Mozart operas. Often when I listen to great music I feel it was not humanly composed but simply dropped down from some celestial heights where it always existed. Great stretches of *The Rake's Progress* make me feel that way.

Old or new, great music will always be contemporary. I cannot count the times that I have heard Mozart's *Marriage of Figaro*, *The Magic Flute*, and his symphonies. Each time, without fail, Mozart's music seems more piercingly beautiful than before. Music that opens fresh revelations at every performance will always be contemporary.

&#8478; I am essentially a lover of lyric music—music expressing its beauties in harmony and melody. Much of the discordant music I find boring. Occasionally, however, a composer will write an opera which is discordant, but because it expresses a discordant idea, that opera is a valid musical composition. But music that attempts to convey a harmonious situation through discord, I find lacking in validity. I firmly support the musical concept stated in *Science and Health*: "To be master of chords and discords, the science of music must be understood. Left to the decisions of material sense, music is liable to be misapprehended and lost in confusion." [7]

The successful composer, in my judgment, is one who uses discord as his servant but doesn't himself serve discord. An illustration of this is *The Devils of Loudun*, a modern opera by the avant-garde Polish composer Krzystof Penderecki, in which I sang the lead role of Grandier at its American premiere at the Santa Fe Opera Company. The opera has no arias; throughout, its music is all discord. A singer is almost never on the same note as any other singer in the cast. The opera conveys a harsh story of cruelty, persecution, crucifixion, rising into final triumph of the spirit. The music is an honest portrayal of the moods of hypocrisy, bigotry, and mercilessness—and in the end, spiritual supremacy. Consequently, while *The Devils of Loudun* departs from the base of traditional opera, Penderecki, using discord masterfully, has created a musical composition of tremendous

[7] *Science and Health*, p. 304.

dramatic impact that stirs an audience as truly as standard opera.

The relationship of discord and harmony in contemporary music is being debated with passionate intensity among today's musicians—as debates have raged in every age when a new musical form has appeared on the scene.

ε➛ Another modern opera which departs from tradition is Lee Hoiby's *Summer and Smoke* based on Tennessee Williams' play of that name. The opera, in which I sang the male lead role of John Buchanan, written especially for me by Hoiby, had its world premiere in 1971 at the O'Shaughnessy Center in St. Paul, Minnesota. The standard opera story revolves around the loves, joys, and jealousies of superbeings. The characters in *Summer and Smoke* are small-town people, and through story and music their lives are portrayed with dignity and touching beauty. Hoiby wrote his music with the knowledge that it would be acted; and faithfully following the story line, his musical composition is romantic and lyrical. Hoiby uses discord, although sparingly, and I believe, appropriately.

ε➛ Opera is conceded to be an artificial art form. Having a story sung is not realistic. On the other hand, the opera repertoire portrays every conceivable human feeling and emotion. The miracle is that through the singing voice, feeling is lifted into a spiritual dimension of beauty and sensitivity, and opera often becomes a very real and exalting experience. In this sense, opera is a valid and enduring art form.

ε➛ In the early history of the Met, singers were not expected to act and opera productions were not directed. People came to hear great voices. Standing at the front of the stage, the legendary singers were themselves the dramatic focal points. Emphasis on acting is a somewhat new development with the Metropolitan Opera Company—with Franco Zeffirelli, the distinguished movie director, and such famous theatrical directors as Tyrone Guthrie, Margaret Webster, and Alfred Lunt having been brought in to direct Met productions.

Opera singing and acting relate to thought. If a singer

understands his role, then his acting is the natural outgrowth of a dramatic situation rather than something superimposed on the music. When Frank Corsaro directed us in *Summer and Smoke*, he gave me only about half a dozen specific acting instructions. Since the music was composed to fit the libretto, my actions had to conform to Hoiby's musical artistry. I simply had to *be* the part, not only sing it. When an opera singer has mastery not only over his voice but also over his body, the audience responds appreciatively.

ॐ A singing career demands utmost discipline. A singer needs familiarity with every facet of the music he is to perform. He must analyze his approach to it, its phrasing, its meaning, and the way he is to articulate it. When his practice is thorough, nothing can interfere with the singer's dominion in performance—there is no chance involved. It is hazardous, as every musician has learned, to go for a stretch of time without disciplined practice—and no one knows this better than the professional singer. In this sense, the practice of Christian Science and the practice of music are to an extent comparable—since the one universal Principle governs both music and musician. You might call practice a form of prayer.

ॐ In my tours, I have sung with the Philadelphia Lyric Opera Company, the Boston, Cincinnati, Dallas, San Francisco, and other opera groups. Usually opera companies give student dress rehearsals or performances. Many students come thinking they won't enjoy opera. But after a performance they frequently have come backstage to tell me, "If we had known opera was going to be like this, we would have come to one before."

An amusing example of this occurred when I was out West doing a production of *Tosca*. The opera company had a policy of selling student tickets at a dollar apiece, but at a private girls' school of 250 students in that area the company had sold only one ticket. So the management asked the tenor, the soprano, and myself to go out to the school and try to sell a few tickets. We appeared at the school during lunch hour. After relating sequences of our opera roles, the tenor then sang the line

"Vittoria, vittoria," from the second act of *Tosca*, ending on a high A-sharp.

Pandemonium broke loose in that dining hall. The students had never heard a human voice making a sound like that. They had grown up listening to transistors. Now they heard the actual sound of a tone so vital they couldn't contain their excitement. Here was proof that when young people have the proper exposure to great music, they respond with vigor. We sold many tickets at the school that day.

This brings me to a matter which I hope will some day be corrected in TV programming—the lack of great music performed on major national networks. When I was growing up, I heard good music on the radio practically every night of the week. When TV replaced radio as a major national entertainment medium, great music was neglected except on National Educational Television. I believe that our young people have suffered culturally because they have not been sufficiently exposed to its exalting influence.

3➤ I have sung in half a dozen operas on TV, several with the old NBC Television Opera Theater, which produced three or four operas a year. Currently the Opera Theater has been replaced by the Public Broadcasting Service, with the same distinguished conductor, Peter Herman Adler.

I have also sung on the "Mister Rogers' Neighborhood" show, which, next to "Sesame Street," is today's most widely watched children's television program. Fred Rogers, who created the program, and I were fellow students at Rollins College, and through the years our musical careers have brought us together. Rogers' philosophy of the program is: love expressed from one person to another. The format revolves around a puppet show. Some weeks the "Mister Rogers' Neighborhood" show ends in a children's opera, in which I sing. Periodically, I go to the Pittsburgh studios for a week at a time to tape the children's operas which are shown on the show several times throughout the year. I have done the roles of an organ grinder, a farmer, and other characters with which children can easily relate.

Many times after a performance at the Met or with other

opera companies parents come to me and say, "My children see
you on 'Mister Rogers' Neighborhood.'" Thus my career is
helped by "Mister Rogers"—proving what Mrs. Eddy says:
". . . whatever blesses one blesses all." [8]

ॐ I have missed very few performances because of sickness.
When I first started singing in New York, I had a small part in
Menotti's Broadway production of *The Saint of Bleeker Street*.
I sang a solo standing on a restaurant table and during a
performance, as I jumped off the table, my leg was scratched by
a protruding nail. A few days later I woke up to find my leg
swollen from hip to toe. The symptoms indicated blood
poisoning. Immediately I began to pray as we are taught in
Christian Science. Opening *Science and Health*, I read: "The
divine Love, which made harmless the poisonous viper, which
delivered men from the boiling oil, from the fiery furnace, from
the jaws of the lion, can heal the sick in every age and triumph
over sin and death." [9] Reassured that only the law of Love, not
the law of matter, was operating in my life, I lost my fear of
poisoning. I also asked a Christian Science practitioner to pray
for me. The next day my leg was normal and I was able to
perform that evening.

Another healing took place years later. When I was about to
go on stage in an opera performance, I couldn't sing above a D,
and the aria called for G's. Holding my thought to the concepts
that "Music is divine. Mind, not matter, makes music," [10]—as
Mrs. Eddy states in one of her messages to The Mother
Church—I was able to sing that aria freely. The audience was
totally unaware that I was having any physical difficulty. When a
reviewer wrote favorably about my performance, I mentally gave
full credit to Christian Science.

ॐ Not long ago a television program pictured aborigines of
New Guinea singing in chorus, in tones recognizable to a
Western ear. Removed from society where music is formalized,
how did these aborigines discover notes? How did their sense of

[8] *Science and Health*, p. 206.
[9] *Science and Health*, p. 243.
[10] *Message to The Mother Church, 1900*, p. 11.

performance develop? To me, the explanation is clear: music springs up in every corner of the earth because the Principle of man is the Principle of music. For that reason, music and man are inseparable. For that reason, song is heard in the wilds of New Guinea as well as in the elegant surroundings of Philharmonic Hall and the Metropolitan Opera House.

ভ In the course of my professional life there have been many moments when the music I was performing filled me with such rapture that I felt especially favored to have a musical career. At other times, of course, there have arisen ordeals that confront every musician. When faced with difficulties, I have had recourse to Christian Science. Working out my problems according to the divine Principle, Love, has led to harmonious solutions. Trials, when overcome, have lifted me higher in the scale of spiritual understanding.

Mary Baker Eddy writes in *Science and Health*: "Harmony in man is as real and immortal as in music." [11] It has always seemed to me that these words flowed from the great love Mrs. Eddy had for all mankind and that they embraced me, as a musician, with special tenderness. Certainly they impressed upon me that harmony in my life was important as a Christian Scientist, and that I could work out a satisfying life-experience with the same precision that one works out a fine piece of music. From this base of metaphysical perception, I have seen details of contracts, the coordinating of singing engagements, and relationships in many parts of the country and with many types of individuals harmonized under the one Principle, God, who is Love.

[11] *Science and Health*, p. 276.

*Former Pittsburgh Councilman James A. Jordon with President
Lyndon B. Johnson at the White House*

# BLACK MAN,
# WHITE MAN,
# GOD'S MAN

### ঌ James Alonzo Jordon

PRESIDENT OF COMMUNITY LEARNING CORPORATION
OF WASHINGTON, D.C.,
FORMER COUNCILMAN OF PITTSBURGH

ঌ I was born in Pittsburgh on October 13, 1923. My parents
were members of an orthodox church, but I stopped attending
at a very early age because religion seemed to me something for
the elderly and frustrated. We were a middle-income family, my
father part owner of the Carter & Jordon House and Window
Cleaning Company. I began to work for him when eleven years
old, and dreamed of building this business into a large corporation.

Though living in a Negro world with a completely Negro
social life, I knew that my work was to be in the world of whites.
There was a drive in me and I believed that no obstacle could
stop me. In my teens I would ride through the neighborhood
where Pittsburgh's mansions stood and decide where I wanted
to live when I grew up. A girl I knew lived in a house facing the
Jones & Loughlin Steel Corporation buildings. Sitting on her
porch I would be enthralled with the teeming activity of iron ore

being converted into steel, and would dream of having such a business.

Fascinated by the lives of leaders in business, industry, and politics, I pored over the biographies of John D. Rockefeller, J.P. Morgan, Jay Gould. Such diverse personalities as Clare Booth Luce, Senator Robert Taft, Thomas Dewey, and Franklin Roosevelt won my admiration. I believed that anyone having their ability to organize could get things done. The fact that none of my heroes was black didn't concern me. They were Americans as I was. They had been reared on the American dream, as I had been. They had a strong sense of purpose; I felt the same stirrings within me.

My elementary and high schools were integrated, but not until high school did I recognize discrimination with its special problems. I always had a need to excel, but realized that as a Negro I had to be even better to succeed. A physical examination revealed I had a heart murmur. Someone was always telling me I couldn't do something. These things didn't stop me. I made the football team, a goal achieved by only two other Negroes in the school, and received varsity letters in football, track, volley ball, and gymnastics. Instinctively I grasped an unseen law which enables everyone to do what needs to be done.

On graduation from high school in June 1941 I won a scholarship to Lincoln University in Oxford, Pennsylvania, just outside of Philadelphia. Lincoln, one of the first Negro colleges in the United States, had the reputation of turning out Negro lawyers and doctors. Law, business, politics—these all interested me, and I decided to prepare for law.

At Lincoln I was in a runoff for president of the freshman class and made the varsity football team, but after a year I looked for a bigger challenge. I wanted to play football at a major college, and transferred to Penn State University. There I studied for a year, until 1943, when the men on campus marched off to the Army. We were going to fight a war to make a free world.

I loved the Army and its uniforms. But there again I encountered discrimination and ended up in an all-Negro company, the first Negro Airborne Infantry Battalion. The Army said Negroes didn't have the nerve to jump out of airplanes so they were generally sent overseas as on-the-ground mechanics, engineers, and quartermasters. Not wanting that, I volunteered for the paratroops. I jumped the very first time in a plane and eventually made 38 jumps, though I never saw active duty. The war ended before a decision was made to send a Negro airborne battalion overseas. On my return from Army duty, I transferred to the University of Pittsburgh.

Hitler's master plan to have his Aryan race rule the world had failed, but service in the United States Army had shown me that democracy needed to be won at home as well as abroad—democracy for black Americans. While still an undergrad, I became actively involved in the battle against racial discrimination, freely volunteering my services with the Urban League to find job opportunities for black veterans. One day I called on the president of a large company. He had been my father's customer for years, and we knew his family well. But when I asked him how many Negroes his company employed, the conference ended. Seeing how people's pocketbooks affected their benevolence, I felt there must be a higher rule than the purse.

Other things began to happen. I was elected to the board of the Student YMCA. Also, as president of the black fraternity at college, I became a new leader on campus and entered campus politics. One day the president of the YMCA asked me to attend a meeting of the National Intercollegiate Christian Council, made up of YMCA and YWCA students from all colleges. At this meeting we passed legislation for setting up the first NICC lobbying office for civil rights in Washington. This occurred in 1946 and portended a national movement. It also indicated my own future.

Shortly after that a YMCA official said to me, "We're having a Second World Conference of Christian Youth to be held in Oslo, Norway. Are you interested in going?" I answered yes. Whereupon my résumé was sent to New York and I was elected to represent the middle Atlantic region—one of twelve students of the NICC in the United States to attend this conference. The YMCA then approached the Pittsburgh churches, which agreed to defray my expenses.

Outstanding religious leaders, including Reinhold Niebuhr,

addressed this conference, which represented 70 countries. For the first time religion's role in great spiritual decisions of the world dawned on me. But I thought denominationalism was hypocritical and a waste.

While rooming with a South African and a Nigerian, I first heard about the problems of apartheid. The South African wanted us to understand the misery of his people, and upon returning home, I organized groups to send clothing. Then the Indonesian students at the conference received word that revolution had broken out in their country, and they circulated statements about Indonesia's right to national independence.

I was surprised to learn that Africa had automobiles and modern buildings, because everything I had ever read or seen in movies portrayed natives doing tribal dances and holding spears. The African students were very upset about a film then running in Oslo that showed English royalty on an African visit watching tribal dancing and chants. They felt the newspapers were not reporting the true story.

Often Norwegians asked the American Negro representatives about racial conditions in the United States, and I was amazed that they knew so much about America's problems. Aware that the world's eyes were on America, I saw that something needed to be done to bridge the gap between America's professed idealism and her actual practice insofar as democratic action for blacks was concerned.

After the conference we left Oslo for Sweden. One day a young Swedish girl asked me to take her canoeing, but I knew a white minister was interested in her and feared that if I dated the girl, this would turn the minister against Negroes. So I arranged for all three of us to go canoeing.

By the time I returned to Pittsburgh, my interest in religion had been fully awakened and I was reading literature on religion in business, law, and politics. But I found no denomination that seemed to relate completely to personal as well as social and economic problems, particularly the many problems of the black community. In my reports to more than fifty primarily white churches which had contributed to my trip, I spoke of the waste and hypocrisy of denominationalism. I was only 23 years old at the time.

Soon after that I was asked to attend the National Students Association conference at the University of Wisconsin. On my arrival I learned that some Southern delegates didn't want any reference to race relations to appear in the NSA constitution, and they packed the writing committee to prevent this. I joined a committee advocating a provision on race relations in the preamble rather than the body of the constitution. We also agreed on a slate of officials, including a Negro. The National Students Association unanimously passed our proposals, and we emerged victorious, arm in arm, with pictures being taken. This was my first political achievement. Deep inside, I felt there was a religious principle operating in all this.

I was the second Negro to finish a graduate course in retailing at Pittsburgh University, and one of the first to work in a department store. Coming into contact with the buying public, I felt the ambivalence of partial acceptance, partial rejection of my race, and it was not a happy feeling. But this job represented a breakthrough for the Negro, and progress was on the march in Pittsburgh.

While studying at the University, I organized the Breakfast Club, a YMCA Students group, and we met weekly to discuss current events and religious views. Because of the publicity I had received, my name was submitted for corresponding secretary of the National Association for the Advancement of Colored People, Pittsburgh branch, and I was elected an officer. Daisy Lampkin, a member of the national board of the NAACP and vice-president of the *Pittsburgh Courier*, a black newspaper, told me about a young lady coming to Pittsburgh. "She is a national field secretary for the NAACP. I think you will enjoy meeting and working with her." That young lady was Marion Bond. When she came to Pittsburgh to organize the NAACP membership campaign, I invited her to speak at the Breakfast Club. She accepted and I was so impressed with what she presented that I invited her home for dinner. A year later, in 1949, we were married. Marion was a Christian Scientist.

The following year I organized the Jordon Supply Company, a wallpaper and paint store. Soon afterward Marion and I, deciding to prepare ourselves for advancement in our careers, both entered law school. Then, for the first time in my life I ran into difficulties. The promised financial backing for my business didn't materialize. I was left with only $140 and some very trying problems. But these problems forced me to search my thinking. I began to realize that I couldn't rely on human drive to make my business work, some higher power was required. Humbled by this realization, I started to attend the Christian Science church regularly with Marion. There I began to understand how our needs could be met through prayer.

One of the first things that impressed me about this religion was its vastly different concept of God and prayer. God was known as Principle, and to my knowledge, no other religion applies this synonym to the Supreme Being. I had long ago realized that the religious conflicts among mankind come from the worship of an anthropomorphic God, a man-made white or black God on a throne watching over us, whereas humanity's need is for an incorporeal God and Godlike man. As an activist interested in law, the concept of God as *the* Principle from which stem all laws governing the universe appealed to me. I saw that this Principle, holding the stars in their orbits and the rivers in their courses, also governs the life of man—not as black or white, but as God's man. In obedience to God's laws, man and the universe are in harmony. In disobedience, man and nature are in trouble.

Six other synonyms for God as taught in Christian Science absorbed my attention: Life, Truth, Love, Mind, Soul, Spirit. These referred to one all-encompassing Being, the All-in-all. Through them I began to understand how it was possible for man to be God's image and likeness. Man expresses Truth in honesty; Love in compassion and goodness; Mind in being intelligent; Soul in beauty, and Spirit in the recognition of the sole reality and power of spiritual values above material considerations. And Life is expressed through a sense of immortal purpose and in the capacity to achieve it. In this way we are the active image of God, and God works through us.

Prayer took on a new meaning as the desire to know God better, to commune with Him as Father-Mother, to understand His laws, to obey His guidance, and to bring healing and freedom to oneself and others.

I was impressed by this statement in the chapter entitled

"Prayer" in *Science and Health*: "Who would stand before a blackboard, and pray the principle of mathematics to solve the problem? The rule is already established, and it is our task to work out the solution. Shall we ask the divine Principle of all goodness to do His own work? His work is done, and we have only to avail ourselves of God's rule in order to receive His blessing, which enables us to work out our own salvation." [1]

The concept of a divine Principle whose reality I could prove in my human affairs held out great promise. Acceptance of God as Principle didn't make Him a distant Deity, but drew me closer to Him as the great creative power and governor of my life—of all reality.

I went to see a Christian Science practitioner who had been a businessman and understood my problems. He talked to me about the Science of Christ and how I could solve my difficulties scientifically. As I began to study this religion, the heroic statements concerning God and man in Mrs. Eddy's writings strengthened me. Often a single line from a page in *Science and Health* acted as a law to solve a problem.

I felt the mighty power of Principle operating in my experience. I accepted the Bible promise: "Thine, O Lord, is the greatness, and the power, and the glory, and the victory, and the majesty: for all that is in the heaven and in the earth is thine; thine is the kingdom, O Lord, and thou art exalted as head above all. Both riches and honor come of thee, and thou reignest over all; and in thy hand is power and might; and in thine hand it is to make great, and to give strength unto all." [2]

Our pressing financial problem was met, we witnessed physical healings, and we had other proofs of God's goodness. Because there is no dogma in this religion, and the God it teaches doesn't divide man but unifies him, I felt I could unite with this church and joined First Church of Christ, Scientist, in Pittsburgh.

After attending law school about a year, I decided to drop out and devote full time to my business, which I operated successfully for five years. Marion and I became active in civic affairs, working to open segregated swimming pools and skating rinks to

[1] *Science and Health*, p. 3.
[2] I Chronicles 29:11–12.

Negroes. We believed that God was no respecter of persons, and had not given any man the right to cut off his brother's joy.

ટે≫ By now I realized that fulfillment of my larger purpose in life required me to expand my work beyond a small business. Again I turned to Principle for guidance toward the next step. Then, as now, my test for measuring any important idea was this: If only I will be blessed by the idea, it is personal ambition. If mankind will be blessed, then the idea comes to me from God.

After weeks of prayer, the idea came to enter big business. As president of my company, I was active in the Junior Chamber of Commerce and knew Fred Foy of the Koppers Company, one of the largest coal and coke producers in the country. One day I talked to him about my joining his company in an administrative position. Neither Koppers nor any other major company in Pittsburgh had ever had a black man working in such a capacity, but Mr. Foy was interested.

After several interviews with five vice-presidents, Koppers offered me the job of administrative assistant to the vice-president of the Traffic and Transportation Department. A year later they advanced me to manager of the Transportation Research and Development Section. I attended Traffic Club dinners, where railroad presidents and other executives met. No black had ever before attended their dinners, seminars, or management meetings. God was leading me, and through me, leading thousands of other blacks into a new field of freedom.

ટે≫ By this time I had decided to complete my law course. When I told Fred Foy of my decision to return to law school, he couldn't understand it. "You're in," he argued. "Why go to law school?" However, I had always wanted to be a lawyer. My religion had led me into the study of the eternal laws of Truth which relate to all men. Now I felt I needed the knowledge of the laws of the land so that I could measure them against God's laws. In business and in the area of civil rights, I felt this was important. I applied to Duquesne Law School and went to school at night for four years.

By now I was totally committed to civil rights, working to get more Negroes employed at Koppers and organizing the first group of black corporate professionals so they might unify their powers. This wasn't so much an effort of human will to break down the white walls of favoritism, rather it was my religious conviction that these walls never had a legal place in the American social system. Although the white man had selfishly and blindly created this unhealthy situation, it now had become essentially the black man's problem. It was he who had to understand God's laws sufficiently to assert his spiritual and moral rights and solve his social and economic problems. Many black leaders saw no improvement except through paths of violence, but Christian Science had taught me that improvement could come through peaceful action by doing God's work in one's field. That was the way I chose.

I conceived a plan by which big industry could open more jobs for blacks, and showed it to Mr. Foy. He presented the plan to the president of Koppers Company, and they arranged a meeting of presidents of all the major corporations in Pittsburgh—Westinghouse Electric, Jones & Loughlin, Alcoa, Fisher, Edgewater, and others. The plan was adopted and we met for a year. Work opportunities for blacks began to expand in Pittsburgh. Later, at a banquet for a thousand people, Koppers then president, Fletcher Byrom, said, "Jim Jordon took me by the hand and led me to my present understanding, and if we had listened to him earlier, we wouldn't have had some of our present problems."

In my job at Koppers, where I supervised more whites than blacks, generally speaking, I was accepted by the white man. Seeing man as spiritual, I could not mentally make racist discrimination about anyone, and as a result the white man had no racist attitudes toward me.

With the exception of one black judge, blacks held no political office in Pittsburgh. My friend Paul Jones, a Negro and a Democrat, had been in politics 30 years but had never been slated for City Council. It was time, I believed, for a black man to be on it. No law of God said that the color of a man or woman's skin determined his or her intellectual ability to function on the councils of government.

Therefore Paul and I organized the Democrats for United Action. Our logo was a wheel with white and black spokes symbolizing blacks and whites working together for unified action. We took our campaign into every ward, and as a result, were able to get jobs for blacks and solve problems for whites—the blacks being interested in jobs and the whites interested in issues. Paul was later elected as the first black to sit on the City Council, his post being a forerunner of other positions in politics for the black man.

After the successful campaign of Democrats for United Action, I became its president. For me, the crowning event of that election year was the chance to accompany Paul Jones to the 1956 Democratic National Convention. Mayor David Lawrence made it possible for him to be appointed an alternate delegate at large, the only Negro in the Pittsburgh delegation. In 1960, before the next National Democratic Convention was held, I read in a newspaper that Councilman Paul Jones would go as delegate, and I as alternate delegate.

Before that convention opened, Paul died suddenly and I was sent as delegate in his place. The question arose, "Who would be selected to take Paul Jones' seat in the Council?" When Mayor Joseph Barr asked me on the convention floor if I would take it, I agreed to do this if my job with the Koppers Company could be continued. The Mayor and Governor, and a few days later, the Koppers Company, consented to this arrangement.

When we returned from the convention, the newspapers listed fourteen or fifteen Negroes who were seeking the Council seat. For weeks, a great deal of crossfire ensued. Since it was unusual for a black Democrat in politics to be keenly interested in business, controversy arose about that factor of my experience. Furthermore, the Council was having its summertime recess; consequently the Mayor couldn't present my nomination to the Council until September. This delay permitted aspirants to campaign against me all summer long. My wife was a Republican, and the newspapers made a great deal of that, saying that if Jim Jordon couldn't control his wife's politics, how would he be able to handle his political affairs.

Facing opposition and jealousy all around, I reached out to God for my peace and direction. With my conviction that God places every man where he belongs in His eternal plan, I knew God would keep me in my right place. I prayed that His will be done, and my faith in His wisdom never wavered. In September 1961 I was appointed to finish out Paul Jones' term as Councilman. When the primaries opened in May of the following year, I campaigned for Councilman and was elected that fall for the remaining two years of Paul's term. In 1963 I was reelected for a four-year term.

In my work as Councilman, in the implementation of laws, in zoning and other questions that arose, I constantly had to turn to Principle for guidance. Frequently I found myself challenged. People would say, "Don't oppose those in higher authority." Sometimes those in higher authority said to me, "You're riding for a fall." This is why the synonym Principle became my favorite name for God. I felt if you applied Principle to a question—political or otherwise—you needn't worry; the forces of God would take care of it. Invariably this proved to be true.

Running for election brought me into contact with the different ethnic communities—Irish, Polish, Jewish. As I came to understand the ethnic distinctiveness, as well as the universal similarities of these people, I realized how narrow my experience had been. More and more I was seeing man as a spiritual, universal being—not as black or white, not as Polish or Irish, nor of any religious denomination or class. I saw that freedoms from economic deprivation were basically freedoms of the Spirit, and that freedom is a deeply felt instinct in man.

When I received my law degree from Duquesne University School of Law and passed my bar examination, the Koppers Company transferred me from the Traffic Department into the Law Department of their company. There I served as legal counsel, one of six lawyers. To my knowledge, there were at that time only three Negroes in the entire country working in the law departments of large corporations. At stockholders' meetings I acted as judge of elections for two years, making decisions on proxies and tallies. This also was unusual for a black.

The three major interests of my life now came into focus—business, law, politics. In these three areas I sought freedom for all people, black or white, and would fight for anyone needing it. Occasional accusations of my being more interested in blacks than in the Koppers Company were not true—and no one knew better than I that benefits had to be mutual. But it was obvious that, as a result of their long exclusion from the mainstream of opportunity and progress, black Americans had the most ground to make up. When I began working in big industry, the only jobs blacks held in large corporations were as janitors and chauffeurs, earning wages so small that their families were in a perpetual state of poverty, and a whole race felt the pangs of humiliation. Now big industry was beginning to see that the black man had to be freed from the racial limitations they had placed upon him. Often a religious man feels the pressures to do God's will, and he must obey. I believe this describes what was happening to me.

🕭 In 1961, shortly after my service on City Council began, unemployment in Pittsburgh rose to 12 percent. One day at a Council meeting I said, "I don't think we should just sit here. I think we ought to do something about it." The newspaper reporters asked me about my plan. I didn't have one, but suddenly I was on TV and radio, and almost daily in the newspapers, bringing the unemployment issue into prominence.

As a result the Mayor's Committee on Economic Development was formed to provide more jobs. We also met with black businessmen. President Kennedy had formed the Area Development Administration, and the Federal Government wanted to go into Pittsburgh and organize there. This took place just about the time President Kennedy was assassinated and Lyndon Johnson became President of the United States.

The Area Development Administration was, I thought, a good thing for black people in all metropolitan cities throughout the country. It proved to me that every man's right to earn a living or establish his own business could be implemented in this country, and I worked closely with the Federal Government. Out of this activity grew the Business and Job Development Administration in Pittsburgh, a nonprofit corporation funded by the Federal Government to provide opportunities for black businessmen. This organization ultimately made the first three loans under the poverty program, and this was announced in the White House Rose Garden by President Johnson.

The Business and Job Development Administration coun-
seled a thousand small businessmen in Pittsburgh. During the
previous fifteen years the Government had made only three
loans to black men; we raised this figure to eighty in one year.
We conducted a training program in small business management and graduated 2,000 blacks. The Mayor's Committee on
Economic Development reorganized the Regional Industrial
Development Administration, creating many new businesses and
resulting in many new jobs for both blacks and whites. Business
improved throughout the entire city. The Regional Industrial
Development Administration has since built shopping centers
and industrial parks in Pittsburgh.

During this time I was taking doctoral studies in public
administration and international affairs at the University of
Pittsburgh as a means of gaining fresh insights into my work.
Although I had organized the Government-funded Business and
Development Administration in Pittsburgh to work with black
businessmen—an organization of blacks to work with blacks—I
was not interested in becoming its president. We tried to get a
member of the faculty of Duquesne University to head it up,
and we looked elsewhere as well, but there didn't seem to be
anyone ready to do this. Finally the organization asked me to be
its president. I asked the Koppers Company if I could have a
year's leave of absence from my job, and they consented.

This was my first experience of working with a minority
enterprise in an inner-city ghetto. I also worked closely with the
Small Business Administration and with the Economic Development Administration of the U.S. Department of Commerce.
This experience gave me a view of proposal writing, of the
process of Government funding of programs, of the political side
of government—further insights into the power structure.

As an elected Councilman, I became part of this power
structure. Working with the leaders of industry and finance in
Pittsburgh, I began to understand how it operates. When you
are not part of the structure, you are on the outside looking in.
But when you are functioning within the structure, you see how
it works to get things done. How and why the power structure
gets things done are important to the moral progress of the
country, and I had ample opportunity to evaluate political

motivation. The national power structure has undergone some changes, with more decision-making done at the community level, to the advantage, I think, of all the people.

As a member of the City Council I came under great pressures, because there were many different points of view, with everyone advancing his own. Since human viewpoints and human knowledge were not reliable guides, I had to rely on higher law, on the Supreme Being. The newspapers, the general community, and fellow politicians were always at odds over some issue, so I constantly had to turn for guidance to divine intelligence. If I was going to provide leadership, I had to be strong and offer sound direction, and that direction had to come from God. I prayed to hear His ideas, and when the ideas came, I also prayed to be able to carry them out. I learned to do this in every major decision of my career. Personal planning produced nothing, but whenever I relied completely on divine guidance, I always saw a solution.

ॐ After President Kennedy was assassinated, President Johnson invited a few black leaders to Washington and took us on a tour of the White House, showing us his personal quarters. He told us what he was going to do for the blacks, and I came away convinced he was sincere.

I remember once finding myself in a swank penthouse apartment in Pittsburgh with leading politicians and captains of industry. All dressed up in a tuxedo, I ended the evening in a kitchen talking to a group of poor people in the neighborhood. The picture of wealth living side by side with poverty made a sharp economic contrast, and I felt that the laws of God and man must bring equalities into this human scene.

On a social level I met with heads of big industry, multimillionaires connected with many philanthropic and cultural activities. One evening I was visiting the home of a business leader and his wife—we were on first-name terms—when the wife, whose family had had a plantation in the South, said to me: "The blacks were very happy there. Wouldn't they have been happier if they had stayed on the plantation instead of wanting to come North? Here they have to compete in a greater society, whereas on the plantation they were not exposed to society's demands." She didn't understand the nature of man, and I told her so.

It wasn't often that I ran into discrimination, but one incident received considerable publicity. I was scheduled to discuss unemployment problems in Pittsburgh with the deans of the School of Business of Pittsburgh University and of the Business School of Duquesne University; we had arranged to have a luncheon conference at The University Club. When we three appeared at the dining room, the head waiter wouldn't seat us because I was black. One of the deans phoned the club manager and said, "This is Councilman Jordon with us." Action was immediate, and they jumped to serve us. But I wouldn't eat there. If The University Club wasn't open to everyone, I didn't want it open for me.

That day I rose in Council to expose this practice. Reporters got hold of the story, which was carried in the newspapers and reported on TV. Many people stopped using the Club facilities. Some weeks later I was invited to dinner at the Croation Club and when I arrived the president greeted me: "Councilman Jordon, you are welcome here though you may not be at The University Club."

૨᎐ After completing my year at the Business and Development Administration, I returned to the law department at Koppers; but I felt my work there was finished. I was also up for reelection to City Council for the third time, but felt that here too I was doing the same things as when I started. Again I searched for direction. Would the next step be in politics or business? An article appeared in *Ebony*, a magazine for blacks, saying that either Carl Stokes, Richard Hatcher, or James Jordon would be the first black mayor.

Asking myself in prayer where I could make the best contribution, it became clear that this should be in industry and business, where there was a need for a major breakthrough for blacks.

After my decision I phoned the president of Westinghouse Electric Company, whom I knew and found to be very fair on the race issue, and told him I would like to work for Westinghouse on an executive level, that the time had come for blacks to operate at a top level in business, and I believed I had the qualifications. He said, "That's interesting because I have been thinking about your working for us."

Westinghouse was about to enter the business area of education. It was a big market, and they wanted me to help them develop it. The president asked me to clear the matter with Koppers, which I did. Six months later, in January 1966, the offer was made to me to be Westinghouse Electric Company's director of educational systems. Westinghouse Broadcasting Company in New York was also working in the education field, so I worked in both New York and Pittsburgh. Out of this activity grew the subsidiary Westinghouse Learning Corporation, and in January 1967 I was made a general manager of the Commercial and Industrial Division of this subsidiary corporation.

Later, when Westinghouse Electric Company decided to enter the area of building low-income houses and formed the Urban Systems Development Corporation in Alexandria, Virginia, they asked me to be vice-president of that subsidiary. I accepted their offer, and we moved our home to Alexandria, twenty miles or so from the capital, although I maintained my law office in Pittsburgh.

&≥ While I was working for Westinghouse Learning Corporation, I became acquainted with the officers of Career Academy, Inc., who were leaders in their field. Career Academy trained people in all fields; hotel-motel management, insurance, investment operations, electronics, etc. They trained not only blacks but anyone who wanted training in these fields. After I had moved to Washington, one of the Career Academy officers phoned and invited me to join their company. The idea of developing men's talents on such a broad base appealed to me enormously. I therefore left Westinghouse and joined Career Academy, Inc. We worked out an arrangement whereby I organized a subsidiary, Career Academy Learning Systems, Inc., in Washington, and I became its president. In 1971 I purchased this Washington subsidiary outright, took over the control of the company, and renamed it Community Learning Corporation, with offices in Washington and Pittsburgh.

But it was not a big company, its services to mankind did not extend far enough. As I sought further spiritual guidance, my boyhood idea to build my father's business into a national corporation returned to me, this time in a new form. I decided to start a minority conglomerate of interstate and national scope. Ten years earlier the idea of minority enterprises had not been widely accepted by either blacks or whites. Now, however, there was a great deal more understanding on both sides, and I felt the time was ripe. Our minority enterprise, Community Learning Corporation of which I am president and chairman of the board, is black-owned and fully integrated, and one of our vice-presidents is a woman.

The services of our minority conglomerate have a wide range. One subsidiary focuses on training the disadvantaged, both blacks and whites. We have conducted training programs in remedial reading and writing, preparing people to work on jobs—in Milwaukee, Atlanta, Philadelphia, Camden, Pittsburgh, with expansion into other cities. The second subsidiary is what I consider an exciting new field in child-care and child-development centers, where we are developing curriculums, teachers' aids and guides, directors' and parents' guides, and also manufacturing new educational materials which help develop parents' and children's skills.

&ᴥ Every man is part of the world, and his work either adds to or subtracts from its harmonies. When a man's work contributes to the spiritual evolution of mankind, it contains elements of immortality, and his individual life becomes structured to conform to God's plan. The prayers and commitments we make to God to do His work place a moral responsibility on us because we are constantly put to the test of proving our sincerity and trust in Him. The tests are challenging, but if we are faithful, the rewards are spiritually satisfying beyond any personal success.

*Mrs. Marion Jordon speaking at Carnegie-Mellon University on the Negro Educational Emergency Drive and some NEED students, 19*

# COMMITMENT TO HUMAN RIGHTS

ﾟ *Marion B. Jordan*

VICE-PRESIDENT OF COMMUNITY LEARNING
CORPORATION OF WASHINGTON, D.C.,
FORMER NATIONAL FIELD SECRETARY OF NAACP

ﾟ As far back as I can remember, my family was deeply involved in the problem of race relations. We lived in Tennessee, and when my sisters and I were quite young, my father was forced to leave our community because he led a movement which would have assured the blacks the right to vote. As the blacks outnumbered the whites almost two to one, this would have changed the balance of political power. My father organized a branch of the National Association for the Advancement of Colored People, the oldest and best-known civil rights organization, which had been prominent in pressing for black people to vote throughout the South. This set off a storm of protest, and we received many threats.

My father was elected president and my mother the secretary of that NAACP branch. Both parents were college-trained, having attended Lane College for blacks (in Tennessee). My mother taught at the high school level, and my father was a funeral director. They had a wonderful sense of compassion for all people, not only blacks. Tenant farmers, the poor whites, and blacks would come to my father when they were in trouble. If they received checks from the Government, the landowners would often take advantage of them because many could hardly read or write and were forced to sign their names with an "X". When they came to my father, he tried to help them obtain the money or land to which they were entitled. On occasion he called in the FBI. He was often commended for his courage and commitment to justice.

The situation reached the danger point when my father picked up the body of a murdered black man that had been placed on the highway. The white man said to have been responsible sent a man to my father warning him that if he testified at the inquest, he wouldn't live to see another day. My father did testify, and I remember my parents and other relatives sitting in our living room with the shades drawn, waiting and prepared to defend our home. My mother thought life was too much of an ordeal in Tennessee so we moved to Kansas.

After our family left Tennessee, some of the whites were determined to make an example of anyone who tried to carry on my father's leadership role in the civil rights field. One night they went to the house of the treasurer of the NAACP branch, woke him from his sleep, and took him away in his pajamas. His body was later found floating in the Hatchie River at the edge of town. The case was widely publicized.

I wanted to contribute to the cause of justice and equal rights, that people might live together in harmony and respect for each other; and I tried to eliminate the hatred and anger and bitterness in my own thinking and wherever I saw it. I reasoned that if God is a God of love, He cannot sanction certain human actions. Searching to find satisfactory answers, I looked into a number of religions. The brotherhood aspect of one of the Eastern religions appealed to me, but it gave me only partial answers. I sought a truth I could apply practically to all my problems, and this I had not yet found. I wanted to know why we were here and what we could do about being born into a condition of hardship and injustice.

When we were still living in Tennessee, I had enrolled in Lane College and continued my studies there after our family had moved to Kansas. When I was a senior at Lane, representatives of a large soft-drink company came to our campus, recruiting prospects to work in their organization. They required preliminary tests, and we were asked to write a paper on "Why American Democracy Should Be Preserved." Much to my surprise, after submitting an essay, I became one of the fifteen finalists. I was anxious to explore the possibility, and my parents agreed that I could accept the job offer.

The finalists were given an expense-free trip to New York, where we met the president of the company and were interviewed by a committee consisting of Mrs. Eleanor Roosevelt, Mrs. J. Borden Harriman (former Ambassador to Norway), and radio commentator H.V. Kaltenborn. On graduation day I received an offer to work for the company in New York City as a national sales representative in special marketing.

The work was interesting. As I traveled about the country, I was learning about business and people. I decided to stay in New York and our family moved from Kansas to this city. Personnel work appealed to me, and I asked the director of personnel for a job in that department. I was told I had done an impressive job in special marketing, but there was no place for a black person in their personnel department. This upset me, so I went to see the president and told him I thought the company's policy was unfair. He wanted me to stay on as a sales representative, but I resigned and went to work for the NAACP in New York City as field secretary, developing and organizing membership drives. I also went on speaking and voting campaigns to end discrimination in housing, employment, and public accommodations. I also was accepted for graduate work in the New School for Social Research.

During this period I looked into Christian Science. The first thing that impressed me about this religion was the fact that it offered healing for all situations and had relevance for the entire spectrum of human existence. I had many Christian Science friends. Among them was a very devoted Christian Science practitioner who stood like the Rock of Gibraltar. The answers she gave me rang true—answers to questions such as: What is eternal life? Can religion relate to social problems? How do we solve human relations problems?

A close friend in Cleveland seemed to be dying after a serious heart attack. Through the prayers of a practitioner in New York, she was completely healed. This proved to me that God's healing power doesn't depend on persons, or the presence of persons. God being everywhere, His power is everywhere available to the thought that understands Him, and it is His ever-present love that heals us.

My first healing, before I met Jim, my husband, was one of human relationship. I had been attracted to a man very different from me. While we shared some mutual goals, our values were not the same. He wanted to change me, and I wanted to change him. I needed to see the spiritual meaning of relationships and marriage. The Christian Science practitioner told me: "You are companioning with God." She explained to me what this meant. I was not to look for human companionship primarily, but in my thought should dwell on the spiritual qualities of man: his integrity, consideration, unselfishness, purity, kindness, and a whole list of spiritual qualities. I was to express this in my daily living until they became my constant companions; and as an effect of such thinking, I would attract companions having similar qualities. I glimpsed what she meant and began to reason this way. I was able to sever the relationship with my friend without ill feeling.

This religion also answered the question of sexual morality for me. Young men often tried to convince me that if I didn't indulge in drink or sex—and I didn't—I wasn't in step with the times. My religion gave me assurance that morality upholds the laws of true love, and that breaking the moral law is not an act of love but an act of bondage.

I had not associated with a church up to this time, because I believed that a churchgoing person isolated himself from life and could not have an impact on the community and the world. But Christian Science showed me that church relates to the whole man, and I united with its universal concept of church as written by Mary Baker Eddy in *Science and Health*: "Our church is built on the divine Principle, Love. We can unite with this church only as we are newborn of Spirit, as we reach the Life which is Truth and the Truth which is Life by bringing forth the fruits of Love,—casting out error and healing the sick." [1]

When the NAACP sent me to Pittsburgh to organize a campaign in that city, I met James Jordon, who was a leader on campus at the University of Pittsburgh. I was impressed by his tremendous sense of principle. A year after we met, Jim and I were married. Deeply in love and with profound respect for each other's individual careers, following the same religion and dedicated to the same goal of winning equality and justice for all people, we began our married life in great happiness.

Jim started his own business, and we both decided to enroll in law school, and use our knowledge of law to win freedoms for our people in Pittsburgh. But financial pressures crowded in on us, so Jim decided to concentrate on his business and make a success of it. We dropped out of law school, and I went to work as executive secretary of the NAACP branch in Pittsburgh.

Many of the city's black problems came to my attention. Jim had grown up near the large municipal Highland Park Swimming Pool, which blacks had never been permitted to use. Groups and organizations had been trying to open this pool but without success. Since no one else would do it, Jim and I agreed to serve as litigants in a suit filed against the city for this purpose. The Mayor of Pittsburgh, who later became Governor of the state, required the City Solicitor to initiate this action, and the swimming pool was legally opened. After we won the case, when Jim and some other blacks went swimming in the pool, attempts were made to hurt them; but finally the pool was fully opened. Then many young people who wanted to use the other public facilities came to the NAACP. Jim and I filed suit against a skating rink and won that case in court. The pattern was set for opening municipal facilities to the blacks.

As the years went by, our commitments to our religious teachings, and our commitments to serve each other in our spiritual goals, grew stronger, drawing us closer. We had many hard decisions to make, but we always made them on the basis of Principle. Jim had taken on a very active role in politics, was serving on the Pittsburgh Council, and his work with the

[1] *Science and Health*, p. 35.

Koppers Company progressed. We were deeply grateful to God.

About this time, housing discrimination was rampant in Pittsburgh, and to ease the situation the Human Rights Commission had interested the Mayor and City Council in a fair housing law. The YWCA, of which I was a vice-president, had decided that I was to present a statement at a public City Council meeting, requesting a strong housing ordinance. A number of other groups participated. Several members of the Council tried to mutilate the bill, and the Human Rights Commission became resigned to having a less effective ordinance. But Jim, a member of the Council, rose and began to ask probing questions of the Housing Commission officials who were testifying. After Jim's speech the entire Council rallied, and a fair housing law was passed.

૱ Politics does not necessarily corrupt a man. We had just purchased a home, and it had a fat mortgage. On the Council Jim had performed a zoning service for a company. One of its representatives called when Jim wasn't home and told me his company was prepared to allow the Councilman to set his own figure for a personal gift. He said he knew a man in public life had to be careful, so he offered cash. The resources of that company were unlimited, but I said, "I know my husband will not accept anything, not even small gifts, as an elected official." The man cynically replied, "Every person has his price. Do you mean to say you don't need money?" I said, "We need money but this isn't the way we get it. But I don't make my husband's decisions for him. I will be glad to give him your message, and you can talk to him later yourself." I told Jim and when the man called later, Jim gave him the same answer.

I have been forced to test the idea of transcending color. Once during a YWCA pre-convention caucus of 500 predominantly black women, just prior to the big triennial convention of 3,000 women, the air was charged with sharp tensions. Gaining the greatest support at the convention was the idea that we were not to vote for anyone who was not black, and discussions in the caucus became belligerent. I thought: Why doesn't someone challenge this racist point of view? You can't correct one kind of injustice with another. Then another thought occurred: There are 22 blacks on the national board; let them speak out. Finally I told myself: You are a Christian Scientist; you understand the nature of man. Why don't you speak?

After praying and beginning to feel calm within myself, I stood up and said that I appreciated the injustices done to the blacks as much as anyone in the room, and we were all entitled to our individuality. But as one member of the group, I couldn't go along with racism in reverse, and only if the group came up with a recommendation I could support, would I work and vote for it. Sitting down, I felt very much at peace, unconcerned with the response to my statements. The truth voiced broke the mesmerism, and the atmosphere changed.

Later a number of people told me I had voiced what they were thinking and asked me to speak on this point at the convention, which I did. The proposal won, and the convention adopted a motion to eliminate racism. This took place in April 1970, and I believe it was not any human power that changed that vote. The YWCA has 2.5 million members who are working toward the elimination of racism in any form. We used the U.S. Civil Rights definition: "Any practice that subordinates an individual to stereotyped notions, whether they be held by a person or a group, is regarded as racism."

ᕫ Following the assassination of NAACP Mississippi field secretary Medgar Evers, in the sight of his wife and children, a great deal of unrest spread among the black community. That was in 1963, while I was serving on the board of the Pittsburgh Urban League.

Seventy-six black high school students who had been accepted at vocational schools and colleges came to the League for financial help. They were good students, but not having scholarship qualifications, they needed money for tuition. I proposed to the League that we find a way of subsidizing their education. The League Board debated the recommendation. Finally a survey was made to see whether industrialists would support this idea. The survey showed that according to the response of the industrialists, the town could not absorb an additional fund-raising effort, and the League decided it couldn't afford to jeopardize its standing with the Community Chest United Fund by launching this campaign.

Concerned about this outcome, I couldn't give up the idea, but kept on praying. It seemed to me that the matter should not be dropped. With unrest rising in the black community and threatening to break out at any point, I felt this was one way of assuring young blacks that all was not lost and that our system could be made to work for them. I thought: Can't the people see this—can't they see they are inviting trouble if we don't find answers for the young blacks?

Jim said, "Why don't you do something about it?" I said, "I can't go out and raise all this money." His answer was, "You could if you put your thought to it." All that night I lay awake thinking about this problem. I prayed: Father, if you would have me do this, then I have to know how you want me to do it. By morning I had a plan. I decided to call a friend who had served on the board of the Urban League and ask her to join me. We would compile a list of people who would respond, and ask them to join with us in raising the money. We needed $30,000 in cash, but I had the strong feeling that this was the right thing to do and that I would have evidence of Christian healing.

Near the Fourth of July my friend and I drafted a letter and sent it out. By September we had the money to send 76 kids to school. Out of this effort has grown an outstandingly successful organization, the Negro Educational Emergency Drive, for the average black high school students who want to continue their studies. In 1973 NEED aided 2,000 black students from the greater Pittsburgh area. Over the ten-year period, more than 8,000 students have been aided.

On August 6, 1965, the Voting Rights Act was passed by the Federal government, and for the first time in the history of our country the blacks in the Southern states won the right to vote. Civil Rights legislation was passed to administer these rights, under Federal supervision in some localities. When this act was finally passed, I realized—as never before—the powerful divine law inherent in Mrs. Eddy's words in *Science and Health*: "God has built a higher platform of human rights, and He has built it on diviner claims. These claims are not made through code or creed, but in demonstration of 'on earth peace, good-will toward men.' " [2]

&#8253; Because of our country's Bill of Rights, people have a right to express freedom of speech and freedom of religion—the rights of the individual. We would hope in this country to escape extreme forms of expression, but not through suppression of ideology. I believe that our system of government and our Constitution are the best that have emerged—because they are founded on basic spiritual laws. It seems to me that the test in the next decade lies in trying to implement to the best of our ability what this country stands for. The challenge we face requires obedience to God's government as revealed in the teachings of Christian Science, enabling the individual to express self-government under the rules of the universal Principle, Truth and Love.

I believe that Christian Science was founded in this country because the philosophy of free speech and free worship provided a soil in which this religion could be nurtured. Ideally our nation follows the same type of government as Christian Science. In the words of *Science and Health*: "The history of our country, like all history, illustrates the might of Mind, and shows human power to be proportionate to its embodiment of right thinking. A few immortal sentences, breathing the omnipotence of divine justice, have been potent to break despotic fetters and abolish the whipping-post and slave market; but oppression neither went down in blood, nor did the breath of freedom come from the cannon's mouth. Love is the liberator." [3]

[2] *Science and Health*, p. 226.
[3] *Science and Health*, p. 225.

*Dr. Rodolfo A. Weidmann of Santa Fe, Argentina, presiding at the First American Interparliamentary Conference in Warsaw*

# SPEAKING
# FOR
# ARGENTINA

## ‌ Rodolfo A. Weidmann

INTERNATIONAL LAWYER OF SANTA FE, ARGENTINA,
FORMER AMBASSADOR TO ORGANIZATION OF
AMERICAN STATES
(TRANSLATED FROM THE SPANISH)

‌ In 1856, in the great surge of immigration toward South America—a huge continent blessed with rich soil, abundant waters, and excellent climate—a contingent of European colonists arrived in Argentina from the Swiss Canton of Zurich. They settled in Esperanza, the first rural colony of the republic. Among them were my great-grandparents Weidmann who, like so many others, opened the furrows of the land. They were farmers and cattlemen to whom the Government gave parcels of land and 21,000 pesos with the requirement that they cultivate their holdings. So they did, planting wheat and barley, corn, nuts, potatoes, also many fruit trees and vineyards. Their houses had roofs made of French tiles and walls of pressed straw. Each family owned horses, oxen, cows, sheep, and pigs, and later operated mills to grind the wheat and manufacture flour for baking bread.

But this was not the land of peace and plenty they had

dreamed of. Theirs was the beginning of the great rural struggle for survival—not only in Esperanza but eventually throughout all South America—that has endured to this day. Those early pioneers clashed with the Indians who saw themselves displaced from their land. They battled against the inflexibility of the rural police and justices of the peace whose tactics often turned to harassment and persecution.

My father was always a farmer and cattleman; and in her younger years, when the family couldn't even think of hiring farmhands, my mother shared in the hard labor of harvest time. Life on the farm was difficult, demanding much effort and sacrifice; agriculture was a mere subsistence economy. Part of the crops were set aside for sale on the Argentine market, but the larger volume had to be exported. Apart from very small factories, no industry existed to process the crops. The Argentines were a poor people with limited purchasing power. The farmers' largest buyers were the United States and European monopolies, which arbitrarily set their own prices and conditions, allowing the growers no voice.

I was the fifth child in a family of eight children, three of whom were boys. Public affairs interested me as I grew up and I became an avid newspaper reader. My father, aware of this, gave me a subscription to the *Record of Sessions* of the Chamber of Representatives. He saw that I had not only a willingness and an ability to help him, but above all, an understanding of our situation.

Desiring to improve the farmers' economic and trade positions, my father entered politics as a candidate for delegate from the department of San Cristóbal. But this experience proved so dismal that he begged me never to participate actively in politics, and for many years his own revulsion was an influential factor in my noninvolvement with activist causes. During my father's unsuccessful campaign he suffered attacks by the clergy from the pulpit; printed leaflets were distributed asking people to vote against him. The leaflets claimed he would close down Roman Catholic churches and persecute their adherents. This, of course, was absolutely false because my father was a peaceable Protestant who respected all religions. On election eve, in February 1928, the committee of the ruling party robbed him of 30 head of cattle, which they roasted and fed to party members.

This harsh encounter was to be followed by an even more severe blow when the great New York stock market crash of 1929, with its international financial effects, brought disaster upon Argentina. Money was scarce, thousands of people were thrown out of work, urban and rural development came to a halt, and moratoriums had to be declared on mortgages. Even though the price of goods dropped sharply, no one could afford them. There were no foreign buyers for the crops, and when the Government bought them to prevent a complete economic collapse, their prices to the farmers didn't even cover production costs. Then, because the Government could no longer pay for imported coal, it used the grain as fuel on the railroads' steam engines. With no buyers in sight, farmers let their cattle loose in the streets but nobody wanted them, not even for hides. Many people lost their properties or incurred debts which burdened them for years. The years 1930 to 1933 were catastrophic.

These financial pressures crushed my father, his health broke down, and he passed on. I was then twenty years old and engaged in the study of social and juridical sciences, hoping that such preparation would enable me to start my life-work under more favorable conditions than my father's. The other seven children were also being educated. On me fell the additional task of supervising and managing my father's lands. My father had been a thrifty, skillful farmer and cattle breeder; consequently at the time of his death he owned 3,900 acres of farmland, some grazing land, 2,000 head of cattle, 200 horses, and 300 sheep. Now that our export trade for cattle and crops was cut off, and our grain being sold to the Government at ridiculously low prices, unpaid bills mounted. Mortgages had fallen due, but there was no money with which to meet them. And certainly there were no funds for college tuition.

My mother became overwhelmed by the problems confronting our family during this national depression. Her health reached a precarious state, and the physicians who treated her held out little hope for her recovery.

In the locality of Grütley lived a Christian Science practitioner, Mrs. Margarita R. Nüssli, a pioneer of the Christian

Science movement in the Province of Santa Fe. She was becoming well-known in the community for her remarkable healing work, and many people, particularly from the department of Las Colonias, turned to her. At this most critical period for herself and her children, my mother learned of Christian Science and went to see Mrs. Nüssli. She began to read *Science and Health with Key to the Scriptures* by Mary Baker Eddy, as well as the Bible, in German. Mother recovered not only her health but also her dominion over the external situation. With confidence and wisdom she assumed command, bringing the whole family back on an even keel. She no longer employed doctors or medicine for help, and she herself performed outstanding healings in Christian Science.

In the midst of the alarm and amazement of relatives, who didn't know about Christian Science or believe in its healing power but repeatedly suggested immediate attention by a doctor, my mother healed my brother of a serious leg infection without any material means whatsoever. My other brother, thrown by a runaway horse, was picked up for dead by a farmhand, who placed him in a wheelbarrow and brought him home to my mother. Alone with the farmhand, untouched by the appearance of death and convinced of man's immortality, my mother prayed according to her newfound understanding of God's goodness. My brother rose up, his recovery instantaneous.

Having been left in charge of his business by my father, I was now very close to my mother and, consequently, keenly aware of her transformation. At this time I, too, was experiencing the fears that had affected her health earlier. I was in my second year of a five-year university course, and I became obsessed by a dread of not being able to complete my education, and this brought me to a state of extreme anxiety. Anguish and insecurity manifested themselves in insomnia, stomach and liver troubles, and all the symptoms of a nervous breakdown. My physical and mental torments made study impossible. Heavily burdened by responsibility, with no financial solution in sight, I was threatened at my most vulnerable point—my university career, which had been my father's great dream and mine.

My mother's spiritual fidelity and loyalty to Christian Science gave me courage. Under her guidance I began reading *Science and Health*—not in German, a language unknown to me, but in French, which I had studied a little in secondary school and more when I was preparing to take the university entrance exams. With the help of a dictionary, I started my discipleship in this religion at a period when we had no Christian Science literature in Spanish and when there were no Christian Science churches or societies in the Province of Santa Fe.

Step by step, my thoughts advanced from a material basis to a spiritual one. Progress seemed slow but sure, and this strengthened my faith, while the study of the Christian Science textbook gave me the understanding needed to secure my new position in life on the strong rock of Truth. My prayers dealt very much with the concept that God made all that really exists, and that God being good, being Love, and being everywhere, there is no place nor space for error of any kind. Abetted by the very effective prayers of Mrs. Nüssli, the Christian Science practitioner, I became physically well again, and my confidence returned. And a way was found to pay for my tuition at the university.

With complete trust in God's goodness, I undertook the administration of our ranch. This meant developing the land, outlining work plans and seeing that they were carried out, directing the sale of the harvests, and the planting of fodder crops. The staff consisted of an overseer and three farmhands, in addition to tenant farmers. Right from the start I gave the overseers and farmhands a share in the profits earned from the land. Much care was required to manage the terms of the mortgages and the cost of working the land. Fortunately, the two mortgage holders offered postponements and reduced interest rates. While we didn't expand our farm, we managed little by little to revitalize our inheritance.

During my years as an undergraduate, I managed the college magazine *Renovación* and was the first student representative on the executive council of the university's College of Juridical and Social Sciences. Upon completing my course, I received a law degree from the Universidad Nacional del Litoral. As I continued to follow the teachings of Christian Science, my working capacity increased and I was able to carry out satisfactorily all the tasks I assigned to myself, both managing the family holdings and practicing as an attorney in civil and commercial law. I founded an active legal practice in the city of Santa Fe, married and established a family, and for many years traveled inland in the province, particularly in the region where we owned lands, to conduct family affairs and to take care of clients, who were mainly rural people.

But my activities soon encompassed more than private business. From my youth I had a burning interest in public problems and, as a student, had already participated in community work. My heritage reached back for generations into the life of the farmer—a life dependent upon what the soil brought forth and what the Government did with the fruits of the farmer's efforts. So in addition to family responsibilities and a law practice, I decided to devote my life to the study of national problems with emphasis on the clarification of the people's legal rights.

I helped organize the cooperative agrarian movement and the Union of Agricultural Producers and Dairy Farmers. Later I became president of the Santa Fe Rural Society, also secretary-treasurer of the Confederated Rural Association of the central and western regions of the province. In this last-named capacity I took part in many conventions and agrarian meetings. From the beginning, I was determined to express my views with complete frankness while maintaining my respect for persons with other opinions.

The philosophy of the Agrarian Movement was: "The land for him who works it, and the products of the land also for him who works it." Unity makes might, I preached, as much for agricultural-producing groups as for labor unions whose power forced Governments to hear their complaints. Agrarian success in the battle against giant monopolies in the meat, grain, and dairy fields, I pointed out, would depend upon united strength expressed through a cooperative. By such activity the farmers would create their own industrial and commercial entities, doing away with the middleman.

I remember an incident that created quite a stir when I was chairman of the Rural Society, since it involved the Governor of Santa Fe. Customarily, at the opening of the annual rural fair, the chairman of the Rural Society would give an in-depth speech setting forth the economic and social problems of the agrarian sector. Because the Governor of the province usually attended these ceremonies and gave a speech stating the Government's views on these problems, it was a matter of courtesy to send a copy of the chairman's speech to the Governor a couple of days before the event.

So this was done that particular year of 1948. Within a few hours before the opening, an official was sent to me by the Governor, requesting that I eliminate certain comments I had made about the Government's agrarian policy. Otherwise the Governor would not attend. I replied that under the circumstances and in accordance with long-established tradition, I owed my allegiance to the agricultural producers' movement, and therefore it was my duty to state our position clearly and honestly. For this reason I was obliged to tell him that the speech would not be changed. There was much apprehension about what would happen, and it was feared that the Government might obstruct our cause or create a disturbance at the event. No official attended the opening of the fair, and the band that usually played on such public occasions didn't appear. Two hundred people opposed to the agricultural producers' cause and carrying huge banners, did attend, however, and tried to thwart the event with their shouts and slogans. Not only did they fail to find any response among the people, who had come in great numbers, but they were drowned out by applause and cheers for democracy and freedom. This display reflected the success of our cause, which reached its climax the following day. I was in my office when I was told the Governor had just arrived. Reaching him before he could enter through the main gate, I welcomed him in the name of the Rural Society. Then I accompanied him throughout his visit and bade him farewell as he left the premises.

૨ As a result of studying more deeply the many aspects of governmental law as they related to the country's social and economic problems, and extending my law practice in these areas, I was made a member of the executive body of the Santa Fe Bar Association, later serving as its president. I also became a member of the governing board of the Argentine Federation of

Bar Associations, attending bar conferences, one conference of the Inter-American Federation of Bar Associations, and various scientific conventions on political and social sciences. I am now a member of the Argentine Institute of Legislative Studies in its section on agrarian and administrative law; also of the Argentine Association of Political Science, the Argentine Institute on Administrative Law, the American Society of International Law, the Inter-American Bar Association, and president of the Center for International Studies of Santa Fe. Also I am currently serving as legal adviser to the Commission for the Advancement of the Human Environment, with headquarters in my city.

In fulfilling the demands of these numerous activities, I have always had the invaluable help of Christian Science. Through it I have been able to practice what Mrs. Eddy says in *Science and Health*: "The term Science, properly understood, refers only to the laws of God and to His government of the universe, inclusive of man. From this it follows that business men and cultured scholars have found that Christian Science enhances their endurance and mental powers, enlarges their perception of character, gives them acuteness and comprehensiveness and an ability to exceed their ordinary capacity. The human mind, imbued with this spiritual understanding, becomes more elastic, is capable of greater endurance, escapes somewhat from itself, and requires less repose." [1] I have experienced all this with great joy and gratitude for the good which has been reflected in my life.

Further, I have followed John's sayings and lean on them: "God is love; and he that dwelleth in love dwelleth in God, and God in him. . . . There is no fear in love; but perfect love casteth out fear: because fear hath torment. He that feareth is not made perfect in love." [2]

Of the seven synonyms for God, as stated in the Christian Science textbook, I have concentrated strongly on Life and Love. I have constantly maintained in thought and action the concept that my life is in God, of whom I am the image and likeness. And this being so, and God being Love, I must reflect

[1] *Science and Health*, p. 128.
[2] I John 4:16, 18.

this Love at all times and under all circumstances. This spiritual standpoint proved very useful to me when, quite unexpectedly and almost against my will, I was first led to participate in the political life of my country.

ॐ The year 1952 was a difficult time in Argentina for the rural community. As president of the Rural Society, I attended many rural fairs and spoke at large public gatherings. Familiar with the hardships of people living in the rural areas, I became the spokesman for small and medium landholders, who only asked fair treatment and the means for bringing technological improvements into their production processes. By uniting themselves cooperatively to industrialize and commercialize their products, thus largely dispensing with the useless and onerous middleman, they would reduce costs for both the producer and the consumer.

Realizing that I could publicize the farmer's plight more effectively in the political arena, I ran for office and was elected representative to the Provincial Legislature from the department of Esperanza. This was the first rural colony of the Republic of Argentina, whose founders included my ancestors.

Triumph on one hand and fierce opposition on the other greeted my 1952 electoral campaign. Two events stand out vividly. One of these was the trip I made to the city of Formosa in a one-seater plane with no equipment whatsoever, flying low over the dangerous route bordering the Pilcomayo and Paraguay Rivers. After the public meeting in Formosa, at which I was the main speaker, I was carried away in triumph. The other incident occurred two weeks later in the province of Jujuy. At the start of a street-corner ceremony in the town of San Pedro, the workers of the local electric plant cut off our current, forcing us to dissolve the meeting and use kerosene lamps in order to reach our local party building.

ॐ The reformation for which the people yearned and which I had hoped to further, didn't take place. The Government was not interested in changes that would have achieved equality for the farmer. Instead it intended to maintain control and place the economy at the service of the governing party rather than that of the national interest. The prevailing climate of violence, the state of siege and internal strife leading to the concentration of power in the hands of the President of the Republic, and the rancor and ill-feeling evidenced at the sessions of the National Parliament—all this made it difficult to consecrate efforts toward a serious and responsible study of grave national problems. Intentionally or unintentionally, all issues undertaken in the parliamentary meetings were brought down to a political level, and there the best of efforts became sterile.

During my three-year term of office as representative in the Provincial Legislature, I served as president of the opposition party. In this role I strove to keep discussions of national problems in the realm of ideas, rather than letting them become personal arguments. Viewing representatives of the governing party as spiritual identities created by God required strict discipline because of the pressure exerted by my group and also members of my political party, who couldn't conceive of any position other than one of outright confrontation without mercy.

But my attitude proved valid. Not only was I treated with respect, but other members of the legislature joined in the spirit of solidarity I sought to pursue when the general interest was at stake. Although the governing party had a large majority in the chamber, their legislators consulted me several times about projected bills, in order to get my opinion and support before presenting them. On more than one occasion, with this support, they were able to obtain advance approval of their own group.

My performance in the Provincial Legislature resulted in my election to the National Chamber of Deputies, as a representative of the Province of Santa Fe. I held this office during a period of great difficulties for Argentina. Acute tension had developed between supporters of the Government and their opposition, with the two great factions dividing the country. A civilian military revolution of great strength, determined to remove the Perón regime, was gathering momentum, and it seemed highly important to reunify the Argentines in anticipation of the Government's fall.

Christian Science was an enormous help to me then in carrying out my duties as a national representative. Following the same line of conduct I had imposed on myself in the Provincial Legislature, I directed my efforts above the disagreements of the moment, toward serving the country. Always I was careful to point out the error to be destroyed, without attaching it to any person.

Though the revolution overthrowing General Juan Domingo Perón's government took place on September 6, 1955, the long-growing civilian and military movement first erupted in June of that year. This released a series of events causing many uncommitted people to champion the revolutionary cause. Realizing that the Roman Catholics were a strong adversary, Government supporters set fire to Catholic churches in the center of the city of Buenos Aires, bringing out a multitude determined to press their opposition to the regime. The most articulate revolutionary leader was Eduardo Lonardi, who took up the theme "Neither victor nor vanquished," in the hope of consolidating both parties. But the actual instigators of the revolution were many. They included members of the opposition in the National Parliament of the provincial legislatures, university students and professors, newspapermen and writers, and many other protestors who had for years insistently called for an end of dictatorship and a return to constitutional government. Both the Perónista party and the General Federation of Labor were dissolved by those who believed—unlike Lonardi, who had been removed from office—that a rigorous program of repression should be instituted against them.

Almost a score of years after the revolution of 1955 deposed the existing regime, those who at that time raised the banner of intolerance were now pleading for national conciliation. How much moral and material injury the country could have been spared if the motto "Neither victor nor vanquished" had been honestly applied from the beginning.

᠍ After the revolution I returned to my home and private business. Within a few months, through open competition, I was appointed senior professor of administrative law at the College of Juridical and Social Sciences of the Universidad Nacional del Litoral. During the two and a half years that I held this position I had many interesting experiences. As my own attitude toward the students changed, I was able to reverse their attitude toward teachers. Discarding paternalism, I gained their confidence and awakened their interest in the study of national problems, which was related to the subject matter taught. As a means of enhancing the importance of the students' classroom role, I initiated a system of promotion without examinations. Classes were pleasant, with few absences, and they achieved excellent results. All the students completed their course with a good degree of competence.

After the reestablishment of order in the institutions, followed by a period of transition, I was called to the National Senate to represent the Province of Santa Fe. Much work needed to be done to reconstruct the country, and we had to start by quieting the spirits in order to open the way for a harmonious and fruitful coexistence. One of the first bills presented by the executive during Dr. Arturo Frondizi's administration was a broad and generous amnesty bill. This bill had been designed to heal open wounds caused by years of fierce political warfare. The concept of the chosen and the damned had to be ended, with a cloak of oblivion lowered over past events.

I had the honor and responsibility of being a reporting member on the amnesty bill. Since its purpose fitted the line of conduct already set for myself in the performance of my duties, I felt spiritually very much at ease. The country urgently needed a change in the mental attitude of its people and above all, its leaders. The motto "Neither victor nor vanquished" demanded immediate, unlimited, and honest application. Minds had to be disarmed, and this required much effort since many still believed that the mandate of the majority gave them leave to subjugate the rights of those who had been removed from power.

Christian Science helped me keep my mental poise when dealing with such unmercifulness and lack of understanding. Many people refused to stretch out the hand of reconciliation to yesterday's adversary, and it was difficult to make them feel or use the Biblical precept "Love one another." After many years of national difficulties, time would reveal that only through the application of this precept, together with the Golden Rule, "As ye would that men should do to you, do ye also to them likewise," could the needed conditions be created for reconstructing the country.

Through the teachings of Christian Science I was able to assist in the very delicate task of strengthening general confidence in the political institution of representative democracy for all—the very effectiveness and survival of which lay in the balance. The people had to realize that whatever promotes the well-being of one social group or individual at the expense of the common good is not good and consequently cannot survive. But it was extremely difficult to win adherence to this principle when personal, selfish ambitions resisted and impeded unity and progress.

The life and works of Jesus, so clearly explained and interpreted by Mary Baker Eddy in her writings, enabled me to understand that changing a nation's mental attitude from a material to a spiritual basis demanded as arduous a labor as that assigned to the Master who, in his mission on earth, endured all kinds of adversities, most of them stemming from ignorance.

I am convinced that only by accepting universal Love as the way of life can we blend in a harmonious effort toward the common good. Thus we understand that the good one person has is available to all, and that it is impossible to build a nation on the quicksand of selfishness and greed.

ও◆ My desire to study and understand international problems led me to accept, in 1958, an appointment to the Inter-Parliamentary Union, which had called a meeting for representatives from the big Western and Eastern blocs, as well as representatives of new African nations. The Argentine delegation, chosen from our National Senate and the National Chamber of Deputies by those bodies, represented all political parties, with the presidency of the delegation assigned to me. Our delegation traveled to many parts of the world and this gave me the opportunity to speak in behalf of Argentina to the world's lawmakers. It also enabled me to view the trend of the different countries' social and spiritual attitudes toward themselves and others.

During my presidency of our delegation, the Inter-Parliamentary Union held meetings in Rio de Janeiro in 1958, in Nice and

Warsaw in 1959, and in Tokyo and Athens a year later. The 1961 meeting was in Brussels, where I spoke on the theme, "Economic and Social Matters," emphasizing that trade is aid. It was necessary to make the industrial countries understand that the underdeveloped nations did not want alms, but stable markets for their goods, remunerative prices, and just conditions in international trade, so that they could stand as equals among all nations.

The international scene revealed the same problems I had observed at the national level, and once again I concluded that only an understanding of the needs of others, with tolerance for their national aspirations, could lead the peoples of all continents to a longed-for peace. Such peace could be strong and lasting only if justice and equality were employed in laying its foundations.

All countries, I saw, are by their very nature opposed to war. This was impressed upon me particularly during my trips to Communist-controlled countries, where I grasped the difference in mental attitudes between the governing and the governed. The governed have a deep desire for peace. When they are sometimes led to armed conflict, they have first become convinced by the governing power that the adversary means to bring them under his authority, subjugating their liberties and taking over their substance.

In my contacts with representatives of countries from behind the Iron Curtain, I was able to prove that Truth alone builds constructively and that understanding draws the nations closer together, finally uniting them in a common destiny. My talks with leaders and delegates showed me that communication must be more intense but absolutely honest and devoid of any intention but that of the common good for all peoples. Only when the urge to raise the standard of living of one nation at the expense of one or more other nations is replaced by the spirit of universal solidarity, will the international community live in harmony and well-being.

The law of universal good is effective only when it is inspired by the idea of man's sonship with God. This idea, which Christian Science teaches, has as its corollary the concept of brotherhood that is incompatible with any unloving act between men. I found that loving treatment, understanding, and goodwill softened the seeming hardness of heart of people in Communist countries.

Upon completion of my term of office as president of the Argentinian delegation, I was assigned to form part of the Executive Committee of the Inter-Parliamentary Union, representing the South American sector.

– In 1962 I was nominated by the executive branch of our Government and approved by the National Senate as Ambassador to represent Argentina at the Organization of American States (OAS) at its headquarters in Washington, D.C. The cause for which I worked during my two years with the OAS had the support of almost all political leaders in Latin America, including Alberto Lleras Camargo, José Figueres Ferrer, Juscelino Kubitschek de Oliveira, Rómulo Betancourt, and others from Colombia, Costa Rica, Brazil, and Venezuela. As Ambassador to the OAS, my debt to the principles and teaching of Christian Science was enormous, and I am grateful for the effective support given me at all times by Christian Scientists in the United States whom I met after my arrival here at the end of May 1962.

Facing the inter-American organization were two basic problems. The political one, with deep socio-economic roots, had been created by Cuba's Fidel Castro, who was infiltrating propaganda into the domestic life of Latin American countries. Castro used ideologic preaching—especially among students—, direct and indirect support of Marxist organizations, guerrilla warfare, terrorism, and other methods. The second problem involved the struggle of underdeveloped nations for a better future, one that might compare favorably with highly industrialized nations; and while this, too, was predominantly a social and economic challenge, it had huge political implications.

To my understanding, both problems are manifestations of the same phenomenon: the explosion of feelings of frustration caused by poverty, misery, ignorance, deficient sanitation, and the general backwardness that characterizes the life of great sectors of this continent. As a result of President John F. Kennedy's inspired idea, the Alliance for Progress was formed to help solve these problems.

కల Latin American nations cling steadfastly to the principle of nonintervention. They cherish their right to exercise self-determination, rejecting totally any direct or indirect outside interference in their domestic life. The strengthening of this principle was a major objective in the creation of the OAS and justified its existence.

Among the basic doctrines set forth by the OAS Charter is one, stating that international order consists of the respect shown to the legal individuality, sovereignty, and independence of the nations; two, that wars of aggression are condemned; three, that victory bestows no rights to dominate the vanquished; and four, that aggression against one American nation constitutes aggression against all the other American nations.

The Alliance for Progress was based on the principle that it is under the shelter of freedom provided through institutions of representative democracy that nations can best satisfy their people's longings for work, housing and property, schooling and health. The Preamble to the Charter of Punta del Este—approved in 1961 by representatives of the American States at a meeting I attended as observer—stated that men and women of the entire continent are reaching for the better life that today's skills have placed within their grasp, that they are determined to have more decent and abundant lives for themselves and their children, to gain access to and enjoy equal opportunities for all, and so to end conditions benefiting the few at the expense of the needs and dignity of the many.

Despite the lofty statements of its charter, and despite its very humanistic philosophy, the Alliance for Progress did not achieve its objectives: to unite the full energies of the peoples and governments of the American republics into a great cooperative effort, accelerating the economic and social development of the participating Latin American countries in democratic societies adapted to their own desires and needs.

To summarize, the experiment which was to be carried out

was that of a political, economic, and social revolution under freedom, declaring that the time had come to give a new meaning to revolutionary action.

ॐ Jesus taught—and as a Christian Scientist I follow this precept—that he who doesn't love his neighbor doesn't love God. Therefore to follow the Master's ideal, we must have respect for the dignity of man, which excludes all manner of exploitation and slavery. I believe that this commandment of universal Love is growing in the minds of people all over the world. Years before, when I attended a meeting of the Second National Congress on Agrarian Law, the subject of tenant farmers was discussed. An agricultural engineer, representing a province where many poor tenant farmers and settlers have only their own arms and very simple tools to work the land, spoke in support of the help the Government should give these farmers. He recommended that credit be extended to them to buy the land they work and make it produce. These people are our brothers, he said, because man was created in the image and likeness of God, and we are all equals. I approached him to express my pleasure and to tell him that because of my religious convictions, I fully shared that concept. He was not a Christian Scientist but on that very important question we thought alike.

Such beliefs need to be made fruitful through preaching and through example—above all through example—because the younger generation alertly watches the actions and behavior of those who represent the established order. When these young people meet someone who lets his religious convictions show forth, they are interested in knowing how that person applies his conviction to the realities of the world we live in, and how effective he is in solving problems.

ॐ In South America the young people want a leading role. Keenly interested in politics, they aspire to take part in the formulation of a new political, cultural, economic, and social order. They want to be heard and counted. That is why they struggle, and sometimes when they are not listened to and heard—though this is not always the reason—they resort to violence, hoping in this way to obtain from politicians and supporters of the establishment what they have been unable to obtain through reason and persuasion. Time will tell if right is on their side—what measure of idealism and purity or how much infiltration of alien doctrines is to be found in these movements.

In my talks with young people I always strive to show them why I believe that violence destroys and does not build up. The democratic social order may have many faults, which sometimes show themselves in the unjust distribution of wealth and power. But this order, these economic, social, cultural, and political entities, are perfectible. Their usefulness will increase as man, acting with intelligence and compassion, devotes himself to building a better order, utilizing his nation's natural resources and human potential. In order for this work to bear fruit, it must be based on conviction reached by paths of persuasion, by emphatically insisting that only through the joint, cooperative efforts of all involved can the goal of general well-being be reached. Social justice is characterized by the application of the principle that we all have the right to equal opportunities, a right that is not achieved by mere proclamation but by definite, constructive action. I have always believed that when people become conscious workers in the building of their own futures, within a system notable for the rule of justice, then the nations will reach their desired goal of well-being, which is the outgrowth of freedom.

Throughout my years of study of Christian Science, I have found that its teachings contain all the rules of behavior that man must follow and practice in order to shape a strong and pure path across humanity's destiny. To me the most outstanding feature of Jesus' life and works was his purpose to save and redeem all mankind. Those who would strive to live in accordance with his teachings, as explained in the great writings of Mary Baker Eddy, must follow him faithfully in the only path to universal peace and salvation.

We all long for a better world, free from fear, from oppression and want, and universal Love is the all-powerful force giving us all we need to achieve this goal. In my prayers for my country and for the world I lean heavily on the promise to be found in these words of Mary Baker Eddy, a promise every Christian Scientist on this earth has seen fulfilled in his life, a promise that is possible in the life of every man and nation: "Divine Love always has met and always will meet every human need." [3]

[3] *Science and Health*, p. 494.

William Howlett, Chairman of the Board and Chief Executive Officer of Ward Foods, Inc., Wilmette, Ill.

# THE SCIENTIFIC
# MAN IN
# BUSINESS

## ᏔWilliam Howlett

CHAIRMAN OF THE BOARD
AND CHIEF EXECUTIVE OFFICER OF
WARD FOODS, INC., WILMETTE, ILLINOIS

ᏔᏔ Before I became a Christian Scientist, I was full of ideas. After studying Christian Science, I was better able to distinguish between productive ideas and nonproductive ones. As I matured in Science and grew active in large business enterprises, I no longer wasted time on ideas that were not productive or impossible of fruition. And this new ability to evaluate ideas stemmed from my understanding of this worldwide religion.

ᏔᏔ My parents were good Christians raised in two different orthodox religions. My mother was a devoted churchgoer, but as far as I can remember, my father never attended church, though he set us a fine example as a man of character, and I saw him on one occasion kneeling by his bed in prayer. He was a talented chemical engineer, an authority on TNT, and during the First World War ran a large munitions plant near Mount Union, Pennsylvania. He put himself through high school and Carnegie

Tech and after marriage attended night school for about ten years, as well as teaching chemical engineering at Toledo University. Upon all of his eight children, six boys and two girls, he impressed the great importance of education.

I was born in Warren, Pennsylvania, but moved to Ohio at an early age. I have the warmest memories of my growing-up years. My parents were honest, decent people who loved their children deeply and taught us the highest moral and ethical standards. We felt secure in their love.

When World War I ended, my father became affiliated with the Egyptian Lacquer Manufacturing Company, and during my childhood and adolescence we lived in Ohio, where my father's work took him. I remember especially our house in Perrysburg, a small village close to Toledo. This little community on the Maumee River was near the locale of General ("Mad") Anthony Wayne's important skirmishes during the American Revolutionary War. In the summertime we swam in the island-dotted river; it was a Tom Sawyer setting, filled with adventure.

Our family survived the 1929 crash, and my dad's remarkable sales development work for his company through that difficult economic period brought him a promotion as head of the Chicago office. With a growing family, he located his house strategically in Evanston, Illinois, halfway between Evanston High School and Northwestern University, so that whether we were in high school or college, we would all have an equal distance to walk to school. At this point I was just entering high school, and my father told me that I could have room and board but that he expected me to earn my own money for everything else, including higher education; and I did.

All through this period I attended my mother's church. But it was a perfunctory kind of attendance, and although I had moments where I felt God's presence, I received no real understanding of what He is. During college I searched in the King James version of the Bible for an understanding of God, but He remained a mystery to me.

I was typical of the boys who grew up in that era of midwestern America. I earned my way through high school by working nights and weekends in a drugstore. When I had some free time, I wrote poetry and played basketball and baseball. By winning a one-year scholarship and doing jobs to pay for my keep, I managed to attend Drake University. My studies continued at Phoenix Junior College in Phoenix, Arizona, on earnings I received from cultivating a little citrus ranch my grandmother owned in that city. And it was in Phoenix College that I began to major in English and started writing a great deal.

Subsequently I enrolled at Northwestern University and worked with my older brother, Grayle, who ran a little news bureau at the University, covering sports for several local and out-of-town newspapers. When my brother graduated, I took over his news bureau, earning my way through Northwestern by writing 10,000 words a week. Working with many of the leading sportswriters of the period, I covered college football, baseball and other sports, and professional hockey. Some of my brothers were majoring in engineering, but I took English, marketing, and advertising courses because they pointed in the direction of my interests. Having thus mixed my courses, I lacked the required credits in any one field and therefore didn't graduate.

Upon leaving Northwestern, I became publicity manager of the Illinois Automobile Club for $32.50 a week and the use of a car. I had an arrangement with *The Chicago-American* whereby I would take trips all summer, write up the tours, and they would give me the back page of the *American* for a feature entitled "Man at the Wheel." As the man at the wheel, I did the driving and writing, the paper had the stories, and the auto club received valuable publicity.

ဢ From childhood I had suffered a number of serious injuries. At the age of three I fell and broke a thigh that was healed after an extended period of medical care. Nine years later, while playing football, I split the main bone in my hip. During the many weeks of suffering which followed, the surgeons thought one leg would be shorter than the other. But I recovered fully, again through medical means. As a college freshman, I had an appendectomy. The following year, while seated in the front of a bus moving along the open highway, the bus collided head-on with a passenger car, but I was only slightly injured. It has always seemed significant to me that after Christian Science touched my life at age 25, nothing of a violent physical nature ever again happened to me.

&◦ While working for the Illinois Automobile Club, I became engaged. One evening I took my fiancée to a dance in Wilmette. There I met a girl named Ruth who had a quality about her that I found very attractive. We had several dances together, and she made a lasting impression on me. Ruth was interested in the theater and was studying at Lake Forest College, and I saw her again briefly when she was rehearsing in a play there. Later I heard that after graduating, she had left to do theater work in New York.

Several months later my fiancée jilted me. Around Christmas time of that same year I was passing through Ruth's home town of Gary, Indiana, and wondered if she was home for the holidays. I called and happily she was there. After dating almost every night for two weeks, we were married. It was the best fast decision I ever made.

Ruth was a third-generation Christian Scientist, and in retrospect I realize that what I loved about her from the beginning was her spirituality, her serenity. Her grandmother had found this religion on a visit to Kansas City, and practiced it faithfully in her home town of Clymers, Indiana. When Ruth was a little girl, her grandmother had healed her of cross-eyes and near-fatal pneumonia through Christian Science. Her mother was also a Scientist, and Ruth had been raised in the Christian Science Sunday School. When we married, Ruth recognized that not only was I seeking the love and companionship of a wife but I was also reaching out for spiritual things.

&◦ Ruth wanted to live in New York in order to pursue her theatrical career. So on my vacation I got a job there with Carl Byoir Associates, the largest public relations firm in New York at that time. They represented several industrial giants, including A & P food stores, B.F. Goodrich, Alcoa, and others. The man who hired me agreed to put me on for three months at $50 a week, "and if you don't make it, you're out." I was 23 years old and somehow it sounded like a good prospect—but I had butterflies in my stomach with a new wife and a new job in that very big city.

We found a little apartment in Scarsdale, and two years after our marriage Ruth became pregnant. One night she started to miscarry. I decided to get a doctor right away, but my wife answered, "No. I have to handle this in my own way according to Christian Science." This was difficult for me, but she was firm and I withdrew my objections, partly because I respected the way she lived her religion.

With the help of a Christian Science practitioner who lived in our building, the healing went forward. Though I didn't understand what was happening, I was conscious that my wife depended upon God instead of medicine. When the healing came, and Ruth later gave birth to a healthy son, my hunger for a better understanding of God took the form of wanting to investigate the religion that could bring about such a healing. I began to accompany my wife to Christian Science lectures and to attend church with her in Scarsdale.

The vestibule to my understanding of God was Mrs. Eddy's use of the synonym Mind for Him. It was easy for me to accept the idea that intelligence is not in the head but comes from a higher source. I had always *felt* God, although He was intangible to me. But He became tangible when I saw that the bridge between God and man is thought. For me, this apprehension let in the first chink of light—an understanding that God is the only Mind, that this Mind is infinite, and that this Mind is man's intelligence from which come all right ideas. The traditional church teaching that God sends disease as well as health to mankind had always troubled me as a theologic inconsistency. If God is good and God is all, why would He cause disease and death? I was delighted to read in *Science and Health*: "The perfect Mind sends forth perfection, for God is Mind." [1] Christian Science began to answer many religious questions for me.

I continued reading the Christian Science books for about a year, during which time the behavior of my boss grew more and more obnoxious to me. I worked in a room with seven other

[1] *Science and Health*, p. 239.

men and my superior made it a practice to come in and insult me before my fellow employees. One night I came home and told Ruth the office situation was so impossible that I had to make a change. She referred me to the statement in *Science and Health* which reads: "Jesus beheld in Science the perfect man, who appeared to him where sinning mortal man appears to mortals. In this perfect man the Saviour saw God's own likeness, and this correct view of man healed the sick." [2]

Then she said, "Why don't you work with this concept of man? You are a student of Christian Science now, and you know our concept of man is different from the usual one." From then on, I held to the spiritual nature of my superior. Gradually, the situation at the office improved until all the animosity disappeared and we became good friends. Proving the effectiveness of Christianly scientific thinking, some ten years later this man who earlier had almost caused me to quit my job offered to make me an equal partner if I joined his business.

૨• When World War II broke out, Willys-Overland Motors, a Byoir client, was producing large quantities of war equipment. They needed to maintain morale among their workers, and the Willys people asked me to join them to assist the chairman of the company on this problem. I had learned enough in Christian Science to know that man really loves to do what is right, and this understanding was helpful in reducing absenteeism and raising morale.

As a father, I had been exempted from active service, and therefore appreciated the chance offered by Willys-Overland to help further the war effort. We moved back to Toledo, where the plant was located. It was there that our first daughter was born. I continued to go to the Christian Science church and was making progress in my study. But I still smoked and drank, actions which precluded my joining a church, whose membership requirements include freedom from tobacco and alcohol. Obviously there were still certain fundamental things that I had to grasp and live.

After about two years in Toledo, the president of Carl Byoir

[2] *Science and Health*, pp. 476–7.

phoned and asked me to rejoin their firm as vice-president in their Chicago office. This meant placing me in charge of Ecko Products (housewares), plus another important account, and of new business as well. So I rejoined Byoir and my family moved to the Chicago suburb of Glenview.

Since Glenview didn't have a Christian Science church, Ruth joined with other Scientists in the community to organize one, an effort to which I gave my full support. Although I knew I had to stop drinking and smoking to be eligible for church membership and all of its opportunities for service, I liked to drink and might have become a problem drinker. I was able to overcome drinking and smoking when I realized this wasn't just an arbitrary church rule, but was based on the vital premise that a Christian Scientist, who depends on dominion over his thought for his well-being, could not afford to surrender this sovereign and vital control for a moment to a drug or any so-called crutch. I reverted once. Then upon my taking the firm position, as *Science and Health* states, that "Man is tributary to God, Spirit, and to nothing else," [3] the appetite left me and never returned.

Free of these habit-crutches and with my church application pending, I received a call from the executive vice-president of Byoir in New York City, who said: "I have great news! We are going to increase your salary by 50 percent, move you back to New York, and put you in charge of promotion on the Schenley Distillers account." There was a long pause. Then I said: "No, I couldn't do that. I couldn't spend eight hours a day promoting liquor. My chart of life has changed quite a bit and what you are suggesting is inconsistent with it."

"If you accept this offer," he replied, "you just might go all the way to the top of the firm. Think it over and call me tomorrow at noon."

"I don't need to think it over," I said, "but I will."

The following day I was driving from Chicago to Milwaukee on another business matter when I noticed a pay-phone sign, got out, and called the executive vice-president back. It was an open phone and the place was busy. After thanking him for the opportunity presented, I found myself declaring in a very loud

[3] *Science and Health*, p. 481.

voice: "As I said yesterday, I won't spend eight hours a day promoting liquor." Hanging up the phone I noticed for the first time that I was in a bar and that thirty rather startled drinkers were staring at me. Apart from the humor of the incongruous situation, I realized how greatly my new freedom had changed my old attitudes. Feeling neither self-conscious embarrassment nor smugness, I walked out of that bar with a new kind of inner poise and self-confidence. That was the first strong stand I had ever taken for the Principle by which I wished to govern all my actions and activities. I knew that I could not gain by urging others to surrender their priceless gift of consciousness—clearheadedness—to intoxicants. Nothing is more cleansing than knowing that one has cast aside expedient material factors for an uplifting spiritual commitment.

Forty-eight hours later I still had received no word from New York. I knew I was in the bad graces of my superior and expected to get my marching orders. Instead of New York, a call came from a totally unexpected quarter. On the line was Arthur Keating, a client and chairman of Ecko Products, who also controlled the Nesco Corporation. Nesco manufactured electrical appliances and did a gross business of about $15 million a year. "I have been up all night thinking this over," Mr. Keating began. "We all have decided that you are the man to come in and head up Nesco."

I immediately recognized that this offer was God's answer to the stand I had taken with Byoir. With no experience in running a business, I progressed in one step from public relations man to head of a large enterprise—and my salary was doubled! Because of my inexperience, I had to look to God alone for answers to difficult financial and business questions—particularly when the Korean War began and we were heavily engaged in producing goods for the U.S. Army. Sometimes we might be bidding on a defense contract for several million dollars, and my Washington vice-president would call me for a quick review of the costs and an okay. Could we go ahead and make a bid at the figure he had calculated? A miscalculation by as little as five cents could, when multiplied, cost the company several hundred thousand dollars. By standing firm on the idea that God was the source of my intelligence and I had the ability to come up with the right answer, we never lost a nickel on one of those contracts.

As the result of studying Christian Science, my whole attitude toward business, and my purpose in the business community, was undergoing radical change. I recognized that it wasn't enough just to hold a key executive position but that one must be impeccably honest with himself and his fellow man to be truly effective and respected. Mrs. Eddy states in *Science and Health*: "Honesty is spiritual power. Dishonesty is human weakness, which forfeits divine help." [4] As I pondered the importance of the moral law in business, these words took on deep meaning for me.

What influence did such scientific truths have on my approach to business? They made me feel that I was, in the words of Jesus, "about my Father's business," that there was in reality no other business, and that I could conduct it only in line with the Father, who is Principle. When you tell an associate that you never want him to do anything that he wouldn't be proud to tell his family, that you never want a dollar that isn't honestly gained, you bring into a business a tremendous moral strength. That strength enables you to ride out difficulties with the courage that is often needed in business. Fidelity to Truth eliminates the fear of the job—the fear of failure.

჻ About a year after I became a church member, I had a Christian Science healing which meant much to me. I came down with a serious case of influenza. At first I was frightened by a lingering memory of my father describing the flu epidemic during World War I, when thousands of people died of the disease. This was the first time I had asked for a practitioner's help. As a result of her prayers, I lost all fear; control of the situation was gained as I became willing to yield my life to God—to the recognition that my life was safe in Him. It was a significant event for me, because I had never before had an illness healed in Christian Science.

Shortly after this, our son, who was eight or nine years old at the time, fell ill with what we later learned were the symptoms

[4] *Science and Health*, p. 453.

of infantile paralysis. On the ninth day of the disease he lost the use of his limbs. My wife engaged a practitioner, one who had helped us frequently, and we prayed deeply, knowing what man divinely is, what this child was, and where his strength comes from. On the tenth day we saw that boy jump out of bed and run downstairs for breakfast. If I had any lingering doubts about the complete dependability of Truth to heal physical diseases, they disappeared right there.

੭❧ During the four years that I headed up operations for Nesco, the company's sales and earnings moved substantially ahead. Then a shift occurred in corporate control, and negotiations began for a merger with another company. Finally Nesco was sold to a company controlled by a man with whose principles I did not agree. My intuition told me not to work for him, and I left the company by mutual consent. He later went to prison for improper business conduct.

Family considerations determined my next business move. By 1951, we had three children. My wife and I wanted them to have the best possible education, and believed they would receive such an education at The Principia, a school for Christian Science children. This fully accredited institution, running from kindergarten through college, is located in two campuses in the St. Louis area. So we moved there, enrolled the children in The Principia, and I established a management-consulting firm. My clients were General Mills, Mississippi Barge Lines, and Magnavox, and I worked closely with their senior officers on a variety of management problems.

The Principia was established in 1921 by Mary Kimball Morgan as a school that approached the entire matter of education from the standpoint of letting that "mind be in you, which was also in Christ Jesus," as Paul said. Because of the universality of Christian Science, students come from many parts of the world. When we moved to St. Louis, The Principia was planning a new campus for the elementary and high schools. I joined a special committee to help raise the money for the beautiful and complete campus, which was started in 1954. I am a trustee of that school today.

After two years in St. Louis, I was asked by one of my clients,

General Mills, to help rebuild one of their companies in Buffalo. Ruth and I talked this over, and it seemed the right thing to do. So we moved to Buffalo, where I became general manager of O-Cello, a manufacturer of cellulose sponges.

We remained there for four years, during which time my wife helped organize a Christian Science Society in Orchard Park, a beautiful suburb. What started as a Christian Science Society when we were in Buffalo is now First Church of Christ, Scientist, Orchard Park.

I served as First Reader in that Society for two and a half years. Working with the Bible and *Science and Health* in preparation for the Lesson Sermons read at the Sunday services, developing from these same source books the lessons for the Wednesday testimony meetings, heightened my appreciation of the teachings and healings of Christian Science and drew me closer to God. Spiritualization was taking place in my consciousness.

ঌ With my work in Buffalo completed, I planned to go back to St. Louis to reestablish my management-consulting business. However, Charles Bell, then chairman of General Mills, had written a letter about me to six of the large banks with which the company had associations. We were staying in a St. Louis motel, and had just placed a deposit on a house in that city, when I got a call from a senior officer of the First National Bank of Chicago saying that Nathan Cummings, head of Consolidated Foods, wanted to see me about joining them. I was all set in St. Louis. Nevertheless I heeded a conviction gained through the years as a Christian Scientist: I had made it a rule to accept at any given time the highest demand made on my services, even though acceptance might be uncomfortable for me. In that frame of thought, I agreed to discuss the Consolidated Foods offer.

At our meeting in Chicago, Mr. Cummings and I felt immediate rapport, and he made me a proposition. He explained that his company's largest division, Rosenberg Brothers, located in San Francisco and up and down the West Coast, was losing money and was in trouble. He said he wanted to sell it, and invited me to become vice-president in charge of operations for Consolidated Foods Corporation. My assignment was to go to San Francisco for a year, sell Rosenberg, and return an agreed sum of money to the parent firm. If this were accomplished, Mr. Cummings agreed verbally that I would be made president of Consolidated Foods, then doing a business of $350 million a year.

I felt I had received a legitimate call for my services as a Christian Science businessman. So we moved to San Francisco. The Rosenberg company, with many plants and warehouses, dealt in dried fruits, nuts, raisins, and diverse food products. Not long after we arrived in San Francisco, a man with a questionable reputation approached me saying he wanted to buy the business. I agreed to meet with him. One day as I walked down from Nob Hill to my office, a thought came to me as clearly as if written on a wall: "If you compromise in any way with your highest sense of right and you get twice what this company is worth, you are a failure. The only way you can succeed is to do this job in accordance with Principle."

After I opened negotiations with the would-be purchaser and his partner, it appeared that I could make a fast deal which would bring Consolidated Foods about $2 million less than the price we had agreed would be acceptable. The Consolidated people in Chicago were agreeable to the arrangement because they were anxious to get their money out. We worked laboriously on the contract, and took a very complicated inventory. On an appointed day I drove to the headquarters of the men with whom I had been negotiating to close the transaction.

On my arrival the man who had first approached me said, "Bill, I hate to tell you this, but my partner won't go along with you." I realized that this was an unprincipled effort to cut our price still further because these men knew I had committed myself to the Chicago people to sell the business. Although greatly disappointed, I remembered the message which had come to me on Nob Hill, and said, "You have made an agreement and have broken it. That ends the transaction!"

Driving back about 50 miles to our home in Hillsborough I felt pretty crushed. The argument for accepting this offer had been: You have been given a year to sell the Rosenberg business, and doing it in 60 days will make you look great. But I knew I had done the right thing. From a little Christian Science

Hymnal on the seat beside me I began to sing the hymn: "Dear Lord and Father of us all, Forgive our foolish ways; Reclothe us in our rightful mind; In purer lives Thy service find, In deeper reverence, praise." [5] By the time I got home, I was confident that Principle was standing with me because I was standing with Principle. And I was beginning to learn that this spiritual feeling was the pearl of great price.

A few days later unusual storms set in and the apricot crops were drastically reduced. But Rosenberg had a very large carry-over inventory of apricots in stock, and this enabled us to move our entire inventory of dried fruits and nuts for their full value—something in the area of $10 million. Within a year I was able to dispose of the Rosenberg business. Not only did the Rosenberg project not lose money, but in the final disposition made a profit for Consolidated Foods, whose actual, net investment was far below the funds received. By refusing to yield to the temptation to make a fast deal that was not right in all its aspects, and by being patient and listening to divine Mind, we had a substantial gain far beyond what would have accrued from that first deal.

֍ With the Rosenberg transaction concluded, we came back to Chicago, where I spent a few months understudying the president of Consolidated Foods preparatory to my moving into that position. During the interim, the opportunity occurred for Consolidated to buy the Lawson Milk Company, one of the original convenience store operators. I was able to assist with the transaction. We took about half the money from the Rosenberg sale and made a cash payment for Lawson.

Shortly after we acquired the Lawson Company, its president passed on suddenly. Mr. Cummings asked me to sidetrack the agreement for me to succeed S.M. Kennedy as president of Consolidated. Since I had helped to negotiate the deal with Lawson and supervised it for several months, I was asked to run the company, which was located near Akron, Ohio. When I took over at Lawson, the company had about 135 stores and was doing around $23 million a year in gross sales. In the course of

[5] *Christian Science Hymnal*, No. 49.

my three years there, by building new stores and expanding and improving the company's service, Lawson increased substantially in size and profitability and became the largest convenience store chain in that area.

As a Christian Scientist, what do you do in a company when you take over its leadership? First, you establish with your people the terms of that leadership. You tell them you are founding your leadership on the highest possible standards and that as long as the company adheres to these standards, their growth and potential are unlimited. Any idea serving people honestly and constructively will grow if it is handled carefully and thoughtfully. The Lawson Company was bringing people milk, bread, and the staples of life with great convenience, cleanliness, quality, and service. All one needed to do was to take the things of value in the business and enlarge them.

During that period Ruth and I again helped to establish a Christian Science church—this time in Hudson, Ohio. We had bought a house in Cuyahoga Falls and joined the church there. One day Ruth came to me and said that Hudson, five or six miles from Cuyahoga Falls, needed a Christian Science branch church, and she had been asked to help. We agreed that we would dispose of our house, move to Hudson, and help organize a church there, which we did. We started as a small, informal group, and I served as First Reader for about six months until it became a Christian Science Society. We first met in the American Legion Hall; now Hudson has a beautiful little Christian Science church.

⁀ In 1962 I signed a five-year contract with Consolidated Foods to be its president, and we moved back to Chicago. Consolidated was acquiring many companies of a diverse nature, so I insisted on a clause in my contract saying that in the event the corporation merged or acquired a company in the tobacco or liquor business while I was its president, I had the right to leave. In 1962 Consolidated Foods had sales of about $500 million and earnings before taxes of about $18 million. When I left in December 1969, sales had reached $1.5 billion and earnings were approximately $100 million before taxes.

A key to this expansion was my confidence in the ability of

the individual to achieve the maximum of his potential. With this in mind, I further decentralized control of the company's operations so that each of its approximately fifteen divisions had its own operating plan and the autonomy necessary for its management to operate freely, with the parent organization giving over-all guidance. Over a period of seven to eight years, with the help of many fine and dedicated officers, Consolidated expanded to more than thirty divisions. Working with my Christianly scientific respect for the spiritual man, I was able to negotiate for Consolidated Foods some of its largest acquisitions, including Electrolux, Fuller Brush, and Booth Fisheries.

We instituted incentive bonus plans on the basis that rewards should be both of the heart and the pocketbook. With fair compensation, high standards, and service as prime stimuli, the essential working discipline is the profit motive. It is as important for a business to enjoy financial health as for an individual to enjoy bodily and mental health. A business without profit or a Christian Science practice without healing would be an abstraction. In this regard, Mary Baker Eddy writes in *Science and Health*: "In the scientific relation of God to man, we find that whatever blesses one blesses all. . . ."[6] And profit is not only earnings before taxes, it is also the profitable benefits that come to all who participate—employees, suppliers, customers, and shareholders.

In 1967 Mr. Cummings informed me that Consolidated Foods planned to merge with American Tobacco Company, with Consolidated becoming a subsidiary. I reminded him of the terms of my contract and my right to leave. At first he preferred not to recognize that I was serious and asked me to reconsider. Whether I stayed or not, he told me, he was going ahead with the merger.

If I withdrew from Consolidated Foods at this point, I was placing in serious jeopardy the first large profit I had ever had an opportunity to realize—some $550,000 accumulated over several years in unexercised stock options. When I came home and told my wife about the position I was taking and the personal loss that could result, her first words were: "Wonderful! Now we are

[6] *Science and Health*, p. 206.

really living!" She had a clear conviction of putting right first! Her support meant a great deal to me in standing firm on my contract. Often through the following months I thought of the Psalmist's words: "I had rather be a doorkeeper in the house of my God, than to dwell in the tents of wickedness." [7] And here wickedness was the suggestion that one can gain by compromising his highest sense of right.

At the board meeting which was to decide on Consolidated's merger with American Tobacco, the vote was 18 to 1 in favor; I was the one dissenting voice. As events turned out, however, the merger with the tobacco company did not go through and I realized again that "one on God's side is a majority." My contract with Consolidated Foods was extended, and the business continued to prosper.

During this period Ruth became Second Reader at First Church of Christ, Scientist, Winnetka. And at the special Lincoln Day dinner, a Republican Party function which is held yearly at the Hilton Hotel in Chicago to honor Abraham Lincoln, Ruth was asked to give the invocation. Usually this is done by a prominent Jewish rabbi, Roman Catholic priest, or Protestant minister. As far as I know, Ruth was the first Christian Scientist chosen to do this, and her being introduced as Reader of the Christian Science church in Winnetka was recognition of Christian Science by the business and civic community.

In late 1969, when I was chairman and chief executive officer of Consolidated Foods, the largest shareholder of the stock failed to back me in a decision which I felt was for the benefit of all our shareholders, and Consolidated and I parted company. Having spent thirteen years helping build this concern into a leader in the consumer goods industry, I could depart in peace because, as my teacher in Christian Science, John M. Tutt, once said: "The substance of a job is the opportunity to be of service." When the opportunity to be of service was no longer present, the substance of that particular human circumstance was no longer my job.

[7] Psalms 84:10.

From the scientific standpoint, there is no dead end in business. Every problem has an answer in Christian Science, and this is not only an answer but a foundation on which to build higher. Mrs. Eddy's words in *Science and Health* are practical and provable: "The very circumstance, which your suffering sense deems wrathful and afflictive, Love can make an angel entertained unawares." [8]

Having left Consolidated, I opened a management-consulting office in Chicago and acquired several small operating concerns. Among them were Mrs. Arnold's and Nancy Keith candy companies, and a Scottsdale, Arizona, restaurant business, Gene's Broiler Buffet.

Then in 1972 the chairman of the executive committee of Ward Foods, Inc., telephoned and asked me to come to New York to head their business, which was in deep trouble. Since I was very happy at the time with my activities, I told him I wouldn't come to New York but might consider the position if they would move the corporate headquarters to Chicago. His answer, after a day or two, was, "We'll move the company to Chicago." I said, "If you do this, I have to be assured of an equity in the company, and I believe Ward Foods would benefit by buying my candy business." I valued the exclusive formulas we owned and felt the business had a fine potential. Ward agreed to my price.

We moved Ward Foods to Wilmette, a suburb of Chicago, and I became chairman of the board and president (later chief executive officer)—titles that had little meaning for me in themselves, but were a symbol of an opportunity to serve. Once again, I laid aside my personal desires (which were to develop my own business) to answer a call for help—a necessary circumstance for Christian Scientists.

As on previous occasions, my approach to the problem was scientific. I reasoned that this business had a legitimate, useful place in the consumer market, and that we would find it. We would redirect this business, and it would grow in usefulness. From the loss of about 20 million dollars in 1972, the company was moved to a profitable operation at the end of the first half of 1974.

[8] *Science and Health*, p. 574.

Business assets are considered to be buildings, equipment, land, inventory—physical things generally—while so-called intangible assets are regarded as ephemeral. From a scientific viewpoint, however, the ideas that go into advertising, selling, the conception of a product, the development of respect for a brand, also are solid assets. If a businessman can realize that *all* assets are ideas, as Christian Science teaches, he can have much greater flexibility in the rearrangement of his assets to better serve a worthy goal. This is what we did at Ward's. Good ideas were retained and expanded, unproductive ones were removed or exchanged, and the whole operation of the company's assets—tangible and intangible—became more vital and productive.

ৎ৽ Shortly after I took over the operation at Ward's, my hearing became impaired. I couldn't hear adequately in meetings or even on a one-to-one basis if there were heavy background noises. Though I worked on this in Christian Science for a few weeks, I didn't receive a healing, and used a hearing aid temporarily in order to carry on my activity. Then I realized that I had a burdened sense about the difficulty of the job I had undertaken, and particularly about the fact that the problems seemed considerably greater than they had been represented to me. I saw I was not grateful enough for this opportunity to be of service. One day I left the hearing aid in the pocket of my shirt, and when it was inadvertently thrown into the washing machine, it was ruined. That incident caused me to think more firmly about the problem and its scientific solution. I knew that nothing can obstruct the scientific man who is about his Father's business, and that all that was true about Ward Foods was the rightful and useful activity of Principle. And I was healed.

ৎ৽ When young people come to me and ask about business, I tell them that what they are doing is not as important as what they bring to the human scene. It is not a job coming to you; it is your thought coming to the job. This eliminates the feeling, "What does Harry think about me?" You don't have to impress Harry; you just have to express God.

Somewhere along the line of his experience, early or late, a

Christian Scientist has to establish his basis of operation. It makes no difference if the job before him is a modest one or the highest office in the land. In the cauldron of business problems, in the area of social pressure—is God really first in his approach? If a young person starts out with the conviction that God is first and everything else is second, this idea is explosive in its implication and its effect on his life. The field of battle is his thinking. His meeting with God is in his thinking, and he can meet Him second by second in his thought.

I used to wonder what Paul meant when he said "Pray without ceasing." [9] Then one day I discovered that to pray without ceasing meant bringing thought moment by moment into the activity of the Christ, Truth. This idea has tremendous practical application in business. With it you cannot fail!

[9] I Thessalonians 5:17.

Elliot O. Yemitan of Lagos, Nigeria, program producer of Radio Nigeria.

# NEW
# FREEDOMS
# IN NIGERIA

## ᖇ Elliot O. Yemitan

RADIO PROGRAM PRODUCER FOR NIGERIAN
BROADCASTING CORPORATION

ᖇ The growth of Christian Science in Nigeria in the past
fifteen years has come against a background of dramatic
political, social, and economic revolutions. In spite of drastic
upheavals and overturnings, Nigeria is rising steadily into a
leadership role in Africa, and progress in all areas is on the
march.

A British colonial possession for more than a century, Nigeria
achieved independence in 1960 after many years of fierce
struggle. A democratically oriented government took over, but
in 1966 surrendered to a military coup. Under the present
leadership of General Yakubu Gowon, Nigeria's distinguished
head of state, the Federal Military Government has displayed a
magnanimous attitude toward religious freedom, permitting
every individual to practice his own religion in his own way, so
long as no other person's interest is jeopardized.

It is noteworthy that General Gowon, a Christian, has on

ᖇ 169 ᖇ

many occasions demonstrated the love inherent in the Christian religion. An example of this occurred after the terrible Biafran Civil War—which raged on mercilessly from 1967 to 1970, dividing and devastating the nation so tragically—when he forgave the instigators of the revolution without exacting reprisals from them. In this action of magnanimous leadership, General Gowon moved the country closer to the concept of "one Nigeria."

The impact of Christian Science on a society like ours, which is consolidating its strengths and assuming its role as an equal among the free nations of the world, can hardly be felt except by someone actually present. There is a dynamism in the air as if a new birth is taking place in our land. Nigeria's population of more than 60 million people dwarfs that of most other African nations. Although 80 percent of our people work in agriculture, Nigeria's oil-based economy provides funds for development that are unprecedented among other black nations of today, and we have considerably more trained professionals. In 1974 Nigeria had a standing army of 250,000 men; she has given some $4 million to neighboring countries suffering from drought, and recently paid for a $3 million road connecting Dahomey's principal cities to the Nigerian border. Nigeria's Commissioner of Trade is heading African trade missions in negotiation with the European Common Market in Brussels.

In these and many other ways, the winds of freedom are sweeping away oppressive, outworn elements. Spiritual values relating to the times and the people are coming to the fore, and religion is receiving a new impetus. Nigerians are deeply religious. Moslems form approximately 45 percent of our population; Christians, approximately 40 percent; and other sects and nonreligious groups, about 15 percent. Presently there is a great searching among the people for new insights into man's spiritual potential—beyond traditional forms of worship. Thousands of Nigerians today look for a living, healing religion, and many individuals are turning to Christian Science.

To my fellow countrymen who ask me, "What is Christian Science?" I explain that this religion, founded on the words and works of Christ Jesus, doesn't rely upon faith alone for its healing, redeeming works. Nor does it ascribe special healing powers to an elect group of men and women. I tell them what Mrs. Eddy has written in her book, *Miscellaneous Writings*: "Christian Science is not a remedy of faith alone, but combines faith with understanding, through which we may touch the hem of His garment; and know that omnipotence has all power." [1]

While most Christian Scientists are in Nigeria's Lagos state (where I live), Christian Science groups have now spread into all Southern states and to a few states in the predominantly Moslem section of the North. Significantly, Christian Science has caught on more rapidly with young people than with adults. I attribute this to the fact that for modern youth in this scientific age, revelation must coincide with logic, and logic must coincide with scientific proof. Christian Science offers revelation, logic, and demonstration to all seekers after Truth.

I know a group of young men who, having endured the bloodshed and suffering of the Biafran War, took up the study of Christian Science when battle ceased, and formed an active Christian Science group in Enugu, the capital of the East-Central State. Bound together by their dedication to universal Love as the Principle upon which they would build lives of freedom and dignity, they decided that Christian Science was too important to keep to themselves. So they carried their newfound religion to the university campuses in their community. (I was able to provide the necessary Christian Science books and give them guidelines in their spiritual mission.) Other Christian Science groups in different parts of Nigeria have done the same kind of missionary work in other universities. Today students meet and hold Christian Science testimonial meetings in five Nigerian universities—in the University of Ife, Lagos University, the University of Ibadan, Ahmadu Bello University, and at the University of Nsukka.

On the political side, youth is taking an active part. Some years ago the Nigerian government planned to enter into a military agreement with another government. The young people, notably the university students, reacted so violently that the government decided to shelve the idea. Presently we have a 29-year-old man serving in the Lagos State government as a

[1] *Miscellaneous Writings*, p. 97.

commissioner—the equivalent of a minister in the British system of government. Also, student bodies have their representatives serving on university committees thus giving them a voice in policy-making in their educational institutions.

A Yoruba proverb says: "A god that is worshipped hidden from the eyes of youth is the one that suffers extinction."

&❧ I was in my teens more than twenty years ago, searching for a spiritual truth by which I could live, when I found Christian Science. This is how it happened.

Abraham Obatayo and Mary Orifunke Yemitan had six children, of which I was the youngest, born on August 1, 1932 in Abeokuta—a Western State town set into a stony hillside 60 miles from the Atlantic seacoast city of Lagos. The Ogun River passed through our town on its way to the sea.

It was in Abeokuta in 1843, coming through the slave port of Badagry, that the first missionaries, sent by the Church Missionary Society of England, introduced Protestant Christianity into Nigeria, which at that time, and for another 117 years, remained a British colonial possession. In April 1973 I visited Badagry and saw the historic landmarks: the iron slave chains now kept as museum relics; the spot where the agila tree once stood to mark the place where the "Word" was first preached; the first one-story house built in Nigeria in 1845.

Radiating out from Abeokuta, the missionaries went forth, planting Christian stations in surrounding districts. Abeokuta was also the place where formal Western education was first embraced, later extending into all of Nigeria. Hence my home town has a justifiable pride in its origins.

For twenty years Christianity surged through Western State. But progress into Nigeria's Northern areas was halted by the Ijaye War of 1860–1862 and by constant internecine and intertribal wars. With hundreds of sick and wounded Nigerians to care for, the missionaries turned their efforts toward relief work. Their preoccupation so interrupted the northward movement of Christianity that to this day the Northern states of Nigeria remain largely Moslem.

As early as 1844, a distinguished Nigerian scholar, the Reverend Samuel Ajai Crowther (later Bishop Crowther) started to translate the Bible into Yoruba, his native tongue—the other major Nigerian tribal languages being Hausa and Ibo. In 1821, as a young boy, Ajai Crowther was captured and placed on a slave ship, but on the high seas he was rescued from slavery by an English vessel and returned to Sierra Leone, where he was enrolled in a Christian mission school. His rare intellectual and spiritual capabilities so impressed his teachers that he was sent to England for higher education. Ordained by the Missionary Society, he was authorized to translate the Bible into Yoruba (also my native tongue).

Crowther started with the first chapters of Luke. Later, other translators took over. What gave thrust to this translation work was the Missionary Society's conviction that the preaching of the Word in the Nigerian native tongue would entrench Christianity firmly into Nigeria's religion and culture. By 1862 the whole King James version of the Bible was published in Yoruba.

People took to the new religion with fervor. Thousands applied themselves to learning to read and write both English and Yoruba in order to understand the Bible, thereby stimulating the growth of schools and bringing all evangelical work into neighboring towns and villages in Western Nigeria. To the British traders and British colonial administrators of the times, Nigeria's Christianization meant economic and political control of the country.

I have dwelt at length on the part my birthplace played in the planting of Christianity in Nigeria in order to show that my native city has witnessed more than a century of Christian experience.

&ᴥ My paternal grandparents did not convert to Christianity. Rich by local standards, my grandfather had three wives, many servants and horses, and my grandmother counted her money in sacks. My maternal grandparents were Christians and owned a farm in a small village 40 miles from Lagos. A narrow-gauge railway linked the capital city with Abeokuta. We children went frequently to the little station to meet our grandparents and see them off after their visits.

As a young man, my father distinguished himself as a

marksman, and his hunting prowess earned him a chieftancy title accorded only to great hunters. Although he was not born a Christian, he later embraced Christianity, becoming a farmer of modest means. At the time of his death, he was president of our local African Church and a highly respected member of our community. My mother was a gentle Christian, devoted to her children and home, working long hours on our farm. As a young boy, I loved to watch her prepare farm products for sale at the weekly market—yams, vegetables, peppers, flour made from cassava, palm oil, and palm kernels.

A mile and a half from our home was the small African Church (Protestant) which I attended from the time I was a very small child, often being carried on the shoulders of my brothers or father as our family trudged along the hot dusty road on Sunday mornings. When I was six years old, the Reverend (later Bishop) J.D. Jiboku baptized me. Oladipo, my native name, being considered improper for baptism, Elliot—a derivative of Elias—was added. In Nigeria at the time, the Christian community didn't consider a person really converted until he acquired a Biblical name.

During my growing-up years my mother insisted that I must have a good education. Space was at a premium in the crowded classroom of the school at Agbado, the nearest to our town. To control enrollment and determine a child's readiness to start school, he had to stretch his arm over his head and touch his ear with his second finger. At a very tender age I was just able to perform this feat. On a memorable January day I became a schoolboy, joining the 250 children at the Agbado school.

Soon I was leading the classes in all examinations. I completed my primary education in record time, graduating with top honors. There were very few high schools in the area and competition for entry was keen. I was among approximately a thousand boys who took the entrance examinations at Igbobi College, a high school owned and run by an Anglican and Methodist Christian Foundation—most high schools of the time were run by Christian bodies. I was one of 30 boys admitted. Igbobi College having high scholastic standards, the six-year course which I completed gave me a thorough grounding in all the usual subjects.

Thus by 1951 I had moved up to the point of university education, my cherished goal. With great expectancy I took the admission examinations for both Cambridge and London universities. While waiting for the results, I found a job as a Kardex clerk with the United African Company in Lagos, a subsidiary trading company of the British Unilever Company of England. United African traded in many commodities, from exporting our native palm products to importing heavy machinery for sale in Nigeria. The nation was already gearing for industrial expansion and exploitation of our mineral resources. (In a decade, Lagos was to become the center of most Nigerian industries, half of them maintaining head offices in this capital city. Modern buildings, heavy automobile traffic, modern paved roads and department stores, a well-designed seaport, and an international airport were to make her a modern metropolis by all standards.)

A few months later the results of both the senior Cambridge University school certificate examination and the London University matriculation examination came. I had qualified for admission to both universities. At that point my dream of higher education was shattered. My parents could not finance the trip abroad. In the Nigeria of that era there was only one university —the University College of Ibadan, which had limited admission. For university education, most Nigerians went either to Europe or the United States of America.

I was overwhelmed by despair. I wanted to be a writer and believed that a university education would prepare me for my career. Ever since I was a young boy, literature had been an absorption. Shakespeare, Dickens, Keats, E.M. Forster had given me a perspective into British thought. But Nigerian writers such as D.O. Fagunwa, Adeboye Babalola, Cyprian Edwensi, Chinua Achebe—whose poetic insights probed the lives of our people— had stirred my imagination. I loved the Nigerian people and it was my hope to contribute to our literature.

So despite bitter disappointment, I refused to yield readily my goal for higher learning, and thought of stowing away aboard a ship to reach England. My relatives discouraged me from taking this foolhardy step, advising me to start saving money if university education was what I wanted. With low subsistence salaries paid to clerks, saving was impossible. Consequently I didn't have a university education. Instead, an entirely different kind of education unfolded for me.

The economic frustrations turned my thoughts inward and made me yearn for an understanding of religious influence in a man's life. Were God's promises in the Bible really true? In the church I was attending, it seemed to me that one thing was preached and another practiced. Wealthy members were treated with deference; those who couldn't parade wealth were held in low esteem. Dissatisfied with this narrow approach to God, and feeling that my spiritual needs were not being met, I stopped going to church.

Quite possibly my state of restlessness reflected what was happening in all Nigeria. I was nineteen years of age, and our nation—with youth in the forefront—was clamoring for national independence. Disenchantment with paternalism was penetrating social and political consciousness, and invading religious concepts as well. Tradition was under fire.

Not far from my home, on the mainland of Lagos, a group of worshippers met every Sunday and Wednesday evening in a room of a small building used as a business school. They numbered only about twelve; half were white Englishmen and women, half Nigerians. As far as I could judge, there was little ceremony in their worship. An hour after the services started, they were gone.

A black gentleman who lived across the road from me was one of the worshippers. A handsome man, advanced in years, at times he would look young and other times would show his age. Fascinated by this aspect of his personality, one evening I summoned up courage, and walking up to him asked, "Sir, who are you and what do you people do when you gather every Sunday morning and Wednesday evening?" He introduced himself as Mr. Renner-Lewis and told me that Christian Science services and Wednesday testimony meetings were held on those days. As I questioned him further, he loaned me a copy of *Science and Health with Key to the Scriptures* by Mary Baker Eddy.

I found the book fascinating and read it avidly, coming across this statement: "A knowledge of the Science of being develops the latent abilities and possibilities of man. It extends the atmosphere of thought, giving mortals access to broader and higher realms. It raises the thinker into his native air of insight and perspicacity." [2]

This and other passages convinced me that here was the truth I had been seeking, and I felt the doors of my thought opening to new freedoms. The realization dawned that Christian Science could become the higher understanding I needed—and that this understanding could develop my ability and possibilities as a writer. I felt deeply comforted in the knowledge that God had not deserted me and that He would guide me in my longed-for career.

The Sunday following my first reading of *Science and Health*, I joined the Christian Scientists in their services. The big step into the study and practice of this religion became the turning point in my life. I read all the available books and literature of Christian Science, making notes of the points I found compelling. As I started to realize my identity as the image and likeness of God, my outlook on man and the universe became spiritualized and a radical change took place in my thinking.

A line of argument in *Science and Health* seemed self-evident: "God, without the image and likeness of Himself, would be a nonentity, or Mind unexpressed. He would be without a witness or proof of His own nature. Spiritual man is the image or idea of God, an idea which cannot be lost nor separated from its divine Principle. When the evidence before the material senses yielded to spiritual sense, the apostle declared that nothing could alienate him from God, from the sweet sense and presence of Life and Truth." [3]

As I acknowledged my spiritual sonship with God, many aspects of thought foreign to His image and likeness began to fade away. First to go was a sense of insecurity, not only about money but also concerning intangible things. All my life, even when I had seemed happy on the surface, I was obsessed with a fear of the unknown. Christian Science taught me that God

[2] *Science and Health*, p. 128.
[3] *Science and Health*, p. 303.

being all Life, and filling all space with His love and power, there was nothing to fear. I began to grasp what Paul meant when he said to the Athenians: "I perceive that in all things ye are too superstitious. For as I passed by and beheld your devotions, I found an altar with this inscription: to the unknown God. Whom therefore ye ignorantly worship, Him declare I unto you." [4] And also what Jesus meant when he told his disciples: "Fear not, little flock, for it is your Father's good pleasure to give you the kingdom." [5]

With fear overcome, a feeling of confidence asserted itself. I began to see myself not as a mortal, but as God created me, spiritual and free. Consequently, daily events became less worrisome; feelings of happiness replaced feelings of darkness and doubt. Within a week after I began the study of Christian Science, I gave up smoking and have remained free of the habit. Soon I became a member of the informal group of Christian Scientists and participated in their church activities.

By this time, the bitterness that often accompanies economic deprivation had been neutralized, and I was writing easily and with joy. I had a new purpose in writing: to emphasize the power of good over evil. I was twenty years old, in 1952, when my first short story was published in English and broadcast over Radio Nigeria. That same year my first short story was published in Yoruba. (Through the years I have continued to be published in both languages. Extracts of my writings have been used to illustrate textbooks in both Nigeria and England.)

  Attending the Christian Science services regularly, I became well acquainted with Theophilus A. Renner-Lewis. Of Sierra Leone extraction, he was the first Christian Science practitioner listed by The Mother Church, The First Church of Christ, Scientist, in Boston, Massachusetts, as practicing in Nigeria. People turned to him for healing, not only in Lagos but in many other parts of Nigeria. I personally witnessed his healing of a young man who went violently insane from time to time, and whose parents had tried many remedies for his cure, without

[4] Acts 17:22–23.
[5] Luke 12:32.

success. Mr. Renner-Lewis took up the young man's case. In two weeks the youth went back to work; he was permanently healed.

Shortly after I joined the Lagos church, I met Beatrice Funmilayo Oluseye, and we were later married. Two Sundays after our wedding, she accompanied me to the services. Later she too became a member of the Christian Science group and has relied solely on Christian Science for the solution of all problems, including healing for herself and our children. When she carried our first child, my wife didn't use drugs of any kind, depending entirely upon Christian Science. At the time of delivery (although we engaged a doctor), we called upon Mr. Renner-Lewis to pray for us, and the birth was completely harmonious. Our other three children were born in similar circumstances.

Grounded in the teachings of Christian Science, my wife and I understood that the birth of a new babe is the human appearing of a spiritual idea created by God, Spirit, before the material world was. God is Father-Mother of all His children, and the spiritual development of our children is a trust conferred upon us. During the periods of birth, my wife and I have studied Mrs. Eddy's words in *Science and Health*: "To attend properly the birth of a new child, or divine idea, you should so detach mortal thought from its material conceptions, that the birth will be natural and safe. . . . When this new birth takes place, the Christian Science infant is born of the Spirit, born of God, and can cause the mother no more suffering. By this we know that Truth is here and has fulfilled its perfect work." [6]

ॐ Although my stories and articles continued to be published and broadcast, my earnings from my writings were insufficient to support our family. Feeling my responsibility to them, I took night courses, hoping to prepare myself for a business career. But my advancement in my position seemed slow. Clearly my income needed to be more representative of what I was metaphysically declaring about the affluence of man's substance, whose source is God—the provider of all good for man and the universe.

[6] *Science and Health*, p. 463.

Soon a job opportunity as audit clerk at a better salary opened up in Ibadan; so our family moved to that city. Since there was no Christian Science group in Ibadan at the time, I found three other Christian Scientists and we started holding informal Sunday services and Wednesday evening testimony meetings. The group increased in numbers and today is functioning as an active Christian Science Society in Ibadan.

ॐ Ever since I became a Christian Scientist, my leading prayer can be epitomized by the words of a hymn in the *Christian Science Hymnal*: "Take my life, and let it be Consecrated, Lord, to Thee . . . Take my lips, and let them be Filled with messages from Thee." [7]

In 1961 this desire began to take tangible form in my career. In a single step, all my experiences came into focus and I was led forward into my present work. I saw an advertisement in a newspaper for a news translator for the Nigerian Broadcasting Company at a salary double what I was earning. Although I was a writer and not a broadcaster, my work was known to the Nigerian Broadcasting Company. So despite the incredulity of my colleagues, who told me that it was ridiculous for me to apply for such a position with its stiff competition—especially since I had no experience in that field—I disregarded the human opinions and followed the spiritual leadings of divine Mind. My study and prayers had made it clear that as God's witness of Himself, I included all right and necessary ideas and possessed the capability to utilize them.

In Psalms I read: "Promotion cometh neither from the east, nor from the west, nor from the south. But God is the judge:" [8] And in *The First Church of Christ, Scientist, and Miscellany* by Mrs. Eddy, I read: "Man lives, moves, and has his being in God, Love. . . . and Love must necessarily promote and pervade all his success. Of two things fate cannot rob us; namely, of choosing the best, and of helping others thus to choose." [9]

After three interviews, I was offered the position of news translator for Radio Nigeria. It was a job translating from English into Yoruba the news that went out to all Nigeria at a

[7] *Christian Science Hymnal*, No. 324.
[8] Psalms 75:6–7.
[9] *The First Church of Christ, Scientist, and Miscellany*, pp. 164–65.

time of crucial changes in our nation and in other developing nations of the world. The whole field of communications came into full view for me and I saw the importance of honest, unbiased news reporting. Universal areas of comprehension, which before I had not grasped, were unfolding before my eyes.

The kinds of ideals which should motivate broadcast reporters and commentators were illumined by Mrs. Eddy in thoughts she expressed about her newspaper, *The Christian Science Monitor.* Her views as recalled by those present at early discussions about launching the *Monitor* appeared in the paper's issue of September 4, 1934. In Mrs. Eddy's opinion, "The test of all *Monitor* news is whether that news is socially important, whether it is news which we all need to know to be informed and alert citizens. It is the goal of the *Monitor* to give to its readers a newspaper which will be vital, realistic and comprehensive, which will give to the good news, to the encouraging news and to the constructive news the prominence it rightfully deserves. At the same time the *Monitor* ignores nothing essential to a penetrating understanding of those aggravated social conditions to which readers of the *Monitor*, particularly, can give healing attention."

᠍ᢦ My work at the radio station brought me and my family back to Lagos, where my wife and I rejoined the Christian Science group—by this time a Christian Science Society—and our children reentered the Sunday School, which now had an enrollment of nearly a hundred children. I held a number of church offices, and eventually was elected First Reader—a post which offered me the opportunity for deeper study into the Bible and *Science and Health* as I prepared the readings for the services. The consequence was further spiritual growth.

In 1959 I had become a member of The Mother Church, The First Church of Christ, Scientist, in Boston. In 1964 I was appointed by The Christian Science Board of Directors to serve as Committee on Publication for all Nigeria, a position which I held until September 30, 1973. Established by Mary Baker Eddy, this office is responsible for correcting in the public press any misconceptions and misstatements concerning the teachings of Christian Science.

In 1966 I visited the United States for the first time in order to attend the biennial meeting held by the Christian Science Committee on Publication in Boston. This conference is attended by the Committees on Publication from every part of the world. I took the occasion to visit New York, Washington, D.C., Pittsburgh, and Chicago—and especially the universities—Boston University, M.I.T., Yale, and Wisconsin State. On invitation, I spoke on Nigeria to a group of students and a community group at Indiana State. The great technological and social advancements in the United States impressed me enormously; but best of all, I enjoyed the warmth and love of Americans and the friendships I made with Christian Scientists in the United States.

Meanwhile, I had also been progressing in my professional career. In 1960, after I had served for several years as news translator, the position of program producer became open, and the Nigerian Broadcasting Corporation appointed me to the job. Later I went to London, where I received my training in radio production at BBC. Following this experience, I returned to Lagos to continue activities as radio producer for Radio Nigeria. The station's policy is "to educate, inform, and entertain" our listeners. I produce five programs weekly in Yoruba cultural and music programs, short stories, quiz programs; I also enlighten listeners on important current and past issues, bringing them ideas designed to uplift everyday living. The Nigerian Broadcasting Corporation also operates a television station. But since only 15 percent of the population now owns television sets, it is radio that reaches the majority of Nigerians.

໒໐ As the years unfolded, the study of Christian Science deepened my concepts of God, man, and the universe. I began to see how the spiritual message I wanted to convey could be developed more fully in novel form. In 1972 the Oxford University Press (Ibadan Nigerian branch) published my novel *Gbobaniyi*.

A work I particularly enjoyed doing was *Ijala*, a collection of traditional Yoruba poetry, chosen in 1967 and also 1968 as a Yoruba literature textbook for the West African school certificate examination (also published by Oxford University Press, Ibadan Nigerian branch). Until the beginning of the twentieth century, Yoruba literature was mainly oral. When Nigerians started to write for publication, they devoted themselves to prose, with very few written poems. So when I started to write professionally, I thought of correcting this imbalance and began a collection of oral traditional poetry in book form.

Literature at its best has always been a major force for turning men's thoughts toward the spiritual and moral values that must govern them if they are to grow, prosper, and find peace and happiness. This universal message runs throughout the Bible, and the literature of Christian Science illumines man's essential purpose in life—his mission to be God's representative on earth.

᠘ After I had been studying and applying Christian Science for some years, people began asking for my spiritual help with their problems. Feeling that I needed to understand more systematically the rules of Christian healing, I applied for class teaching to an authorized Christian Science teacher in London, was accepted, and flew to that city in 1966 for instruction. As my plane carried me northward over the wide expanse of the Atlantic Ocean, I couldn't help thinking that my youthful aspirations for higher education were about to be fulfilled in this important step in a way that divine Love alone could provide. (In 1971 my wife had similar Christian Science class teaching.)

Over a period of twenty years as a Christian Scientist, I have very seldom been absent from work due to ill health. However, I recall with special gratitude a healing of some years ago. I came down with a severe case of pneumonia. For two days I worked metaphysically for myself, without relief. Then I realized I had to be more thorough in my prayers. Pneumonia being inflammation of the lungs, and inflammation being a mental state of fear and anxiety, I began systematically to eradicate these errors of thought by replacing them with the concept that man, God's spiritual idea, is not subject to material suggestions or conditions of fear.

Opening *Science and Health*, I read: "Have no fear that matter can ache, swell, or be inflamed as the result of a law of any kind, when it is self-evident that matter can have no pain nor inflammation." Also: "It is well to be calm in sickness; to be hopeful is still better; but to understand that sickness is not real and that Truth can destroy its seeming reality, is best of all, for this understanding is the universal and perfect remedy." [10] Within a few hours, I was completely healed.

My metaphysical prayers in Christian Science have healed others who sought my help—in cases of hemorrhaging and other physical complaints, also in connection with finding proper employment. In all my prayers, I follow the teachings of Christian Science: that it is divine Principle, not person, that does the healing work.

My reverence for Mary Baker Eddy's accomplishments increases daily as I consider the magnitude of her life-work in establishing her Church, a movement which now spans all continents. This—together with her foresight in founding the Christian Science religious periodicals and also the international daily newspaper, *The Christian Science Monitor*—makes me realize that her energies came not from any human source, but from "the mind that was also in Christ Jesus." Her love for all mankind can be found in these words in *Miscellaneous Writings*: "I desire the equal growth and prosperity of all Christian Scientists, and the world in general; each and every one has equal opportunity to be benefited by my thoughts and writings." [11]

It is difficult to estimate how many Nigerians are today studying Christian Science; but there is hardly a part of Nigeria where the words "Christian Science" have not been heard. They have come to the attention of my countrymen, women, and children through press news; notices of services published in the newspapers; distribution of Christian Science literature in public places; person-to-person communication, and through Christian Science lectures. Further, the Christian Science radio series "The Truth That Heals" has been broadcast weekly on radio station WNBS.

---

[10] *Science and Health*, pp. 393–94.
[11] *Miscellaneous Writings*, p. 291.

⟩⟩ The missionary spirit is strong in Nigeria, and Christian Science is being discussed in many homes, universities, and offices of our land. Mrs. Eddy has written: "Christian Science reinforces Christ's sayings and doings. The Principle of Christian Science demonstrates peace. Christianity is the chain of scientific being reappearing in all ages, maintaining its obvious correspondence with the Scriptures and uniting all periods in the design of God. . . . God is Father, infinite, and this great truth, when understood in its divine metaphysics, will establish the brotherhood of man, end wars, and demonstrate 'on earth peace, good will toward men.'" [12]

[12] *The First Church of Christ, Scientist, and Miscellany,* p. 279.

Mrs. Adele Simpson with her "Simpsonian Institute" collection.

# FASHION

## ஃ*Adele Simpson*

FASHION DESIGNER AND MANUFACTURER, NEW YORK

ஃ My parents had taught their children to fear God, but I could never accept this idea. From the time I was a small child, I instinctively resisted the concept of a God to be feared. At the same time, I didn't know how to go about finding a better understanding of Him. So as I grew up, while I honored God and the Ten Commandments, I was not pursuing religion. I was in pursuit of a career that would establish fashion trends and lead me to the top in my field. This had resulted in a frantic pace of activity difficult to maintain, creating tensions at home and business. At this point, I learned about Christian Science and began to know God as the universal Principle, Love.

ஃ My birthplace is New York City, the largest garment manufacturing center in the United States. I was the youngest of five sisters in the days when it was the custom in many New York homes with large families to buy one bolt of blue serge material and call in a dressmaker. She would make middy blouses and skirts for the older girls, which would subsequently be passed along down the line. As the last recipient of these hand-me-downs, I rebelled and decided to make my own clothes. By the time I reached fourteen, I was designing and sewing all of my sisters' clothes as well.

One of my older sisters, a gifted artist, had a job as a sketcher with Ben Gershel & Company, a clothing manufacturer. Her employer, admiring what she wore, wanted to know where she got her clothes. When she told him that her little sister made them, he sent for me and gave me a job. I was still in grade school, so I went in on Saturdays to sketch and pin buttons on the clothes so the factory hands could sew them on.

One day the Gershel Company's designer became sick, and Mr. Gershel gave me the opportunity to show what I could do. Clothes at that time were made with a heavy hand, involving layers of interlinings, and one could get into a dress only by pulling it over the head. I began to develop a scientific approach to fashion design. I felt there was a need for clothes that would be beautiful but also easy to get into, and would require a minimum of care. Simplifying the whole process of dressing women seemed important even then, and has continued as my governing fashion philosophy. As it turned out, I became the first to design clothes that women didn't have to put on over their heads.

In the beginning, I didn't have much expertise or a professional approach to fashion designing, but I wanted passionately to make good. Although my early sketches were legible and readable, I needed to know more about the techniques of fashion designing. So I left the Gershel Company to take a dressmaking and art course at Pratt Institute.

Mary Brown, who taught me the principles of dressmaking, instilled in me a certain lasting discipline—as essential in the art of dressmaking as in the art of life. It became a precept of mine that, in order to accomplish anything of value, one must have meticulous follow-through. Besides the day classes, I took special night courses in draping. These were given by dressmakers from established companies like Henri Bendel—a shop catering to some of the most fashionable women in New York—who taught

Pratt students how to work with fabrics. For me, draping had all the excitement of sculpture as I saw a flat piece of material suddenly take shape and a third dimension. Because I was tiny—I am four feet, nine inches—I developed a philosophy of "thinking tall"—of having big ideas in order to accomplish something worthwhile in my life.

After finishing my course at Pratt Institute, I returned to Ben Gershel & Company. There my sister designed the suits and I designed the dresses. A year later an opportunity came to be designer for William Bass at a salary of $30,000 a year. To a twenty-year-old, the offer of so much money, not subject to today's taxes, was staggering. Under the William Bass label, my clothes were successful and were much talked about in the trade. Then Al Lasher offered me a job with his firm. Since the Lasher Company used more expensive fabrics of a better quality, I took the job.

One day a salesman named Wesley Simpson called at my office to show me his new line of beautiful fabrics. After I had made my choices, he invited me to dinner. My answer was, "No, thank you, I never go out with anyone in the trade." Mr. Simpson knew one of my friends and arranged with her that I be invited to dinner at her home. On arrival I found that my dinner partner was the fabric salesman I had refused to date. After a whirlwind courtship of three weeks—and in spite of my being practically engaged to another man and Wesley to another girl—we were married. The years that have followed have brought deep happiness, expanding horizons, and spiritual growth to both of us.

ࢌ Shortly after our marriage, my husband and I started our own dress manufacturing business. However, the emotional pressures of such a close and constant marital-and-professional relationship proved too much for us. So after a year my husband went into factoring in the textile business (an involvement with fabrics which has continued to this day), while I returned to Mr. Lasher's firm.

But the commercial world continued to crowd in on me. I found myself turning to God in prayer. But what was God? Was prayer to Him answered—if so, how must I pray? My husband's sister was a Christian Scientist, and sensing my spiritual need, she began to talk to me about this religion. What she said about the healing, calming power of Love impressed me to the extent that I decided to look into the teachings of Christian Science.

In the chapter entitled "Marriage" in *Science and Health*, I read: "Science inevitably lifts one's being higher in the scale of harmony and happiness. . . . Kindred tastes, motives, and aspirations are necessary to the formation of a happy and permanent companionship." [1] I saw in these words an ideal by which my husband's and my talents could be harmonized, each supporting the other spiritually in our home, each free to fulfill his individual purpose in life. The ideal grew to be fully shared when my husband, too, became a Christian Scientist.

Mrs. Eddy's writings enthralled me. Although I had known the Bible all my life, it had been a closed book. Now, with *Science and Health* as my guide, I began a search into its hidden wisdoms. Mrs. Eddy's words impressed me: "The central fact of the Bible is the superiority of spiritual over physical power." [2]

Since I was considered a young fashion leader in the trade, the whole subject of leadership fascinated me. So I began to research the Bible, to analyze the laws of God, to probe the character and vision which made Moses a great leader. I came to the conclusion, as *Science and Health* pointed out, that there is a fundamental Science of Life—of man and the universe—with rules and laws which, if applied, would bring achievement and spiritual satisfactions to men and women. I decided that to the best of my ability, I would apply these scientific, sacred laws of God to my own career. And Christian Science would show me how to do this.

It was also fascinating to find that—from Genesis to Revelation—clothes often symbolize a man's concept of himself. When Job sat in sackcloth, demanding from God reasons for his desolation, the Lord answered Job out of the whirlwind, and

[1] *Science and Health*, p. 60.
[2] Science and Health, p. 131.

said: "Deck thyself now with majesty and excellency, and array thyself with glory and beauty." [3] Therefore I concluded that according to the Bible, even in their garments, men and women should express their highest spiritual selfhood.

᭞ In the first years of studying Christian Science, I would go off by myself early in the morning with the Bible and *Science and Health* and, following the citations in the *Christian Science Quarterly*, read the weekly Lesson-Sermon, the study which Christian Scientists pursue daily and which comprises the sermon at our Sunday services. Soon my thoughts would be filled with the realization that "In the beginning, God. . . ." *God* created the heaven and the earth; *God* governed man and the universe. *God* was first! A sense of peace would flood my consciousness, continuing through many hours of the day.

I began to see the distinction between creator and creation. God is the creator, and man and the universe are the creation. The answer to the question, "What is man?" in *Science and Health* became a governing rule in my creative work. It reads in part: ". . . that which has not a single quality underived from Deity; that which possesses no life, intelligence, nor creative power of his own, but reflects spiritually all that belongs to his Maker." [4]

The tensions which accompany the egotistic belief that man is a personal creator left me. I saw that the work of the artist was to image forth the ideas that came from God, the one creative Mind. And as a manufacturer, I realized that, fundamentally, my job was to do the will of the Father—in the words of Jesus, "to be about my Father's business."

᭞ Mr. Lasher operated his dress manufacturing business under the trade name of Mary Lee. At the time I rejoined him shortly after my marriage, I became a full partner, and we changed the name to Adele Simpson. When Mr. Lasher passed

[3] Job 40:10.
[4] *Science and Health*, p. 475.

on a few years later, I acquired the business. I was then 29 years of age and had two children. I turned fully to Christian Science for inspiration and courage to carry on with the added business responsibilities, and God's love sustained and led me forward.

ᔡ Several years after our marriage we bought a small house in Greenwich, Connecticut. During World War II, when we wanted to help people under Nazi attack, we sent for nine children to come from London. Because an English ship had recently been torpedoed, there was some fear that the children might not be safe in an Atlantic crossing. So only two children and their mother arrived. They lived with us for four years during the war's duration, the children attending the Christian Science Sunday School with our son and daughter. Since our home was too small to accommodate us all comfortably, we bought a large, wonderful house in Greenwich. Today, with our children having homes of their own, my husband and I still enjoy this lovely house, with laurel growing inside and outdoors. Full of happy memories, it continues to be a haven and a place where our children, grandchildren, and our friends—among them writers and artists—are always welcome.

ᔡ During my early years as designer-manufacturer, Paris was the style-setter of the fashion world, and leading fashion designers and clothing manufacturers found it imperative (most of us still do) to visit that beautiful city and view the new collections of the great fashion houses. Later, when other capital cities also became fashion centers, I visited them as well, always with my husband. Thus together we began our world travels.

During this period my husband, under his own name, was conducting a textile converting business. He conceived the idea of introducing the work of leading artists into the textile field, and became one of the first in the United States to commission artists like Vertès, Dali, and Bemelmans to create—under their own name—exquisite *croquis* (designs). These works of art were reproduced by textile manufacturers in silk, wool, cotton, and synthetics for use in fine quality clothes. In that romantic era, beautiful art in textiles was part of the American scene. Today the paintings of these artists hang in the Metropolitan and Brooklyn museums.

Beautiful and unusual fabrics have always been an absorption for me. The study of fabrics has drawn me to many faraway places where they are produced. Responding to their possibilities has enriched and extended my own expression and output.

Often my friends in America have given me letters of introduction to their friends in different lands. So I go into a country not as a stranger, but as a friend. Through the eyes of my new friends, I see a country from within and come to understand a people's most prized treasures and artistic riches. And sometimes its economic needs. My religious teaching that there is one universal Father-Mother, and therefore one family of man, has led me to share with several countries abroad my knowledge of manufacturing techniques and fashion trends— helping them in their efforts to produce for a world market, especially for the United States.

This sharing of ideas has brought me into contact with leaders and artists in other lands involved with the production and merchandising of their native fabrics, clothes, and crafts. My husband and I have been graciously received at the palace of President and Mrs. Ferdinand Marcos of the Philippines; in India by Mrs. Indira Gandhi and Mrs. B.K. Nehru; in Nairobi by Mrs. Kenyetta; in Tokyo by Mrs. Yanagitto, painter and kimono designer. In turn, many of the fabrics, jewelry, and artifacts of these nations have been the inspiration of the fabrics I design for my clothes. Friendship and love are talents which all artists need—and already have as the children of God.

᠔᠍ Early in my travels I began to collect fabrics, costumes, books, and dolls that represent a country's art and culture. These are housed in a special studio I call my "Simpsonian Institute." My doll collection speaks a "language of the eye"; it represents the ambience of the countries I have visited, the artistic heritage and lifestyle of a people.

Every country expresses its own special beauty. Japan has its pure silk kimono fabrics, woven obis, brocades loomed by its ancient finger-weaving; Indonesia has its batik designs of cottons and silk, the sarong, beautiful bracelets and necklaces, and stunning headdresses; France, its exquisitely designed silks; England, its woolens and tweeds; Switzerland, its embroidered cottons; Turkey, its caftans and carpet designs; Italy, its Como silks and knits; Kenya, its Swahili printed designs and cottons; India, its saris; Argentina, its gauchos and riding clothes; Spain, its clothes of softest leathers and luxurious suedes; Russia, its furs and boots. And this expression of art extends throughout all nations.

Many museums throughout the United States maintain a special division for the exhibition of costumes. These illustrate in design, fabric, and detail something of our nation's evolving culture. In order to contribute to this record in fashion, I have donated fabrics, books, and costumes to the Costume Institute of The Metropolitan Museum of Art in New York City, to the Drexel Institute in Philadelphia, Historical Museum of Chicago, Dallas Costume Museum, Brooklyn Museum, and the Fashion Institute of Technology of New York. Eventually I plan to turn over to the Fashion Institute of Technology my entire studio collection, which is in the process of being catalogued and evaluated for this purpose.

In 1967 The Metropolitan Museum of Art held an exhibition of dresses from the eighteenth century to the present, and one of my costumes was exhibited in the section of Contemporary Design. This was one of the museum's most successful costume exhibits, with 200,000 people attending. In *The New York Times* of October 25, 1967, John Canaday wrote: "The Metropolitan Museum's new exhibition 'The Art of Fashion' is a high-styled spectacular. Posing the question, Is fashion an art? the museum answers with a convincing affirmation. . . . It is a beautifully staged exhibition, filled with luxuriously beautiful objects. And . . . it establishes the validity of fashion as an art. . . ."

To young people who are thinking of fashion designing as a career, I say, Drink in the world's beauty. You cannot possibly see a collection of beautiful paintings and then do something ugly in color or form or design. Mrs. Eddy's words in *Science and Health* can be an inspiration to young people: "Beauty is a thing of life, which dwells forever in the eternal Mind and reflects the charms of His goodness in expression, form, outline, and color." [5] When fashion designing is approached from the understanding that the divine Mind is the creator, it becomes more beautiful—as the hand of the artist attempts to approximate "the charms of His goodness."

 

ఌ Fashion in America is big business and must be run in a businesslike way. It is highly competitive and it must bring a profit, not only for oneself but for the many talented and specially gifted people who are indispensable to an organization whose function is to create, manufacture, sell, and deliver quality clothes for the American woman. The artist cannot simply please himself, he must design for the world he lives in.

Several times each year I visit many American cities to present in person each collection I design. I meet and talk with women of many ages, occupations, interests, tastes, and attitudes. I listen to what they say, I experience and learn. I visit museums and small galleries, go to book shops, food markets, factories, schools, libraries, and universities. I sense the changing beat of life in America—the change that the exciting and wonderful world of fashion reflects.

I wear two hats in my business—one for the artist and another for the manufacturer. They somehow combine in my overall approach. When designing, I feel a responsibility to the people in my organization who must earn a living. I think of the shopkeepers who buy the clothes and must sell them at a profit. I keep in mind the fitness of things—the right clothes for the right occasion. Where will the woman wear the clothes? Will they fit into her wardrobe? Will they fit into today's way of life? Clothes must relate to all these things. What I have learned from my world travels, from visits in shops, from conversation with women in this and other parts of the world—all these

[5] *Science and Health*, p. 247.

factors contribute to the fabrics I design, the clothes I fashion, manufacture, and sell.

Christian Science sets a standard of excellence for its followers, in whatever field they may be working. I believe that as a result of our organization maintaining a high standard in design, fabric, and manufacture, our clothes have had the distinction of being worn by famous ladies and internationally known models —among them Twiggy, Marissa Berenson, Audrey Meadows, Margot Fonteyn. And famous photographers have photographed them—Avedon, Horst, Penn, and Hiro—for *Harper's Bazaar, Vogue,* and other leading fashion magazines.

All through its existence, even in the Depression era of the thirties, our company has never had a losing year—a record of prosperity which I attribute solely to Christian Science. The words of Proverbs have guided me: "Trust in the Lord with all thine heart; and lean not unto thine own understanding. In all thy ways acknowledge him, and he shall direct thy paths." [6]

᭟ Dealing with 60 or 70 people a day in my manufacturing organization, I have found that the harmonizing factor in human relationships is divine Love. If I arrive in the morning to find an employee doing something wrong, I don't confront him before his co-workers, but wait for the right opportunity, usually at the end of the day. Then I explain what was not right, ask him to think about it overnight and see how it can be corrected. This practice has won for me many loyal and thoughtful workers.

In the garment manufacturing business, with its temperaments and pressures of seasonal deadlines, people tend to be excitable. The teachings of my religion that all is under the government of divine Love has not only helped me remain calm under stress, but also helped bring an atmosphere of calmness to others. One of the typical crises that arise at fashion shows is caused by missing dress packing-cases. By realizing that in the infinitude of Mind, nothing is lost, I have remained calm. And inevitably the cases have turned up in time.

[6] Proverbs 3:5–6.

ཙ In 1960, on a visit to Washington, I met Mrs. B.K. Nehru, wife of the Indian Ambassador to the United States. Then as now, India's economy needed strengthening, and Mrs. Nehru was trying to promote hand-loomed textiles and other handicrafts from India. In sympathy with her efforts, I designed a collection of beautiful summer evening "garden party dresses," using Indian cotton saris, some woven with threads of gold. These clothes were featured in fine shops throughout the United States.

In 1964, just before the opening of the New York World's Fair, Mrs. Nehru invited me to India to help choose the fabrics for exhibition at the Indian Pavilion. While there, I met Prime Minister Mrs. Indira Gandhi. I visited the weaving and printing centers of Calcutta, New Delhi, Benares, Agra, Madras, Jaipur, Ahmadabad, and Bombay, and after my return, designed a collection of clothes using the exquisite Indian saris and brocades. Then I gave a fashion show at the Indian Embassy in Washington, which United States government officials and friends of Mrs. Nehru attended. Later, at the Indian Pavilion of the World's Fair, I gave another fashion show for the visiting American fashion editors. In this way, the Indian fabrics were widely publicized for their beauty and practicality—and I hope to some degree helped that country's economy.

In 1965, at the request of the Turkish Travel Bureau, I went to Istanbul, visiting the Turkish embroidery and dressmaking schools, and found their students greatly influenced by Italian fashions. When I returned to America, I sent back paper patterns from *Harper's Bazaar, Vogue,* and *Mademoiselle,* plus my own designs, so that Turkish students would have ideas for dressmaking and designing for the American market.

A great artistic exchange is going on in the fashion world, an appreciation of all national art and culture. This is drawing mankind close to the realization that we all have "the same Principle, or Father."

We have beautiful cottons in America. Although cotton has been an important industry in this country since the beginning of the nineteenth century, it was long overlooked as a quality fabric by American designers, and even by fabric people themselves. The Italians claimed they made the best silks, the French the best prints, and the English the best woolens, but nobody recognized that the United States made the best cotton. In the 1960's cotton manufacturers were searching for ways to expand the industry. My use of cotton for daytime and evening dresses "took cotton out of the kitchen," as the Cotton Institute stated, and created a fashion trend in this country. I became the first fashion designer to receive a Cotton Council Award, presented to me in 1962 at a Washington fashion show by the then Secretary of Agriculture, Ezra Benson. The show was attended by many of the senators and government people from cotton-growing states. Subsequently, a high-quality cotton was developed in western Texas and California. Economically, cotton became very important. Today the Swiss and Italian cotton manufacturers come to this country to study the kinds of cotton we make—the different weights, their suitability for different climates, and their crease-resistant qualities.

ॐ I am grateful for the privilege of having dressed several first ladies—Mrs. Dwight D. Eisenhower, Mrs. Lyndon B. Johnson, and Mrs. Richard M. Nixon. It is a challenge to dress officials' wives and other women in the public eye, who are always open to criticism. They lead very busy lives, are constantly traveling around the country, and must have packable clothes—clothes that behave well, photograph well, fit well—clothes that they can feel safe in, clothes that give great pleasure and enjoyment and that are made in the best taste and quality of fabrics. I dressed Pat Nixon for her trips to China, Russia, and Africa; for her campaign tours; and also for her second inaugural ball. I dressed Lady Bird Johnson for her daughters' weddings, for the Beautification program trips around the country, and for her trips abroad, and have made sports clothes suitable for wear at her Texas ranch. Friendships have developed with these outstanding first ladies, and my husband and I have had the honor of dining at the White House.

❧ In the summer of 1974, in Salt Lake City, the American Academy of Achievement presented Golden Plate awards to fifty honorees; and I was one of the recipients. The awards were given to individuals who had made contributions in the fields of the automotive and aerospace industries, finance and business, medicine, the United States military services, education, chemistry, broadcasting, movies, conservation and environment, and others. As a contributor to the fields of fashion and textiles, I felt deeply honored to be included among this distinguished group.

❧ Some years ago, on one of my buying trips to Switzerland, I had a few hours to spare before leaving for Paris and decided to visit an Oriental art exhibition in a small Zurich museum. It was November, snow lay on the ground, and I wore knee-high boots. While enjoying the beauty of the collection, I looked at my watch and realized it was nearly plane time. Turning quickly to leave, I slipped and fell on the highly polished floor. When a museum attendant picked me up, I found I couldn't take a step without great pain in my ankle and knee. The attendant helped me to a waiting car that I fortunately had hired to take me directly to the airport. On the way there, my prayers centered on the Ninety-first Psalm: "He that dwelleth in the secret place of the most High shall abide under the shadow of the Almighty. . . . For he shall give his angels charge over thee, to keep thee in all thy ways." [7]

Upon arrival at the airport, the driver commandeered a wheel chair that enabled me to board the plane. When finally strapped into my seat, I noticed about a dozen passengers—skiers on their way back from St. Moritz—either on crutches or with their arms or legs in casts. When we arrived at the Paris airport, an ambulance was backed up to the door of the plane to receive the injured passengers. But I refused to go with them in the ambulance, making my way through customs, hobbling and in great pain. When I reached the hotel, my ankle and leg were so swollen that the house doctor had to cut my boot open in order

[7] Psalms 91:1, 11.

to remove it. He suggested that I go immediately to the American hospital for X-rays; he was sure my ankle was broken and my kneecap splintered.

However, I refused to go, praying all that night to prove the healing power of Christian Science. Turning to *Science and Health*, I read: "Realize the presence of health and the fact of harmonious being, until the body corresponds with the normal conditions of health and harmony." [8] The next morning I asked for help from a Christian Science practitioner. The following day the swelling was gone, the discoloration disappeared, and I was able to walk easily and without pain. The healing was complete.


ॐ Everywhere I travel, I seek out Christian Science branch churches and attend the Sunday services and Wednesday evening meetings. I never cease to be impressed by the fact that all over the world—whether in Italy, France, South America, Germany, England, the Far East, the Near East, Beverly Hills, Dallas, New York, Greenwich, Boston—the Christian Science services are the same. Whether conducted in English, French, Italian, Spanish, German—I am grateful to Mary Baker Eddy for her provision for a worldwide church. With communications as they exist today, no place is remote. Always I am inspired by the spiritual beauty of the services in all the Christian Science churches I have visited, and the elegant simplicity of the churches themselves.


ॐ All my working life I have been in the business of fashion. But it has been more than a business, it has been a fascination with the way people all over the world express their sense of beauty, and it has been a way for me to contribute to this expression. In *The People's Idea of God*, Mrs. Eddy has written: "As our ideas of Deity become more spiritual, we express them by objects more beautiful." [9]

[8] *Science and Health*, p. 412.
[9] *The People's Idea of God*, p. 14.

Christian Science is as fresh in my thought and alive today as when I first began its study many years ago. It has enriched me, spiritualized my approach to man and the universe, and brought me great happiness. For this, I am profoundly grateful to Mary Baker Eddy.

*Ellis Gulliver at his Dimby Downs ranch.*

# EXPANSION IN AUSTRALIA

## ❧ Ellis Gulliver

CATTLE BREEDER AND FARMER OF
NEW SOUTH WALES, AUSTRALIA

❧ I was born on a dairy farm about ten miles from Maitland, a town 130 miles north of Sydney, Australia. Its population numbered about 4,000. Only a neighbor's wife attended my birth, because doctors and hospitals were not then available in country districts.

Dairy farming provided a mere subsistence living, and my parents were in poor circumstances. We depended largely on the land, having our own ducks and fowls, making our own butter, and shooting wild ducks and other edible birds, plus hares and rabbits when possible. The only major items to buy were bread and groceries. At the early age of six I was already helping to milk cows and do other farm chores.

As the youngest of four sons, I seemed to be left a good deal to my own resources in my early years and consequently led a somewhat lonely existence. But looking back I can see that this gave me an opportunity for independent thinking. I would walk around the fields by the hour, wondering what life was all about. Some people were happy, others in the depths of misery. Some were sick, others healthy. There were some living in luxury, others in grinding poverty. I perceived that everything appeared to be governed by one's mode of thinking or understanding, and so I felt that there must be a law or principle underlying thought. This law, when understood, would enable one to have an abundant life, would enable one to be healthy instead of sick, happy instead of miserable, successful instead of poverty-stricken.

With supreme confidence I made a solemn vow to myself that somehow, somewhere, some day, I would discover this secret, and like Mary of old, kept this assurance in my heart. Only in later years did I learn that this desire was the prayer that led me to Christian Science. My only early religious training was attendance at a Church of England service or Sunday School.

Not until I was nine years old, when we moved to a farm nearer town, could I go to school. It was a three-mile walk each way, and I well remember the traumatic experience of first attending school at this age and catching up with the school system. At the end of the first term I was last in the class, but by the end of the second term stood second, and remained in that position during all my school years. The son of a Welsh coal miner always managed to top the class. In four years I completed eight years of primary schooling and received my qualifying certificate to go on to high school at the age of thirteen. But I was eager to earn a living and started as an assistant in a drapery store at $1.30 per week. My thirst for knowledge continued, however, and this was satisfied through correspondence courses and, later, university extension courses.

After two years' work in the drapery store, I looked for wider horizons. So I left the store, and with a hired horse and cart, started selling surplus pumpkins from my parents' farm. A number of coal-mining towns lay within a radius of ten miles from home, and it was toward these I drove each day to sell my goods.

After some months, when our supplies ran out, I became apprenticed to a pastry-cook baker in Maitland, about three miles from where we were living. My working hours started early—at midnight or at 3:00 A.M. or 5:00 A.M.—and I rode a bicycle to and from work, later a motorcycle. I well remember the cold, frosty winter mornings, when my hands would be almost frozen to the handlebars of the bicycle. On such days starting the fires in the bakery ovens was a welcome relief from the cold. Everything was reversed in the summertime, when it was essential to keep the doors closed a good deal because of the yeast. (Yeast requires even, warm temperatures—extremes of heat or cold will spoil the leavening process.) Maitland is located on a river system that is subject to flooding after heavy rains, and sometimes we had to use sandbags to keep the flood waters out of the bakery. On such occasions I had to row to work and tie up the rowboat near the bakery.

At age 21, having served my five years' apprenticeship in the pastry-cooking trade, I decided to seek my fame and fortune by opening my own business in one of the suburbs of Sydney. As a raw country lad with $200 in my pocket and a burning desire to succeed, I arrived in the capital of New South Wales. That was in January 1931, at the beginning of the Great Depression, so it was not difficult to find empty premises. I soon located, at a low rental, a vacant shop having a bakehouse with a built-in brick oven in which to bake my goods. Large electric and gas ovens belonged to the future.

A period of great hardship followed. I had much to learn about the baking trade and also about business practice. The long hours of work yielded very little profit; but I refused to accept defeat. The conditions I faced only increased my overwhelming desire for some basic truth to guide and direct my life. Sometimes on a Sunday I would attend three Protestant church services. The ministers were fine men, doing their best as they understood it; yet they didn't provide any answers to my deep searchings and longings.

It was about this time that I read a magazine article strongly critical of Christian Science and its founder, Mary Baker Eddy. In my own simple way I could see that Mrs. Eddy's statements, criticized most vehemently by the writer, contained the truth I sought, and I made up my mind to investigate for myself. I searched in several book shops for a copy of *Science and Health with Key to the Scriptures* by Mrs. Eddy, but none of them knew about the book. Finally someone told me that I could get it at a Christian Science Reading Room, which I did. The study of this book, along with the Bible, was to change the whole course of my life. But Christian Science was not something I could devour in one gulp. My apprehension of it was a slow and gradual process, each human problem forcing me to deeper study and understanding.

ॐ After about five years at my original location, during which time I opened a second shop in an adjoining suburb, I received an offer for the business at a good profit and decided to sell. While awaiting an opportunity to reopen in business, I requested a Christian Science practitioner to help me, through prayer, to be guided to the right location.

Meanwhile I was working for the Sydney electricity authority, demonstrating electric pastry ovens at a pastry cook's exhibition in the Sydney Town Hall. One day a lady came in and asked if I would care to rent, for use as a bakery, one of the shops in a building she had just erected at Edgecliff, a wealthy suburb. She had been walking past the Sydney Town Hall, noticed there was a pastry cook's exhibition inside, thought she would like a cake shop in her new building, came in to look around, was attracted to me—and I had found my ideal place.

Coincidence? From the progressive events that followed, I tend to believe that it was my prayers in Christian Science that showed forth God's plan for me. The next day I met the lady, and arrangements were made for me to fit out the new shop; she even allowed me three months' free rent to help me become established. With the equipment installed, the business opened and soon began to prosper.

But though I could produce and organize the flow of baked goods behind the scenes, I had difficulty in finding the right girl who would be competent in both selling and displaying the goods attractively. I had come to rely on a statement in *Science and Health* which read: "Divine Love always has met and always will meet every human need." [1] So I duly advertised, knowing that Love would meet this need. Since Depression conditions

[1] *Science and Health*, p. 494.

still prevailed, about 25 or 30 girls applied for the position. When the businessman next door wondered what all the girls were doing about the shop, I jokingly told him I had advertised for a wife. The girl chosen proved to be the right one, and within four months did become my wife! This marriage has been a great blessing, and at that time provided the teamwork necessary for our progress in the business.

〰 Owning the Bible and the Christian Science textbook did not mean that I had much understanding of their contents. I hadn't found the time to do any in-depth study, and now I realized that I could no longer remain on the fringe of Christian Science. Until this period, my life had been a busy one with no health problems. My testing and proving time came when I began to suffer severely from dermatitis, a painful skin condition that made food handling very difficult.

Over a period of about twelve months I was treated by three medical men without relief. In desperation I finally visited a skin specialist. For two weeks various raw materials with which I worked had to be taken to him, and he tested them on my skin. After this he was able to prove conclusively that according to medical science I was allergic to flour. That is, flour coming in contact with my skin set up an infection. The verdict was that never again would I be able to work with flour, and if I didn't get away from it I would not be able to eat anything containing flour. Had I been an employee, a certificate would have been supplied for permanent worker's compensation. This sounded like a death sentence to all my hopes and ambitions.

A tarlike substance was applied to my body and limbs each night for temporary relief, but how to get between a pair of sheets in this condition is best left to the imagination. Attempting to escape from the flour, I took an extended holiday in the snow country of New South Wales, and there the condition became worse than ever. I had reached the end of the medical road.

But my extremity proved to be God's opportunity. In a hell of suffering I commenced to read through the Christian Science textbook. One short sentence stood out like a searchlight to my yearning thought: "In the quiet sanctuary of earnest longings,

we must deny sin and plead God's allness." The marginal no
was "Effectual invocation." [2]

I disposed of the tarlike substance in the snow and gained
clear, spiritual concept that I had to deny the reality of th
condition and plead, or understand, God's allness. This ment
discipline was undertaken with a zest that excluded everythir
else from consciousness. I realized with all my heart that suc
consecration was vitally necessary. Every time the itch, the pai
the discomfort presented itself, I denied its spiritual reality an
pleaded God's allness. This was my first thought before going t
sleep at night, and my first on waking in the morning. It was a
earnest longing and thirsting after righteousness, or a righ
understanding of God.

After three days of my persistent prayer in this fashion, "th
Word was made flesh"—rendered practical. My raw skin ha
been renewed. I was completely free. Touching the hem c
Christ's garment, I had been able to prove that Christia
Science heals. What medical science could not accomplish i
more than twelve months of suffering, this religion had achieve
in three days. As Mrs. Eddy states in *Science and Health*: "Th
rays of infinite Truth, when gathered into the focus of idea
bring light instantaneously, whereas a thousand years of huma
doctrines, hypotheses, and vague conjectures emit no suc
effulgence." [3]

More significant than my physical healing was the mental an
spiritual freedom gained—a surety that despite any huma
verdict, there is no obstruction or separation between man an
his Creator. An entirely new manner of thinking had given m
an added mental dimension. I returned to my cake-manufactu
ing business and though often covered with flour over the year
my body suffered no further ill effects. I had gained th
realization that God, and not a material substance, governs th
universe, and that no error of thought can bind us beyond ou
belief in it.

I don't mean to imply that as a result of this healing
immediately achieved human perfection. There were many trai

[2] *Science and Health*, p. 15.
[3] *Science and Health*, p. 504.

of character that still needed correction, many qualities of thought that needed spiritualization. But whatever one does prove of Christian Science is the reality because it is firmly anchored in its source, God. Though my understanding of Christian Science at that time was "as a grain of mustard seed," it had accomplished much.

&❧ After my healing the business continued to grow and prosper, and I received and accepted an excellent offer to sell. Following a three months' holiday, we found an empty shop in the suburbs of Randwick, about five miles from Sydney, which we opened for the same type of business. Very soon we outgrew this shop and expanded into an adjoining one. When we outgrew this, a third shop next door was acquired—all three premises being interconnected by our opening up adjacent walls.

But again I found that my understanding of Christian Science was to be fully tested. By this time World War II was in progress, and Japan had entered the war by the bombing of Pearl Harbor. Australia faced the direct threat of invasion. With the country operating on a full wartime basis, and all manpower placed under government control, a decree was issued that any industry not essential to the war effort should be closed down to release men for the armed services.

When the cake-manufacturing industry was classified nonessential, it appeared that my lifework would be wiped out overnight. I must admit to being completely mesmerized by the thought of loss, and this kind of thinking is fatal. Then I realized that I had to gain, as never before, a clearer understanding of God and true substance. My study included the definition of God in *Science and Health*: "The great I AM; the all-knowing, all-seeing, all-acting, all-wise, all-loving, and eternal; Principle; Mind; Soul; Spirit; Life; Truth; Love; all substance; intelligence." [4]

While studying this, I saw that because God is "all substance," man, His reflection, must ever be at one with substance. There is never a moment when man could be separated from the divine consciousness, God, so substance must be as omnipresent

[4] *Science and Health*, p. 587.

as God. Walking the streets at night after business, I was conscious only of the fact of God's presence, and consequently, the ever-presence of substance. This substance was just as close as honesty, and honesty could not be taken from me, nor could one have just a small portion of honesty. We claim it in its wholeness.

After about three weeks of this way of thinking and reasoning, I was appointed to the advisory committee dealing with the cake-manufacturing industry to advise the Government minister whether this trade was really redundant and should be closed down or whether it could be altered to assist in the war effort. The committee was well aware that workers in munitions factories, as well as the general work force, had to have food and someone to supply it.

As a result of my holding fast to divine Principle, those products that were not helpful to the war effort were prohibited, and those that were helpful were retained. The industry was allowed to continue, not only with benefit to myself and others in the baking industry, but also to the general work force and the public as well. (I remember providing food for the first American troops that landed in Australia under General MacArthur, to help repel the threatened invasion from Japan.)

This action proved to me the truth of the Master's promise: "Seek ye first the kingdom of God, and his righteousness; and all these things shall be added unto you." [5] How often mankind puts the cart before the horse, seeking the human things first and forgetting or not understanding the basic Principle underlying all good, which is universally available.

Not long after this time, the business I had sold at Edgecliff was resold, failed, and closed down. The owner of the premises requested that I return and reopen it. This was done in conjunction with the Randwick business, and both grew and prospered until they became the biggest home-style cake business in Australia. The term "home-style" or "homemade" meant that baked goods were prepared in electric ovens on the premises where they were sold, and arrived hot on the selling counters.

[5] Matthew 6:33.

&❧ About this time a great leavening occurred in my consciousness. One of my childhood dreams had involved the romance of Australia's great inland, with its sheep and cattle ranches and their vast flocks of sheep and herds of cattle. Australia is an island continent almost as large as the United States of America, ranging in climate from the tropical north to the temperate southern zone, with some desert in the center. In sharp contrast with the 200 million population of the United States, Australia numbers about 18 million people spread over this enormous territory. Shearing annually about 170 million sheep, Australia produces the largest amount of wool of any country in the world, practically all of it for export. We are also the largest cattle-breeding country.

While I had a great desire for sheep and cattle raising, I didn't see how it could be fulfilled at that time since large amounts of capital were required. But the idea behind my desire seemed a constructive one, and I was sustained by a beautiful statement in *Science and Health*: "Hold thought steadfastly to the enduring, the good, and the true, and you will bring these into your experience proportionably to their occupancy of your thoughts." [6]

In my profession, I had always been fascinated by the process of working with yeast. I have seen large masses of dough in which the yeast had been forgotten; they were lifeless and of no use. But with the addition of a small amount of yeast, leavening started, chemical changes took place, and very soon it became food for man's use. To me this presented a practical illustration of the way a progressive idea could become an expanding influence in my life.

With this concept firmly fixed in thought, I began to look at properties within a hundred miles or so of Sydney, but nothing in that locality worked out. After making inquiries at the Rural Bank of New South Wales, I was introduced to a client of the bank who offered to sell me his sheep and cattle property. It was about 300 miles from Sydney, near Quirindi in northwestern New South Wales. Its broad rolling plains with hills in the background reminded me of the type of country I had always

[6] *Science and Health*, p. 261.

dreamed about. Clearly, divine Love had led me to this place. With bank assistance I was able to purchase this beautiful ranch.

The property was unimproved, so a home was built and a manager installed. This done, I set about acquiring about 3,000 sheep and approximately 400 head of cattle, bought at public sales or privately within a radius of 200 to 300 miles. At that period, large motor trucks were not available for stock transport, so the herds had to be walked to the railhead nearest purchase, then delivered at the railhead nearest our property. Sometimes we employed drovers to walk the stock from the point of purchase directly to the ranch. In the case of sheep, this would take three to four weeks, with the drovers sleeping out with them at night. Finally, equipped with stock, I was in the sheep and cattle business!

Much prayer and work was required to get the organization running smoothly, since I still operated the cake business in Sydney. My grasp of every phase of the cattle business was essential—the kind of staff needed for an efficient operation; the type of sheep and cattle that would thrive best on my property; when to buy and sell; familiarity with fodder, and also weather conditions. Gathering information from neighboring cattlemen and from the State Department of Agriculture, I was determined to utilize the most progressive techniques.

A couple of years later an area of about 6,000 acres, twenty miles away, became available for lease. This lease I acquired, and after a few months felt a strong impulsion to purchase the property. I was able to do this, not long before the seller passed away. Had I not followed my intuition, the property would not have been available to me after the owner's death. This has turned out to be one of the finest properties in New South Wales.

I was very green in my new ventures, so different from my boyhood experience with dairy cattle. But as I turned to God, the one divine intelligence, I always found my answers to problems. Often these were not the generally accepted methods of doing things, but such new ways sometimes proved very successful.

ᔒ The first property I had bought contained a portion of a dry lake bed that filled only every twenty or thirty years. During heavy flooding in 1950, this lake filled up overnight. One morning I received a telephone call in Sydney from the manager, stating that he had been moving sheep to higher ground all night, but 1,500 had been cut off in a back field. These had been washed away and drowned, along with many belonging to neighbors. The whole countryside, a flat plain, was inundated by a sea of water. My first reaction was to try to be physically present, but I was 300 miles away, the road and rail links were cut by floodwaters, and all airdromes were closed. Remembering that the Master spent many days and nights in prayer to God, I resolved to discipline myself to spend all that day in prayer.

Turning to *Science and Health*, I read: "There is no vapid fury of mortal mind—expressed in earthquake, wind, wave, lightning, fire, bestial ferocity—and this so-called mind is self-destroyed." Also . . . "The material so-called gases and forces are counterfeits of the spiritual forces of divine Mind, whose potency is Truth, whose attraction is Love, whose adhesion and cohesion are Life, perpetuating the eternal facts of being." [7] Applying these statements as spiritual law to my circumstance, I knew that God's provision for man was perpetual, and that His laws, understood, protect man and beast from disaster. At the end of the day I was absolutely certain that God's laws of preservation prevailed in my experience, and no malicious argument could convince me otherwise.

The next day a telephone call stated that the sheep had been found in a portion of the lake with their heads just above water. The volume of water coming down from the surrounding hills could have filled this area of the lake many feet deep had it not been that the water cut itself a new channel against the natural slope of the land and entered the lake at a lower point. Had it followed its normal course, there could have been no hope for the sheep. God's law of preservation had indeed prevailed! After much hard work the sheep were all rescued from the water and taken to higher ground. These sheep were later sold for $20,000, so the loss would have been considerable.

[7] *Science and Health*, p. 293.

⏂ The floods left a semipermanent lake about fifteen miles long by about eight miles wide, a portion of which covered about half the property. It appeared that this would involve considerable loss, since the land covered had been rendered ungrazable. Considering a statement from Proverbs: "The blessing of the Lord, it maketh rich, and He addeth no sorrow with it," [8] I knew that what God gives with one hand, He certainly does not take away with the other.

My area was on the eastern end of the lake with a two-mile frontage to it. We get strong westerly winds in this part of Australia, and when these blew they drove the water over the flat plain for a distance of about half a mile, only one or two inches deep. After the wind subsided, this water soaked into the ground or receded back into the lake. Thus was acquired a self-irrigated area about two miles long by about half a mile wide. Because of this we were able to carry more stock than before. Birds came, nested on the water's edge, and multiplied. Wild ducks appeared by the thousands, as did swans, pelicans, seagulls, snipe, cranes, plover, ibis, and all types of wading birds. It was a joy to behold so much expression of life.

⏂ The other property was unimproved, and it became necessary to build houses for the staff. Four houses were eventually built, plus a church for staff and district worship, a shearing shed, a cattle shed, hay sheds, and about 40 miles of internal fencing. We erected 10 miles of telephone line to be connected to the telephone exchange. Fifteen bores (waterwells) were sunk to depths of 40 to 200 feet to get water for stock. Windmills placed on these wells pumped water into 10,000-gallon storage tanks. This supply was then reticulated to watering points in various fields. All these improvements were carried out in a postwar period with rationed building materials, when every nut and bolt was hard to obtain. Nearly everything had to be organized from Sydney, since I was still involved with the cake-manufacturing business. When taking time to travel 300 miles for supervision of the properties, I had to travel 20 miles between each one.

[8] Proverbs 10:22.

Following my election as First Reader of First Church of Christ, Scientist, Sydney—this meant conducting services—I decided to sell the first property and concentrate on the second. In this way I could travel by night train after the Sunday evening service, arriving in the country early Monday morning, and return on the Tuesday train. This would clear Wednesday for my preparation of the Wednesday evening testimonial meetings. During my three years' term as First Reader, I made this trip each fortnight, carrying on my Sydney cake businesses as well.

& I have said there were no buildings originally on the farm property, and the land itself was overrun with noxious weeds. To start building we had to have water. This meant having to put down a well, equipping it with a windmill and storage tank, then piping it about half a mile to the building site. We also had to install our own generating plant to supply electricity. In all this development I was mainly in uncharted waters and had to rely continually on divine intelligence for direction.

I had seen a couple of lucerne (alfalfa) plants growing where lucerne hay had been fed out to stock. This was not considered country where this plant would grow, but I tried a small area and found that it did well. So sharecroppers were engaged to cultivate some of the land bearing these weeds and to sow wheat. As the farmers cleaned out the noxious weeds with the wheat crops, larger areas were sown to lucerne until we had 3,000 acres sown down. This increased by five times the carrying capacity of the land with sheep. In turn, the value of the land, and its economic capacity to produce, were increased. Not only was I enormously benefited, but so were hundreds of other landholders within a couple of hundred miles who did the same thing. The living standard of some thousands of people had been raised.

& In 1951 we started a cattle stud, beginning with registered pedigree cows and a registered stud bull. There were many cattle breeds to choose from, but I decided to start with Poll Herefords—a breed that was in its infancy in Australia. Some experienced breeders treated my venture as a joke. Contrary to their opinions, Herefords grew to be one of the most popular breeds in Australia; my cattle were able to command premium prices, not only because of their fleshing, but because their being hornless prevents damage and bruising when the cattle are in the yard or being trucked. (Top quality Poll Hereford imported from the United States lifted the standard of our local breeds, and the improvement has gone on.)

Seven years later I went to New Zealand to purchase a bull, but was frustrated at every turn. The right quality seemed unavailable. Then Mrs. Eddy's statement from *Miscellaneous Writings* came to mind: "Self-renunciation of all that constitutes a so-called material man, and the acknowledgment and achievement of his spiritual identity as the child of God, is Science that opens the very flood-gates of heaven; whence good flows into every avenue of being, cleansing mortals of all uncleanness, destroying all suffering, and demonstrating the true image and likeness. There is no other way under heaven whereby we can be saved, and man be clothed with might, majesty, and immortality." [9]

Again it became clear to me that any activity that departs from a spiritual base of thought limits man and leads to frustration, whereas his identification as God's image and likeness opens his thought to infinite possibilities. I changed my base of thinking from material getting to spiritual being. Immediately I felt renewed assurance that man never reaches a dead end in his spiritually unfolding experience. In this attitude of thought, I again took up my search.

I had no intention of buying females, but three heifers in calf to a top imported Hereford bull were offered to me, and I felt an inner urge to buy them. On my last day in New Zealand a bull that only then became available was purchased and proved a most successful breeder. The three heifers in due course produced three top bull calves, one of them becoming a Senior Champion at Australia's premier beef cattle exhibit, The Sydney Royal Easter Show. At that time an offer was made for him that would have set an Australian record, but he was taken home for breeding. The stud has continued to grow and prosper, ranking

[9] *Miscellaneous Writings*, p. 185.

with the top Poll Hereford studs in Australia, whose Poll
Hereford cattle are of world standard.

We have exported cattle to South America and Korea. Our
biggest success occurred at the 1972 Sydney Royal Easter Show,
when our reserve Senior Champion bull sold at auction for
$36,000. This represented an Australian record price for a Poll
Hereford.

&sect; We had a very bad drought in the years 1965–1966, when
we were heavily stocked with 10,000 sheep. This necessitated
costly hand feeding and finding fodder for them in other parts of
the state. Even so, we lost quite a number of our stock. With
deep spiritual understanding, I had to see that infinite substance, being as omnipresent as God, could not be destroyed by
drought or any other manifestation of material substance. In the
fullness of time I obeyed an inner conviction to sell most of the
sheep and concentrate more on cattle and cropping. I grew
wheat, barley, oats, grain sorghum, and sunflowers, the latter to
be crushed for oil. Some time later this decision was proved wise
when the wool market went flat and sheep became almost
worthless. Only during the past several years has wool come back
into favor, making sheep valuable again.

As the American, Japanese, and European markets opened up
for almost unlimited supplies of Australian beef, our cattle
prices soared. Japan, China, Russia, the Middle East, and other
areas started taking more of our grain. Consequently Australia's
supply of grain for export could not equal demand, and the
price increased. By taking a positive approach to the problem of
drought, and realizing that true substance cannot be affected by
any material circumstance, I saw apparent defeat turned into
victory.

&sect; During the war years, when manpower was short and I was
working long hours, I seemed to be enslaved within four walls.
At that time I began to appreciate that man as the idea of God
could no more be held in bondage than his Principle, God,
could be. This understanding had its concrete manifestation. As
business grew, I was lifted from its manual side to the purely
managerial side. This change has brought me a freedom that I

never before thought possible, and has enabled me to utilize my comprehension of Christian Science in a broader and wider way.

Having maintained my connection with the baking industry, I am presently treasurer of the Master Pastrycooks' Association of New South Wales. As such I deal with industrial awards and payments to union members. This is done through the union secretaries and government conciliation commissioners. I am grateful for the prevention of many strikes, and for the instances where justice has replaced injustice, whether it be on the employers' or union's side. In dealing with all industrial matters, I have found the Golden Rule more powerful than all legal wisdom brought to bear on these often very contentious matters.

After finding traces of oil and gas in a well put down for stock, I was led to take out oil leases in Australia, and consequently gained experience in the oil exploration field. This was followed by mineral exploration leases in search for gold, silver, sapphires, lead, copper, zinc, etc., and eventually led to a directorship on the board of an Australian mineral exploration company.

ஜ Anything that I have attained has been brought about, not by any personal ability of my own, but through the study of the Bible and its spiritual interpretation as set forth in Christian Science. I have only reflected, or expressed insofar as I was able, the divine intelligence of my Father-Mother God.

The cake-manufacturing businesses have been sold gradually over the years, and although I still take an active interest in the trade, I suppose my first love is the boyhood dream of wide open spaces, including the various birds and the Australian kangaroo. At the present time we run about 1,700 head of cattle and a few hundred sheep, farm about 1,000 acres to wheat, 1,000 acres to grain sorghum, 500 acres to oats, and allow about 600 to 700 acres to lie fallow or be planted to other crops. There is a great deal of satisfaction in working with nature and watching crops spring from the soil.

We have three sons. The two eldest, with their wives and families, live and work on the ranch, along with a stud manager and other staff. Our youngest son, after taking his economics degree at Sydney University, is with an Australian oil exploration company, although still interested in the land. My wife and I live in an apartment fronting the beautiful waters of Sydney Harbour, and commute to the ranch every two or three weeks, also attending to city business interests. We live as a small village on the ranch property. In this way we all enjoy our family around us, yet each has his own home and personal responsibilities.

Any successful business must have the right personnel, and I express gratitude for the many wonderful people who have been so faithful over the years. Only too often we like to see ourselves as the ideas of divine Mind, sometimes forgetting that the other fellow also reflects this one Mind. But I feel very strongly about the dignity of man and have seen wonderful examples of men being lifted up by this simple process of spiritualized thought. Maybe for the first time in their lives someone has seen them in their spiritual identities, and this recognition frees individuals to manifest greater ability. This is not simply mawkish sentiment whereby we allow ourselves to be imposed upon, but by a reverse process, we find that those who are not ready for a higher way of thinking and understanding remove themselves from one's environment.

How provable is Mrs. Eddy's statement in *Science and Health*: "Through discernment of the spiritual opposite of materiality, even the way through Christ, Truth, man will reopen with the key of divine Science the gates of Paradise which human beliefs have closed, and will find himself unfallen, upright, pure, and free, not needing to consult almanacs for the probabilities either of his life or of the weather, not needing to study brainology to learn how much of a man he is." [10]

[10] *Science and Health*, p. 171.

N. Leonard Alderson, *Senior Vice-President of Tradax, Geneva, Switzerland.*

# GRAIN
# FOR THE
# WORLD

## ‌ N. Leonard Alderson

SENIOR VICE-PRESIDENT OF TRADAX,
GENEVA, SWITZERLAND

‌ Cargill, Incorporated—with its affiliate Tradax, Geneva, of which I am senior vice-president in charge of international operations— is one of the two largest grain-trading organizations in the world. I am responsible for all the international trading, warehousing, and transportation operations of the Tradax group, including those carried out by the companies in the group which now extend to Argentina, Brazil, Japan, Thailand, Australia, the United Kingdom, Holland, Germany, Belgium, Denmark, France, and Italy.

We buy grain, oil seeds, and allied products anywhere in the world where they are in surplus, own and charter ships to transport them, and sell them anywhere in the world where they are needed. Cargill's head office is in Minneapolis, Minnesota— the United States being the largest grain-exporting country in the world. I have worked in the head office and also in Peoria,

Chicago, Montreal, London, and for the past fifteen years at the Tradax headquarters in Geneva.

I have spent much of my time buying and selling grain in many countries. Some of these deals have been relatively small; the largest have involved millions of dollars worth to countries like the Soviet Union and China. The risks in this business appear to be enormous. Often we sell the crop before it is planted; at other times we have afloat on the high seas cargoes of grain for which we cannot find buyers.

Many are the factors we have to take into account in making trading decisions—economic, political, climatic. How does someone placed in a position of such responsibility make his decisions? As a Christian Scientist, I rely on the rule that God, the one divine Mind, alone governs man and the world. The concept that man is controlled by a personal mind is limited, whereas the idea that God is the Mind of man frees him from limitation.

From the time I was a small boy growing up in England, I have put into practice the scientific law that the one Mind governs, and this law has led me forward progressively.

ࢦ I was born in Reading, Berkshire, a city of about 140,000, forty miles west of London, and home of Huntley & Palmers, one of the largest biscuit factories in the United Kingdom. My paternal grandfather was a Methodist minister. Both my parents were brought up as strict Methodists. They heard about Christian Science when I was three years old and suffering from severe eczema. A friend suggested Christian Science treatment, my parents responded to the idea, and a very rapid healing followed. Impressed by this result, Father and Mother took up the study of Christian Science, and soon thereafter joined First Church of Christ, Scientist, Reading. They enrolled my elder brother and me in the Christian Science Sunday School.

At the local grammar school I was a good average student with no particular flair for academics, my major interest being sports—football, rugby, tennis, and particularly cricket—an interest that continued all through my academic years.

When I was ready to enter secondary school, my parents hoped that I could attend Leighton Park, a public (fee-paying) school run by the Society of Friends, for whom they had much respect. However, my father's earnings as a bank clerk with Barclay's Bank did not permit private tuition for his sons. My mother, however, kept an open mind about the matter. She refused to believe there is a limitation to God's goodness. She didn't tell God what to do, nor did she allow herself to wish for more money to bestow upon her sons. She simply left all planning to God's wisdom, and meanwhile appreciated the good points about the school I was already attending.

When I was thirteen, Barclay's Bank announced a new scholarship program for the sons of employees to a select list of schools. Leighton Park was one. I entered my application and was accorded a special bursary. The sum awarded was not sufficient for me to be a boarder at any of the schools on the list, but made it possible for me to attend Leighton Park—within cycling distance from our home—as a day pupil.

At Leighton Park I immediately excelled at cricket. The month following my fifteenth birthday, I was among the top eleven best players in the school. This meant that I could expect to play in the school's cricket matches for four more years— quite an unusual achievement. However, my form deteriorated, and for three years I was in and out of the team, never able to command a regular place. My last year at Leighton Park I again failed in the early games and was in danger of being dropped altogether.

Finally I came to grips with the problem. I saw I was being hampered by pride in personal ability—and pride is one of the cardinal errors in any religion! I decided that my performance on the field had to reflect the qualities of God, Mind. Precision, accuracy, strength, intelligence—all requirements for good performance in the game—were basically attributes of God, and as His image and likeness, I had the ability to express these qualities completely and satisfyingly. Suddenly the years of frustration were over. The promise of mental and physical freedoms about which I had read in *Science and Health* and the Bible was fulfilled. I scored runs every time I went to the wicket, finishing with a century in my last match, and was awarded the bat as the best player in the school. The lesson I learned on the Leighton Park field was to stand me in good stead in the years

ahead, namely, that one must turn to divine Mind as the source
of all ideas and hence of all achievement.

ﻬ Graduating from Leighton Park in 1948, I served twenty
months in the Royal Air Force as clerk in the education office,
spending the entire time at the headquarters of Signal Command near Henley-on-Thames, about twenty miles from Reading. This proved to be a completely uneventful time in my
life—except for one outstanding experience.

Early one morning I awoke to find that an illness from which I
had suffered occasionally had returned in such a serious form
that I was unable to move from my bed. I asked a friend to
telephone a Christian Science practitioner to pray for me and, in
accordance with regulations, to inform the station sick quarters.
He returned to say that the practitioner was helping me; he also
said that the ambulance would not be able to come for half an
hour. Although the pain continued to be severe, I clung to the
rule in Christian Science that in God's control of man there is
no lapse from the harmony He ordains. By the time the
ambulance drew up, an immense sense of relief and joy had
filled my consciousness, and as the orderly opened the door of
my billet, I knew I was healed. I rose and went in the ambulance
to the sick quarters, where I informed the medical officer that
Christian Science had healed me. He examined me and declared
that I was indeed perfectly fit.

ﻬ During my last year at Leighton Park, my mother had
gone to see the headmaster to discuss the possibility of my going
to university. He informed her that my academic standards were
not high enough to qualify me for admission. As in former years,
my mother again refused to accept any suggestion of limitation.
We had long discussions about the possibilities for infinite
development with which God endows His children. My mother
*knew*—not just hoped—and helped me to know, that if it was
God's will for me to go to university, He would open the way. If
not, a better course would be revealed. But in any case, as His
image and likeness, I would not be limited. As it turned out, I
was admitted to Cambridge University on my record.

࿔ Leaving the RAF in the spring of 1950, with several months to fill in before going to university, I took a summer job as an associate master at Fan Court in Surrey, England, coaching cricket and tutoring a group of boys. Founded by Geith Plimmer (who later became a Christian Science lecturer) and Guy Snape, Fan Court is a primary school (from nursery school age up to thirteen) for the children of Christian Scientists. It was exciting for me to see Christian Science applied every day in the field of education. No child at Fan Court was mentally bound into a concept of being slow or backward. Instead, the unlimited qualities of God's spiritual children were stressed and built upon, and the children responded! This activity so impressed me that I seriously considered becoming a teacher. Although my career eventually developed along totally different lines, Fan Court gave me an interest in young people that has influenced many of my nonbusiness activities in recent years.

࿔ In October 1950 I appeared at the opening session at Cambridge University. However, my two years' service in the RAF had left me mentally rusty, and for the first two or three weeks I felt academically very inadequate. I would read a history book without retaining what I had read. After about three weeks of mental struggling, I heard that a Christian Science lecture was to be given nearby, and I attended.

The lecturer pointed out that the power and intelligence of God, divine Mind, are infinite, constant, and eternal. They cannot be at a high point at one time and at a low point another time. Man, as the image and likeness of God, reflects intelligence, now and forever. The light broke through, and I saw that I could claim this intelligence now just as much as I could have two years ago—or in twenty years. As this spiritual law became clear to me, I was able to retain what I read. I also realized that examinations were an opportunity to express my God-given intelligence, and anxiety over exams left me. The results of the exams proved successful.

࿔ I played a lot of cricket and rugby at Cambridge, representing my college in both sports. Soon a number of other activities began to absorb my attention. Through the United

Nations Student Association I developed a keen interest in international affairs, to such an extent that I was elected chairman of the Cambridge University branch and subsequently became president of the United Nations Students Association of Great Britain. This association was formed to spur interest in the activities of the United Nations at university levels throughout the country. Distinguished leaders, including members of the British Parliament, came to Cambridge and lectured on the merits of a united world. I remember especially hearing Sir Gilbert Murray, the great British statesman-scholar.

Although there seems to be quite a wide gulf between the idealism of the student working for the UN Student Association and the businessman making decisions based on economic realities, I have no doubt that this early interest in a world community of nations opened my thought to its possibilities, and eventually led me into international trade, specifically the area of food distribution.

But basically, I believe that the underlying support of all my activities was my work with the Christian Science College Organization, where I served as president and twice as Reader. My two terms as Reader were both summer terms, during which time the examinations take place. Calculating materially, one might believe that the many hours required for developing the readings for the weekly testimony meetings would have diminished my academic achievements. Quite the opposite was the case. By delving deeply into the nature of Life, Truth, and Love, my use of the time for academic studies became more productive, and I graduated with honors.

ॐ Having graduated, I now needed a job, and called on the adviser of the university appointments board. I told him I didn't know what I wanted to do but I made one stipulation: I didn't want to work outside England. I was sent on interviews with a few English companies, but nothing worked out. Then I was offered an interview with a large American company looking for someone to train in the United States for about two years and then to work anywhere in Europe thereafter. At first I was surprised at being offered something that seemed to me so unsuitable. Then I realized that the limiting, personal mind was putting up barriers. Human will as to what my career was to be, or where I was to go, must yield to God's will and way. I decided to listen to what divine Mind was unfolding for me. I had never heard of the company, knew nothing of its activities, and when the type of work was explained during the interview, I simply didn't understand what was involved. But I *knew*—as one so often knows in Christian Science—that this was what Mind was revealing as my right activity. I was offered the job with Cargill, Incorporated, in Minneapolis, Minnesota, which I accepted—and I have since had not five minutes' regret.

ॐ Cargill at that time was the largest domestic grain-trading company in the United States. It was planning to enter the field of international trade through an affiliate named Tradax. Company executives knew this would require large numbers of non-Americans in the future. In 1953 they hired three Europeans, of whom I was one. I spent two years in training in North America—in Minneapolis, Peoria, Chicago, and Montreal—learning the business from the ground up.

I spent several weeks in the Minneapolis accounting department, learning the process of billing, costs, and payments. From there I moved out into Cargill's processing plants. I sampled and unloaded grain in a country elevator in a small Minnesota town; worked in a mill where animal feeds are processed and in a soybean-processing plant (Cargill being the world's largest processor of soybeans); journeyed west to San Francisco and worked in the copra-processing plant. Following this, I transferred to Peoria, spending several months placing telephone orders with small dealers for individual carloads of grain. I left Peoria for Chicago, the world's largest grain futures market—which operates like a stock exchange—learning how grain is bought and sold for future delivery. Then I went back to Minneapolis to work as a junior merchant, trading in cottonseed oil, which we bought in the United States for sale abroad.

By this time, the management office of the newly formed Tradax international organization had been established in Montreal, and I was transferred to that Canadian city to work as an assistant merchant putting out offers of grain to Japan and Europe.

In 1955 Tradax, England, opened its offices and I returned to London as manager of the department selling feed grains to manufacturers of animal feed compounds in the United Kingdom. This was not an easy assignment. Twenty-five years old at the time, I was representing a large American corporation that had previously worked through an English agent. Most of my customers were twice my age. So once again, it was essential that all kinds of humanly imposed limitations yield to God's laws of good, where neither tradition nor age can impede man's progress. Gradually our market in the United Kingdom increased, until eventually we accounted for the largest share in this area of grain trading.

In 1956 the international head office for the Tradax group was established in Geneva. In October 1958 I was appointed assistant to the vice-president in charge of the wheat and barley trading department. So I moved to Geneva, where I have lived ever since.

&～ In January 1958, while I was still stationed in London, I went skiing in the Austrian Alps and met Sally Heard of Wolverhampton, England. Sally was a Cambridge graduate in history, although we were not at the University at the same time. After I moved to Geneva, with Sally remaining in Wolverhampton, I found a number of reasons for making frequent trips to England! Sally and I were married in August 1959 and set up home in an apartment in an old mill just outside Geneva.

Sally's parents were devout Christians of a strict orthodox faith. While Sally respected her parents' religion, there were aspects of it which she couldn't accept, although she had found nothing to replace it. When we first met, she had never heard of Christian Science. After we were married, she met many Christian Scientists and felt they all had "something" which was worth investigating further. But for a considerable time she was hesitant to commit herself to a religion which seemed such a demanding way of life. Even to many practicing Christians, Christian Science can appear almost ascetic. Like adherents of some other faiths, Christian Scientists do not use tobacco, intoxicants, or drugs. Yet what can seem at first glance restrictive proves to be a freedom—a release from leaning on material crutches to achieve a sense of joy, mastery, and confidence. Sally gradually recognized what Christian Science had already taught me about freedom from limitation. The time came when we both realized how deep must be one's commitment to the Science of Christianity if one is to remain spiritually free.

Helen Patricia was born to us in 1960, and in 1962 Caroline Sally was born. The children, being born in Geneva, had the priceless opportunity of receiving their early education in the French language, and so are bilingual.

In October 1961 I was appointed vice-president in charge of Tradax's wheat and barley trading department. In the next several years there were many occasions when I was put to the test of proving the principles of Christian Science in my personal and business life.

One day I had indications that the Government of a country with whom we had never done business was about to buy a large quantity of wheat. I decided to fly there immediately. On the plane I studied in depth a pamphlet published by The Christian Science Publishing Society, entitled "Being Is Unfoldment." The article contained such statements as: "Unfoldment is divine Mind's mode of expression. . . . It is the activity of Love making divine facts manifest in human affairs; it is, to human sense, the showing forth of what is actually and continuously taking place. . . . It cannot be going on here and not there; nor can it mean that 'this' unfolds and 'that' does not."

With these spiritual truths at the forefront of my thinking, I was ready on arrival to prove them in my practical experience. I was soon led to exactly the right official, and although I had been told that in this particular country negotiations would be long drawn-out, within four days I had concluded a sale of wheat worth about $11 million.

The next morning, the official with whom I was dealing phoned to say that the Minister of Foreign Trade was refusing to authorize the contract, as he now had a cheaper offer from another source. (I should perhaps explain that in my business a verbal agreement is always accepted as binding, so that the signing of a contract is only a formality. This is an essential code of ethics, since prices in grain trading fluctuate up and down on an hourly basis.) I refused to accept this decision and so advised the official. At the same time I realized that this problem was not just an occasion for achieving business success, but more importantly an opportunity for the people with whom I was dealing to illustrate the highest moral standards. In refusing to consider a price reduction, I based my argument on the one point that to do anything less would be accepting that man can spiritually fall below the standards of Truth. As a Christian Scientist, this was unacceptable to me. It took two more days of firm discussions, but finally the deal was concluded at the original price, and the contract signed.

ঐ Notwithstanding such proofs of the efficacy of Christian Science, I was not at the time living my religion as faithfully as I had learned it in Sunday School, adhered to it as a university student, and made it the guiding force of my life. After entering business, I enjoyed many years of success. But as time went on, I began putting more and more effort into my business, and less and less into the study of Christian Science. In 1964 my company offered me a large insurance policy. This necessitated my having a medical examination. The doctor who examined me said that I was suffering from dangerously high blood pressure, and that if I was to have any hope of being acceptable to the insurance company, I must follow a course of medical treatment. This treatment involved the taking of tranquilizers which I was told would reduce my blood pressure. Shocked and made fearful by this diagnosis, and not being spiritually fortified by reliance upon divine Mind alone—a conviction that the daily living of Christian Science brings—I agreed to the medical treatment. I considered it only a temporary measure. My insurance was accepted, though at rates much higher than usual. Soon I found myself taking increasing doses of tranquilizers. After a few months I was completely dependent on these pills, to such an extent that on one occasion when I realized I was running out of a supply during a visit to an Eastern European country, I had to return home earlier than planned.

Then one day while lighting a bonfire in the garden, I was badly burned and was taken to a hospital for treatment. By the time I returned home two hours later, I had reached the decision to stop the drug-taking and to turn completely to Christian Science which had proved effective all my life. I telephoned a Christian Science practitioner and asked him to pray for me. In humility, I opened *Science and Health* and read: "The blood, heart, lungs, brain . . . , have nothing to do with Life, God." Also: "All that really exists is the divine Mind and its idea, and in this Mind the entire being is found harmonious and eternal." [1]

The burns showed rapid improvement and within a week I was back at work. But something infinitely more important was being healed. I was proving to my full conviction, as Christian Science teaches, that man, God's image and likeness, does not need to depend on drugs for the harmonious functioning of his body. The road toward my complete recovery was not easy, nor was it short. But gradually the nervous strains lessened, the high blood pressure was reduced, and I was able to feel again the peace, joy, love, consideration for others that come with the awareness of God's unceasing care for me and all.

I had learned another important lesson: If one believes that business success is achieved because the human mind is aggressive, hard-working, and smart, one becomes vulnerable to the condition that the human mind and system can be overstrained. But if one knows that God is the omnipotent Mind governing man—and turns daily to the divine intelligence for guidance—then he is free from physical pressures and physical problems. The months when I was struggling with this serious physical condition were a trying time for my family, and I shall always be grateful for my wife's spiritual steadfastness in encouraging me to rely wholly on Christian Science for healing.

I had been a member of The Mother Church, The First Church of Christ, Scientist, in Boston, since 1948. Now, in 1965, wanting to make my full commitment to the Christian Science church organization, I joined First Church of Christ, Scientist, Geneva. Sally joined with me. We both became active in church work, for which I had formerly thought I was too busy. A year later, in 1966, my wife became a member of The Mother Church. That same year, Sally and I attended the centenary

[1] *Science and Health*, p. 151.

Annual Meeting of The Mother Church, signaling 100 years since the discovery of Christian Science by Mary Baker Eddy. In profound gratitude, we knew that our lives attested to the healing, saving influence of this worldwide religion.

Also in 1966, feeling that I needed further enlightenment in the teachings of my religion, I took class instruction with a Christian Science teacher in England—a systematic course taught from the Christian Science textbook, *Science and Health with Key to the Scriptures*—which gave me fresh insights into the laws of God governing man and the universe, and the healing ability that accompanies such understanding.

Three years elapsed, and the company offered me additional insurance. Before taking the required medical examination, I talked with my teacher in Christian Science. He pointed out to me a verse from Romans 13: "The night is far spent; the day is at hand." [2] Also Mrs. Eddy's definition of "Day" in *Science and Health*, which reads in part: ". . . Mind measures time according to the good that is unfolded. This unfolding is God's day, and 'there shall be no night there.' " [3] As explained by Mrs. Eddy, night is "darkness, doubt, and fear."

I saw that as the image and likeness of God, I could only reflect His radiancy, in which there is neither doubt nor fear. The personal, mortal mind had no power to limit God's measurement of good for me. My spiritual selfhood reflected His energies—stability, tranquility, calmness, vitality. These were the only conditions that any measuring device could find. So I went to the examination knowing that God had already heard and answered my prayers. The results showed such improvement in health that the insurance company not only offered me better terms on the new policy, but offered to improve those on the policy written four years previously.

&❧ Throughout this narrative I have often referred to divine Mind. Indeed this synonym for God used in Christian Science is the one I employ most frequently. Since there is only one God, there can be only one Mind. This Mind is not exclusively mine,

---

[2] Romans 13:12.
[3] *Science and Health*, p. 584.

but is the Mind of all. Thus I can readily understand that the flow of ideas that Mind is sending forth is not only to me but to all those around me. This is a marvelous basis for acquiring the ability to delegate responsibility, which is so essential if one is to succeed in business. The egotistic concept that only the head of an organization has special insights into the flow of good ideas limits a company, whereas the viewpoint that it is possible for all men to receive limitless ideas from the one infinite Mind removes limitations and enables an executive to delegate his work fearlessly. Consequently I have developed a splendid team to work with me. I make few decisions relating to their areas of responsibility, but rather support them in their decisions.

In 1969 I was appointed merchandising manager for Tradax, Geneva, responsible for all trading decisions made by the group worldwide. By this time Tradax had become very large in the international field. In December 1972 I was appointed director-general—senior vice-president in charge of operations of Tradax, Geneva.

 🐦 Since the operation of international grain trading is not widely known, it might be useful to detail its general activities.

The work of the international grain trader covers an extraordinarily wide spectrum—from the grass roots to international politics and high finance. In the United States we buy grain from the farmer, sometimes even before it is sown, sometimes long after it has been harvested. We store it at our country elevators and transport it to our seaboard elevators in barges and railway hopper cars. We also purchase grain at the rural level in Argentina and Brazil. But in countries such as Canada, Australia, and South Africa, government-sponsored marketing boards take over the crops, and we buy the grain we need from them.

The grain we buy is sometimes sold at the seaboard of the country of origin, with the foreign buyer sending his own ship to pick it up. At other times, we sell it delivered to the country that needs it. To service our foreign customers in this way, we have to charter many millions of tons of ocean shipping each year in the European, American, and Japanese freight markets. Some of our sales are made in quantities of a few hundred tons to small flour millers, animal feed manufacturers, or oilseed crushers, while others are made to governments in quantities worth more than $100 million a transaction.

The grain trader can seldom buy and sell simultaneously with a profit margin. He must therefore assume a risk by either buying first and selling later or by selling first and buying later. If he makes the right decision concerning "which leg to take off first," he will make a profit; if he makes the wrong decision, he will take a loss. In dealing on a big scale, the risk that the trader must take can obviously be enormous. How does the trader analyze this risk before making his decisions?

Knowledge of climatic conditions, crop conditions, the economic state of different countries of the world, political factors which may result in wars, revolutions, or such matters as export embargoes, are clearly essential to him. He will probably be buying and selling in a variety of different currencies, so he must be expert in predicting fluctuations in exchange rates.

Such knowledge will be accumulated by different individuals in different places throughout the world. Speed of communication to those making the key decisions at the head office is essential. My own company has a worldwide private telex network, which makes us the largest customers of the Swiss Telephone Company.

Good information is a start, but the trader still has to analyze and draw conclusions from it. He must decide what he wants to do and try to do it at once, for it is no use having a good communications system if one doesn't take advantage of it with quick decisions. In fact, many major decisions are often made in less time than it has taken to describe the process in this section of the chapter!

In this complex and often exciting business operation, I have learned to rely on divine intelligence and intuition for my decisions, and for the decisions of my team.

ॐ The 1972–1973 crop year was a unique one in the history of the international grain trade, a year in which news of our business moved from a few inches in the business columns to the front pages of the world's press. The problem began with the purchase of 28 million tons of grain by the Soviet Union.

The procedure of the Russian purchase was one which the United States had no way of anticipating.

Prior to the arrival of the Russian buying mission in Washington in July 1972, the United States was concerned about the extent of its grain surplus, particularly in wheat. The arrival of the Soviet mission appeared as a great opportunity to alleviate the problem. What no one in the United States apparently knew—and given the secrecy with which the Russians conducted their operations, they had no adequate means of knowing—was the full extent of the Russian demand. By the time the Russians had bought 28 million tons of grain, accumulated from many countries, the world supply-and-demand structure had been completely changed. Fears of shortage had replaced fears of surplus, resulting in an increase in the price of wheat over a twelve-month period from $60 per ton to more than $200 a ton. A shortage of cereals appeared in many countries and a whole series of problems arose throughout the world. The wild price fluctuations from day to day, even hour to hour, exerted unusual pressures on the international grain-trading market. Some firms were forced into liquidation, spreading fear in their wake.

A good deal has been written alleging that certain United States trading groups favored by the Nixon administration had foreknowledge of these vast purchases. As a European, I do not presume to comment on an internal American controversy. But in view of the piecemeal way the orders were placed and the secrecy surrounding a whole series of individual deals, I find it impossible to believe that anyone but the Russians knew of their intentions beforehand—and in particular the complex timetable under which they contacted numerous grain suppliers all over the world. In fact, I suspect that at the beginning of the negotiations the Russians did not intend to buy as much grain as they finally finished up purchasing. The quantity was increased as crop conditions at home deteriorated on account of adverse weather.

During this period, it was essential that I conduct my business transactions with fearlessness and freedom from limiting concepts. It was time for me to ponder again what *Science and Health* says: "The human thought must free itself from self-imposed materiality and bondage." [4] I saw that it was vital that I not allow any set of circumstances, however complex they might seem to be, to impose limitations on my thinking and actions. The immutable truth is that nothing can prevent God's man from seeing opportunities for expressing the ideas of Mind—ideas which are wholly limitless and good. My objective was to follow the leadings of divine Mind. What appeared as a condition of limitation was turned into a period of spiritual growth for me and growth in our business. I approached each day expecting this to happen; and it did.

ခ In twenty years of traveling on business through all the continents, I have found wide acceptance of the fact that I neither drink nor smoke. But there has been one country where my non-drinking caused a certain tension and on several occasions made me feel uncomfortable. One day it became clear that the problem would not be solved by avoiding it; what was needed was healing. On my next visit to this country, at a banquet I attended, one of the hosts got to his feet and sarcastically proposed a toast to me, expressing the hope that by the time of my next visit my health would improve sufficiently for me to join him in a drink.

Here was exactly the opportunity I had been waiting for. I explained that it was time that they understood why I did not drink. It was my religious conviction. I was a Christian Scientist and Christian Scientists don't take stimulants of any kind. The man looked at me very hard for a few seconds and then said, "I'm sorry. I understand, and the matter will never be mentioned again." The tension immediately disappeared and I am sure that the difference in our drinking habits will never again cause a gulf to exist between us.

ခ Wanting our young daughters to feel the influence of Christian Science at school as well as in their home, my wife and I enrolled them in Claremont School in Esher, Surrey, England. Claremont is a school of 300 girls from the ages of eight through university entrance. All boarders are Christian Scientists, al-

[4] *Science and Health*, p. 191.

though girls of other religious denominations attend the day school. The main building is a magnificent Georgian mansion originally built for Clive of India, set in a lovely parkland. Since 1970 I have had the immense pleasure of serving on the governing council of Claremont School—an activity which brings me into contact with children of school age.

My wife and I are also members of the organizing committee of "Arc en Ciel," a two-week summer camp for Christian Scientists between the ages of 16 and 25, held in Leysin in the Swiss Alps every other summer. Founded in 1968 by Marc Engeler, the camp is attended by young people from Europe, India, the United States, and New Zealand who know sufficient French to understand most of the talks and discussions. Some campers arrive as what we call "Tunnelites"—those who are temporarily in a dark tunnel of thought, not sure what they want out of life. Many of these go home convinced that Christian Science is a practical religion of universal scope and application. Often these young people are looking for the truth—the light at the end of the tunnel—and they find it amidst other young people in a constructive atmosphere of social activities and sports, as well as serious discussions on the meaning of Life, Truth and Love, that often last late into the night.

ॐ Jesus said: "Verily I say unto you, if ye have faith as a grain of mustard seed, ye shall say unto this mountain, remove hence to yonder place; and it shall remove; and nothing shall be impossible to you." [5] Christian Science has helped me fulfill—in a measure for which I am profoundly grateful—Jesus' promise in my life.

[5] Matthew 17:20.

Dr. Homer E. Newell (at desk) at Smithsonian Institution ceremo
celebrating the completion of an ultraviolet sky survey by NAS,
Orbiting Astronomical Laboratory. At left is Dr. Fred Whipple, form
Director of The Smithsonian Astrophysical Laboratory.

# MAN AND THE UNIVERSE – MATTER OR MIND?

## ৯ *Homer E. Newell*

FORMER ASSOCIATE ADMINISTRATOR OF NATIONAL
AERONAUTICS AND SPACE ADMINISTRATION,
WASHINGTON, D.C.

৯ In my career as a space scientist, one of the early group to agitate for the creation of NASA—the National Aeronautics and Space Administration—I was assigned responsibility for the unmanned science and applications program. And my role in the Apollo program was to lay plans for the scientific research to be done relative to launching a manned vehicle to the moon. The success of the Apollo mission, when astronauts walked on the surface of the moon, was not only a tremendous achievement for the physical sciences but also proved the Scriptural premise that the man whom God created has dominion over limitations of time and space and environment.

At the turn of the twentieth century the great Russian space scientist Konstantin Tsiolkovsky said, "The earth is the cradle of humanity, but mankind will not stay in the cradle forever." For centuries men have thought they were trapped on earth. Going to the moon, Mars, or Venus is a way of expanding our concept of man's unique place in the universe.

A hundred years ago in her textbook *Science and Health*, Mary Baker Eddy predicted a time when "The astronomer will no longer look up to the stars,—he will look out from them upon the universe. . . ." [1] Already thinking in universal terms, she knew that men would eventually accept the fact that Mind, not matter, pervades all space.

The import, the grandeur, of Christian Science lies in the premise that there is infinite Mind, infinite Life, infinite Love, which never ends. But if one adopts the premise that all is matter, the postulate is—it ends. Right premises can open up a wide variety of careers for young people, whose experience becomes a never-ending unfoldment of new opportunity for growth, enjoyment, enrichment. Anyone who enters into a particular mode of thought or action is practicing that mode of thought or action, whether he recognizes it or not. One always comes back to his initial premise. It is therefore important for a young person to decide early whether his premises will be matter, limitation, finiteness—or Mind, infinitude, and abundance.

&ᴥ I have known Christian Science all my life. From the time I was a young boy, the thing that appealed to me in Christian Science was the sense of order and completeness manifested in the universe. The study of nature, and of mathematics, too, conveyed to me a sort of poetry and beauty and art.

While in the seventh or eighth grade, I happened to pick up a book on astronomy by Martha Evans Martin called *The Friendly Stars*. It belonged to my grandfather, an electrical engineer and contractor whose variety of interests included science. The book presented a whole new world and told of stars and constellations that were hundreds of thouands of light years away. This was the period when astronomers were beginning to perceive that space is populated with billions and billions of galaxies besides our own, and that our Milky Way is in itself a galaxy. I sensed in this the combination of order, beauty and

[1] *Science and Health*, p. 125.

magnificence that attracted me to Christian Science as well as the physical sciences. From that book I proceeded to study all the other books on astronomy I could lay my hands on, went out at night to identify and locate different stars and constellations, and thought about the wonders of God's creation.

Later my father, who was also an electrical engineer and contractor for motor repair in the local mills of Holyoke, Massachusetts, brought me some chemicals that someone at a wood pulp mill had given him. That started my interest in chemistry, and here again I found the same order and beauty: if you did certain things in a certain way, you knew that the results would always turn out the same. I learned to crystallize chemicals out of solutions and got the most beautiful geometric forms and colors in those crystals. Another new world had opened, expanding thought and feeding it with poetry.

I got all kinds of books on chemistry, built up a chemical laboratory and did a lot of experimenting, so that when I entered high school I had already studied the material covered in the high school course. During the first few weeks the chemistry teacher gave me the final exam, which I passed, and reversing the usual procedure, passed the course. In that first year I did advanced things in chemistry, helped in the classroom, and experimented at home. Again, my whole forward thrust was toward new frontiers of thought about the nature of the universe.

Chemistry led to geology. My grandmother had books on that subject, and in them another new world appeared. Here, too, through minerals, crystals, and rocks, I found poetry and beauty. Progressing to physics, my experience was the same. Wherever I looked in these studies I saw orderly thought, open-mindedness, and receptivity to new ideas—insights into fields with which I wanted to be associated in my life work.

About this time I discovered another new area of order—mathematics. I had a wonderful teacher, Miss Barry, with a universal approach to everything. She knew the sciences, understood advanced mathematics and relativity, read the classics in their original Greek and Latin, and could quote Shakespeare at length. Under her teaching, my study of geometry flourished.

Again my interest transcended the school course, and Miss Barry helped me grasp the theory of relativity.

The fascinating aspect of relativity was its challenge to what have been regarded as common-sense notions about the external world of time and space. The behavior of objects moving at high speed differed from what was originally thought. Like the other sciences, the appeal of mathematics was its orderly process of thought, insight, and analysis concerning the world about me. The popular belief that only about twelve people understood relativity was not true. Relativity was and is understood by thousands of students everywhere.

Of all my studies, I found mathematics perhaps the most exciting. It was my major in college and graduate school at the University of Wisconsin, and I took both undergraduate and doctorate degrees in that area. Teaching as a career, with its opportunities for mathematical research, seemed a way of keeping me in close touch with a field that again appealed to my love of universal symmetry. A carefully worked out mathematical theorem showing how initial assumptions inevitably lead to certain conclusions—here, too, was a sphere of poetry and beauty.

Throughout these years of maturing, I found myself turning daily to Christiain Science for direction, protection, and healing. The revelations of my religion deepened my insights into ultimate reality and kept my vision trained upon the high realization that God, Spirit, alone determines the nature of man and the universe. My parents' interest aided me in following my chosen course. None of us anticipated the turn my career would take, but I was convinced of God's guidance and place for man.

After taking my doctorate at the University of Wisconsin, I joined the mathematics department of the University of Maryland; there I enjoyed teaching very much. But when I went to Maryland, World War II had already broken out, and teaching Army Engineering and Air Force cadets seemed closer to the nation's purposes.

About the middle of the war this program for special Army courses ended. So I searched around at various laboratories that were doing work to support the war effort, and wound up at the

Naval Research Laboratory. In the NRL the greatest need was in the field of physics, so I began applying mathematics to physics problems. Among other things, I worked on the propagation of radio waves for communication purposes.

Germany had made great advances in rocketry, an enormous challenge to scientists all over the world. My group recommended to the Navy that we study the upper atmosphere by means of rockets, and when this idea was accepted, we started a rocket-sounding project. In January 1946 I gave a series of lectures to the group, on artificial satellites, the kinds of orbits one might put them into, and the properties of orbits. Others in the group gave lectures on their special fields—propulsion, aerodynamics, guidance and control, atmospheric sciences, and so on. In that way we forwarded our program of studying the upper atmosphere.

About that time, the Army made available to us some V-2 rockets captured in Germany. This enabled us to equip the giant rockets with instruments for studying the upper atmosphere and the sun, and gave us a means of starting our high-altitude research right away instead of having to wait until we could build our own rockets. The different agencies involved in this program of upper-air research united to form the V-2 Panel.

From these early beginnings evolved the program that everybody knows about today. New rockets were built, and almost every month new records were established—altitude records and new discoveries—until finally, during the International Geophysical Year of 1957–1958, the Soviets, and then the United States, launched the first artificial satellites. Thus we moved from capabilities developed before and during World War II to our present exploration of an entirely new frontier for mankind. And in that process I switched from mathematics to physics.

&ordm; External and internal forces spurred the advancement of space exploration by the United States. The Soviet launching of Sputnik I in October 1957 caused consternation in this country that Russia, rather than the United States, had sent up the first satellite. There were predictions about possible Soviet domination of the world, and much agitation for the United States to do something specific to meet the competition.

The Rocket and Satellite Research Panel—a new name for the original V-2 Panel—had already mapped out plans for greatly increased activity in the development of rockets and artificial satellites. A committee, of which I was chairman, had been created to work out thoughts and ideas for a national space establishment devoted, first, to scientific investigation and application in space and second, to exploration by means of manned space flight.

Now with public sentiment behind us, we started to promote the idea of a national space establishment. Members of my committee—William Pickering, Wernher von Braun, and William Stroud—and I visited Vice-President Nixon and outlined our thoughts to him. He quickly grasped what we were saying. Agreeing that the country needed basic research and advancement on new space frontiers, he arranged appointments for us with five Atomic Energy Commissioners: with George Allen, head of the United States Information Agency; with Senator Clinton P. Anderson, chairman of the Joint Committee on Atomic Energy; with then Senator Lyndon B. Johnson; and with Congressman John W. McCormack, head of a special House Committee to draw up a bill on space. We told our story to these people. The time was ripe. Many other agencies were pushing for the same sort of thing. And all the different forces led to the creation of what eventually became known as the National Aeronautics and Space Administration. We were in the formal business of opening up and exploring a vast new frontier!

〜 Long before we got to the Apollo program, our office, then called Office of Space Science and later Office of Space Science and Applications, was launching unmanned satellites, deep space probes, and sounding rockets. As the manned vehicles became available, we continued our scientific research with the unmanned devices, and out of these early years of planning and work has grown the tremendously productive and fruitful research of the Apollo exploration.

As an example: We arranged with the Geological Survey to build up a program in the field of geology for studying the moon and the planets. They developed a strong group of people working at Flagstaff, Arizona, who have contributed heavily to the groundwork by making geological maps of the moon, and helping astronauts to train by means of field trips here on earth. Prior to our first moon landing there were unmanned missions by Rangers and Surveyors, spacecraft which came under the surveillance of my office. As a result we had tens of thousands of pictures and some analyses of the moon. Lunar orbiter spacecraft had mapped almost the entire surface of the moon, helping to lay the basis for the astronauts' successful moon exploration.

NASA also gave grants to a host of scientists to develop equipment for analysis of rock samples when they were brought from the moon. We organized experiments and developed instruments to be set up by the astronauts on the surface of the moon. In all of this, we worked hand in hand with the Office of Manned Space Flight, which was running the Apollo program.

Through these years of planning and work, we have collected a vast amount of information on the universe—the moon, Mars, Venus, the sun, and stars—all of which finds its practical application in a variety of ways. We have created satellites that help to predict the weather, that offer weather information for farmers and construction engineers, and provide pilots with pictures of cloud formation they will meet along their routes. Communication satellites have been created to cut transoceanic telephone costs by half and make transoceanic television possible. Other satellites help us to survey and explore natural resources and monitor the earth's environment.

But most importantly, I think the activity has given everyone a better picture of the immensity of the universe and of the beauty of the world we live in, while pointing up reasons for being more thoughtful, wiser, and more considerate in the way we use our own planet.

࿎ Space exploration has moral, economic, and spiritual implications. The great progressive periods in modern history have almost always been times of war, leading many to conclude that war is necessary for technological and economic progress—a very immoral point of view. But suppose nations become so involved in the challenging problems of exploring the solar system and the universe that they don't have need for wars to

spur on mankind's progress? Then conquest of space replaces
conquest of nations as a productive adventure in the human
economy.

Realistically speaking, man must meet the challenge of space.
It has appeared in his line of reason, and he must find the answer
to the nature, substance, and identities of the universe. It is in
meeting and overcoming such challenges that he grows and
progresses. The struggle to know, to understand, to extend his
domain is what keeps the spirit of man alive. Wherever his
imagination roams, man seeks also to go.

Glimpsing the true spiritual nature of man, the Psalmist sang:
"When I consider thy heavens, the work of thy fingers, the
moon and the stars, which thou hast ordained; What is man,
that thou art mindful of him? and the son of man, that thou
visitest him? For thou has made him a little lower than the
angels, and hast crowned him with glory and honour. Thou
madest him to have dominion over the works of thy hands; thou
hast put all things under his feet." [2]

ᢜ▶  When working in Christian Science as well as the physical
sciences, one comes face to face with the question of how to
relate the two. The premise of Christian Science is that God,
Mind, is all. The premise of the physical sciences is that matter
is all. So you can't reconcile the two premises. The question can
be resolved only in one's interpretation of what the universe is.

As a lifelong Christian Scientist, I have made these statements
from Mrs. Eddy's textbook *Science and Health* the premise on
which to base my viewpoint concerning the fundamental nature
of man and the universe: "The universe, like man, is to be
interpreted by Science from its divine Principle, God, and then
it can be understood; but when explained on the basis of
physical sense and represented as subject to growth, maturity,
and decay, the universe, like man, is, and must continue to be,
an enigma. . . . Spirit is the life, substance, and continuity of all
things. We tread on forces. Withdraw them, and creation must
collapse. Human knowledge calls them forces of matter; but
divine Science declares that they belong wholly to divine Mind,

[2] Psalms 8:3–6.

are inherent in this Mind, and so restores them to their rightful home and classification." [3]

Christian Science presents unfoldment and progress. And the physical sciences offer mankind opportunities for unfoldment and progress. In this sense the purposes of my religion and the physical sciences seem to coincide. The basic divergence between the two comes from the limitations and finiteness which the physical sciences would impose upon man and the universe by classifying them as matter. This is the dark side of the picture—a picture that I am convinced the Science of Mind is destined to change. At the present time my participation in the physical sciences is to help spur inspiration, development of insight, and increasing understanding in the field of space exploration. I have a role to play here even though I know that there is another, more direct way to reveal the forces of the universe.

ॐ Many people misunderstand what Christian Science means when it says there is no matter. They think that without matter there would be a great emptiness where neither man nor the universe exists. Nothing could be further from the truth. Christian Science says that God being the creator of the universe and pervading all space, all that exists is Mind and its infinite manifestation; that what one sees depends upon one's mental perceptions and insights. The physically minded man will see physicality. The spiritually minded man will see the perfection, harmony, and loveliness of the universe and will exalt God. What God, Mind, sees is the reality. Therefore the Christian Scientist endeavors to see out from the divine Mind to the perfection of spiritual man and the spiritual universe.

At our present stage of perception we see this reality of Mind's creation only faintly. The order and beauty that we see in the sensuous universe are the promise of what we shall clearly see some day as the unmarred and spiritual perfection of reality. If God, Spirit, and His spiritual universe did not exist, you would see nothing. Paul understood this when he said: "For now we see through a glass, darkly; but then face to face: now I know

[3] *Science and Health*, p. 124.

in part; but then shall I know even as also I am known." [4] When you relate the human that you see physically with the divine reality that is unseen to physical view, you touch God, Life itself. You feel His love expressed. You know His creation is perfect and spiritual. You understand intuitively that health and well-being are your natural states.

The world needs to break through the dark dream that accepts imperfection as a natural and inevitable thing. We must wake up to the fact that good is real because good is God expressed by man and the universe. We are all moving inevitably toward a clearer understanding of this reality because the one Mind, God, moves us that way.

Physics simply assumes the existence of matter and ignores such questions as: "Why am I here? Who created the universe?" Therefore physics leaves unsolved the problem of being. Metaphysics is the Science of being that seeks to define man's origin, nature, purpose, and place in the universe. When one discovers that Mind, not matter, is the power that controls and heals man, he begins to perceive that metaphysics is not just an interesting academic subject, but actually the Science of Life. One of the arguments often heard against philosophies is that, while interesting, even fascinating, they are impractical because they are not usable in certain instances. The discovery that metaphysics raised to the spiritual level is the Science of reality immediately brings with it the challenge to prove its premise in actual practice.

When I was in college, I had an experience that absolutely convinced me that Christian metaphysics is Science. All during my youth I had been bothered with what might be called rheumatism. Whenever I exercised too much I would be stricken with excruciating pain. But I enjoyed sports, especially swimming, hiking, and tennis. At college one day I returned from rowing feeling terribly sick. I couldn't sit, stand, or lie down. I tried to help myself metaphysically but didn't seem to get any relief. Then about three o'clock in the morning I realized that, although I had been praying conscientiously, I had really been thinking, 'There is no pain like this pain in my body.'

[4] I Corinthians 13:12.

Then I thought, 'Really, this kind of praying won't heal. I know that God is Spirit and man is His image and likeness, therefore man is spiritual and perfect, not material and imperfect. All that is going on here is that matter is making its plea for reality and you're listening. But matter can't say a thing to you!' And just like that, all the pain was gone permanently. Metaphysics had proved itself to be above physics.

Matter says, "I am the kind of stuff that is real. I have medical laws and physical laws, and you just can't do anything about me because I am substance. Because I am real, spiritual healings cannot happen." This silent argument can be extremely vigorous and obstinate. But all you need is one instance of Mind-healing to undo the argument and to prove that matter is not what it says it is. And that becomes the turning point from matter to Mind.

If you play the game entirely within the rules of physical science, you know that nothing is accepted that cannot be proved by experiment. Your body of scientific knowledge is built up by observation. This parallels what Mrs. Eddy said must be the way of establishing Christian Science: through proving its premises. You don't know anything solely by theoretical reasoning in science; you prove it by demonstration. If you accept the physical science concept of man, an animal made up of atoms, molecules, and so on, this means that the metaphysical healing of Christian Science is impossible. But if you have just one case of Mind-healing, that is enough to dispute all the laws of physics and matter. And we have vastly more than one case—we have thousands and thousands. Here, using the physical scientists' own ground rules, we discover a very powerful argument that reality is not what it is generally believed to be. Reality is something else: it is Mind and its infinite expression.

You are always being tempted to identify your current concept of yourself with the material, with matter. The demand is not to yield to that temptation, but to identify yourself with the reality, with Spirit and with Truth. In that way you see your own identity not as a material being, born according to laws of physics, but rather as a complete and infinite expression of divine Mind, without beginning and without end. The human interpretation sometimes goes awry. The fact is always there.

Some people want to mix matter with Spirit; they have an idea that a study of the physical sciences and the physical universe will lead to the understanding of spiritual causation and creation. But this is not going to happen because the study of matter and mortality is the constant study of an enigma.

As I see it, the constant frustration of trying to find an answer to the material universe will eventually force the individual to turn elsewhere, and that change of viewpoint generates a new willingness to perceive the divine reality. But the amassing of tons of information about atoms, molecules, and strange particles leads nowhere but back to where one started from— matter.

੨๛ Some physicists think of the material universe as infinite in extent; others as finite. But finiteness may not be so much a question of the extent of the universe as a question of evanescence, that nothing can last forever. You think of the sun. The sun has lasted now for ten billion years and that is a long time. It will probably last for another billion years or more. But physical theory says it will eventually die and become a white dwarf about the size of the earth, and the earth will become a clinker too cold to sustain physical life. Here a finiteness of time enters into the picture, so you don't have to argue whether the universe extends out into space. Finiteness has a beginning and an end. Time is a great measurer of finiteness. To understand eternity, one has to reject the limited human mind and accept the divine Mind, or supreme intelligence, as the source of man's consciousness. Then thought accepts this divine, infinite calculus—the height, depth, breadth of infinite Life and Love which fill all space.

The variety that we see, the constant evidence of new things that we experience as we explore the universe, are but indications of the infinitude of Mind, which never stops unfolding and revealing itself. The material scientist would interpret these discoveries as newly discerned aspects of matter or energy, whereas the metaphysician would interpret such evidence as pointing toward the constant unfolding of infinite intelligence bringing new views of reality to light. When a man understands that Mind's infinitude fills all space, he loses his terror of the unknown and overcomes the fear of mortality, loss, and death.

᠔ "Progress is the law of God," writes Mrs. Eddy in *Science and Health*—never dependent on matter or materiality.[5] The infinitude and revelations of Truth are something to keep in mind—Truth being synonymous with God. The history of mankind, when considered from this spiritual standpoint, takes on a different meaning than the one derived from the belief that progress is the result of the interaction of chance and material forces.

Throughout history wonderful truths have been discovered that have contributed to mankind's progress. Let me go back to mathematics for an example. Many people today may be surprised to realize that the concept of zero was a very difficult one for men to learn. It developed many centuries ago among the Hindus. When it was introduced, the use of zero with positive and negative numbers gave us the basis for our modern algebra. Zero became the central point for mathematical calculations, and now we are accustomed to thinking about such concepts as 30 degrees above zero and 30 degrees below zero. But many years passed before zero in mathematics became a part of the thinking of the race.

Christian Science is a system of calculation whose numerals are infinity, with divine Mind as the center and circumference of the universe. Starting with Mind, new perceptions unfold to mankind, and new dimensions of reality appear in which error and matter are obsolete. Since nothing can endure which is not immortal, I believe the time will come when mankind will accept this truer, more precise system of calculating from God, the perfect cause, to man and the universe, the perfect effect. Such acceptance will produce increased harmony among races and classes, progress in all fields, and better health for mankind.

᠔ One of my mathematics professors in the field of algebra, Professor Cyrus Colton MacDuffee of the University of Wisconsin, gave a wonderful course. I remember how he stood up one day and said, "We are going to go through the proving of

[5] *Science and Health*, p. 233.

this theorem. We have a rigmarole we go through. Step by step we go through the logic which proves that the theorem is true. But what really counts is whether you see it or not. When you see the truth, it is clear, it is right, you have it, whether you have actually worked out the proof or not. On the other hand, to convey it to somebody else, you have to go through the steps and move through the logic of establishing the theorem."

I think this is interesting as it relates to the Christian Science textbook, *Science and Health*. Mrs. Eddy experienced the full revelation of Truth. The divine Principle and range of reality were clear to her, from the infinitesimal to the infinite. And it took spiritual discernment and courage in those days of immersion in material thinking—alone, having nobody else with whom to exchange her thoughts and ideas—to go out and say that in reality the world is not material but spiritual, a manifestation of God, Spirit. This was her premise and she needed to prove it. So starting with that revelation—with the truth that she knew—she produced a textbook. This book gives the series of steps people need to follow in developing for themselves the inspiration that perceives the healing truth, and frees them from matter and materiality.

To me the important thing is to receive the inspiration, the revelation, because that is what really gives you the answers. Many times in teaching mathematics and in working out mathematical problems, I have discerned the right answers at the beginning, and of course that is a remarkable feeling—you have found the solution. But to convey it to others, I have had to go through the problem step by step, working it out for them, showing how I arrived at the answer—and it takes time to do this.

I remember back in Harvard when I was taking a course in mechanics from one of the world's greatest mathematicians, Professor George David Birkhoff, somebody asked him about a very difficult problem. After he wrote down the problem on the blackboard, he stepped back, looked at it, and then said, "It seems to me that the answer must be such and such." And he wrote the answer down. He then proceeded to develop, step by step, the solution to the problem, but it took him the rest of that period and all of the next day's session to show how he arrived at the answer. That is the difference between instantaneous answers and healings in Christian Science on the one hand, and answers and healings on the other hand that have to go through step-by-step arguments in order to prove the basic premises. But either way, this is what *Science and Health* enables one to do metaphysically.

Not long ago I was talking with several Christian Scientists who are also working in the physical sciences, and we commented that almost a hundred years ago, before the development of modern science, Mrs. Eddy presented her insights into the fundamental nature of science, theology, and medicine. And even today, after a century's change, these insights continue to be accurate.

໒ Mankind makes both moral and immoral uses of its scientific discoveries. Here again one needs to establish premises. It is characteristic of matter that for every action there must be a reaction. That is one of Newton's famous laws of physics. Such a law finds expression in the following inconsistencies: that physical progress may generate the ability to improve health but also to conduct biological warfare; to move mountains but also to destroy cities and countrysides. If you accept matter as real, you have to take the reaction with the action, which is another way of saying you have to take the bad with the good. But if you have solidly based your premises on Spirit and spiritual man, then you have the good without the law of reaction.

Christian Science is not just a theory but rests on what Mrs. Eddy describes as demonstration. If you can make it work, you have it. If you can't make it work, no matter how well you talk about it, you don't have it. The challenge to the young person is to make it work, and the encouragement to the young person is that thousands have shown that it does work. So when one approaches the problems of poverty, of human rights, of the environment, and of the myriad human activities, we can know there is a solution of Mind that matter and limitation cannot reverse. Today's demand is to eliminate from the international scene the basic immoralities of warfare and of human exploitation. The opportunity to those who understand the Science of being is to take up this challenge and eliminate these evils by applying Christianly metaphysical thought and Christianly scientific action.

It was clear to us who were part of the Apollo program that going to the moon was easier perhaps than solving some of the problems here on earth—because we agreed that it could be done. That was our premise, and the country gave us the utmost support in proving it. In problems of food, environment, the cities, and human rights, mankind must agree that there are solutions, then work to find them. The Christian Scientist knows that these problems can be healed and contributes daily toward that end.

ৈ People often view morality as something relative. Morals tend to be related to time, place, circumstance. As a consequence, there is a tendency to undermine behavior by asserting relative arguments: "You have to look out for yourself." "What you do can't hurt anybody." But if you find the basis of morality in Principle, in the fact that the universe is the expression of Mind, calling for consideration, honor, the Golden Rule, perfection, goodness—then you have a basis for morality that cannot be undermined; you have a reason that is permanent. If your premises regard matter as real, then morality is hard to sustain. If your premises consider Spirit as real, then morality is easy to sustain and is easy to live by.

ৈ For most people, truth is most closely identified with reality. So when one is searching for what is real, what is close to one's life, to his being, he is searching for truth. And to reach it, one has to be honest with oneself, one cannot hide from himself what he is trying to do and what his motives are. Don't let limited, material thinking and a limited material sense of self shut you out from the spiritual sense of who you really are.

Young people are trying to find their identity. Many say they don't know where they are at. But if you identify yourself as God's image and likeness, you immediately have a basis for your real being, for what you are in the universe, and where you are going. Identifying yourself with the divine, you immediately rise higher in your concept of yourself, and that higher idea unfolds in a variety of ways, pointing up the right course in your career, your associations, your sense of being.

This need to identify yourself with the divine reality is at the heart of the problem that everybody is struggling with. One is constantly tempted to take sides with limited concepts. It is well worth resisting that temptation and instead identifying oneself with Mind, not matter, reaping the abundant harvest that goes with that premise.

To one who is struggling with any form of limitation, whether it is sickness or deprivation of any kind, you can always know that "in Him you live and move and have your being." No matter what path you are taking, it cannot take you away from God; and the time will appear when the right action will be clear to you, the mists will disperse, and you will see that your pathway always was with Him. God is everywhere, and nobody can be outside of Him. The poetry of the universe, its hidden beauty and sensitivity, and all its joys are yours.

Christian Science has been a source of support, discernment, guidance, and understanding in everything I undertake. It has been my link to what I regard as the reality of being in an era when it is very difficult to perceive what reality is. It has been a source of orderly thought in a period of confusion and concern. In a day and age when it is hard to find a path, it has been the pathway to follow.